# Montana

# Also by Keith Dunnavant

# Montana

## THE BIOGRAPHY OF FOOTBALL'S JOE COOL

# KEITH DUNNAVANT

Thomas Dunne Books ♨ New York
St. Martin's Griffin

THOMAS DUNNE BOOKS.
An imprint of St. Martin's Press.

MONTANA. Copyright © 2015 by Keith Dunnavant. All rights reserved. Printed in the United States of America. For information, address St. Martin's Press, 175 Fifth Avenue, New York, N.Y. 10010.

www.thomasdunnebooks.com
www.stmartins.com

Designed by Steven Seighman

The Library of Congress has cataloged the hardcover edition as follows:

Dunnavant, Keith.
    Montana : the biography of football's Joe Cool / Keith Dunnavant. — First Edition.
        p. cm.
    Includes bibliographical references and index.
    ISBN 978-1-250-01784-0 (hardcover)
    ISBN 978-1-250-01786-4 (e-book)
    1. Montana, Joe, 1956–  2. Football players—United States—Biography.
3. Quarterbacks (Football)—United States—Biography.  I. Title.
    GV939.M59D86 2015
    796.332092—dc23
    [B]
                                                                            2015019171

ISBN 978-1-250-01785-7 (trade paperback)

Our books may be purchased in bulk for promotional, educational, or business use. Please contact your local bookseller or the Macmillan Corporate and Premium Sales Department at 1-800-221-7945, extension 5442, or by e-mail at MacmillanSpecialMarkets@macmillan.com.

First St. Martin's Griffin Edition: November 2016

D  10  9  8  7  6  5

*To my late brother, Robert Dunnavant, Jr., an outstanding journalist who profoundly influenced my development as a writer and as a man*

# Contents

# Montana

# Prologue

THE QUARTERBACK GATHERED THE SNAP and rolled left, scanning the horizon for an open man. It was a beautiful day at Tampa Stadium, the air thick with September hope, when the Super Bowl tantalizes every team, even the woeful Buccaneers. It was a day Joe Montana would never forget.

By the time the San Francisco 49ers reached the third quarter of their 1986 season opener, headed for a decisive 31–7 victory over Tampa Bay, Montana owned two Super Bowl rings. He was the most efficient passer in the history of the National Football League. He was the man of countless heart-pounding rallies, including the memorable Cotton Bowl victory over Houston, when he overcame hypothermia, brutal cold, and a 22-point deficit to pull off the most stunning comeback in Notre Dame history. He was the man who sent Dwight Clark into the clouds to beat the Dallas Cowboys, turning a page in NFL history. He was Joe Cool. But he was not yet the man he was supposed to be.

One of the attributes that made Montana so tough to stop was his ability to get rid of the ball in a flash, often rolling left or right and contorting his body to send a perfect spiral soaring in the opposite direction, defying not just clawing defenders but immutable gravity. This time, as the quarterback drifted left, he could see Clark, his close friend, moving into the open to his right. In an instant, the window would close, and Montana's career had rested to a large measure on his skill in exploiting such small intervals of time and space. With the rush approaching, he twisted his body, cocked his right arm, and threw back to his right. Just as the ball drifted toward Clark's outstretched hands, he felt something in his body pop.

In a way he could not possibly comprehend, the quarterback had reached a turning point in his career.

Imagine Picasso without his blue period, Sinatra without the Capitol years, Cosell without *Monday Night Football*.

In September 1986, Joe Montana was not Joe Montana yet.

Not *that* Joe Montana.

Not yet.

# CHAPTER ONE

# The First Crack

THE FATHER WAS A PUSHER. It all begins with the father, a Navy veteran who managed a local finance company on Main Street in Monongahela, a thriving blue-collar town near a bend in the big river, in the pulsating steel and coal corridor of western Pennsylvania. It all begins in that volatile cauldron of affection and ambition and vicarious thrill that so often goes terribly wrong. It all begins in a very dangerous place, where love so often turns to hate.

Joe Montana Sr., the descendent of Italian immigrants, played competitive sports in the service and was known around town as a decent backyard athlete who battled for every basket in pickup basketball games with teachers at the local high school. But every man approaches fatherhood in a reactive state, influenced, often unwittingly, by the lingering shadow of his own childhood. "When I was a kid I never had anyone to take me in the backyard and throw a ball to me," he once said. "Maybe that's why I got Joe started in sports." Sometimes it's just that simple: a twinge of regret reverberating across the generations.

"Every guy wants his kid to be a better athlete than he was, and Joe was no different," said family friend Carl Crawley Jr., who became the son's youth league football coach. "Joe pushed and pushed and pushed Joey, because he wanted his son to have what he couldn't have and because he could see the kid wanted it."

The son, Joseph Clifford Montana, was born on a Monday, June 11, 1956, the year of Elvis, the Suez Crisis, and the Hungarian Revolution. His mother, Theresa, the daughter of Italian immigrants who had been lured to the new world by the great industrial expansion of the early twentieth century, eventually divided her time between homemaking chores and her employment at Civic Finance, where she kept the books down the hall from her husband. Joe Sr. had traded a career as an installer for the telephone company for the office job, which allowed him to spend more time with his family. The future Pró Football Hall of Famer was their only child. The Montanas were a tight-knit family, and in the years to come, in those adrenaline-filled days of the late 1960s and early '70s, when Joey was starring in three different sports for local teams, often traveling across Pennsylvania and beyond for youth-league and public school tournaments, she was almost always in attendance—alternately manning the concession stand or cheering her boy on at the top of her lungs.

The son began his life in a modest two-story, wood-frame house on Monongahela's Park Avenue, a working-class street of tight contours and steep lots located just blocks from the central business district. The first hint of athleticism could be seen—and heard—when Montana was still an infant. "He used to wreck his crib by standing up and rocking," his mother, who died in 2004, told *Sports Illustrated*. "Then he'd climb up on the side and jump to our bed. You'd hear a thump in the middle of the night and know he hit the bed and went on the floor."

Animated by dreams—encouraged by his father—of someday becoming a professional athlete, young Joe began gravitating to the front porch at the end of the workday, ball in hand, waiting for his dad to arrive home so they could continue his athletic education amid the creeping late-afternoon shadows. Even when he was exhausted, the father always made the time. It didn't take him long to see that his son was gifted: fast afoot, able to throw farther and more accurately than other kids his age, capable of sinking a jump shot from long range. It didn't take him long to start investing a measure of his own self-esteem in his son's budding athletic career.

The elder Montana was the first to school him in the fundamentals of football, basketball, and baseball; the first to try to hone his raw talent; and the first to cultivate the competitiveness that would prove central to his success. Sometimes he taught by example, challenging the son to furious games of one-on-one in which he "grabbed . . . pushed . . . [and] threw his elbows." Sometimes the pushing was tactical, like dangling a tire from a tree limb and making sure the son fired a certain number of tight spirals each day, so he could develop his arm. (Like many other Catholic boys across the land, he imagined himself as Notre Dame great Terry Hanratty, quarterback of the 1966 national champions, leading the Fighting Irish to another victory in the House that Rockne built. The father and son rarely missed an Irish game on the radio, and frequently watched the Sunday television replays.) Sometimes it was strategic, like fudging the paperwork so the eight-year-old could play nine-year-old midget league football. Even though he was a year younger than all the rest, the skinny kid with the closely cropped blond hair and the earnest blue eyes was immediately recognized as one of the best players, so naturally, he became a quarterback.

Unlike many of his teammates, he did not approach the game as an outlet for his boyish aggression. The chance to hit somebody was not what made him tick. A rather timid player who tried to avoid contact, he earned playing time by the projection of his superior athletic skills and a widely admired competitive streak. Even then, the coaches and players could see how much he hated to lose. Childhood teammate Keith Bassi recalled, "Joe thrives on competition. He lives for it."

Two years after joining the youth league, when Joey, in a moment of youthful distraction, considered quitting the Monongahela Little Wildcats so he could join his cousins in the Cub Scouts, it was his father who manipulated his perseverance by insisting he complete the season—simultaneously teaching a valuable lesson about the importance of not quitting something he had started and protecting him from the consequences of a hasty decision.

"The father was a driving force," said Crawley. "You take him out of the equation, I think you have a very different story."

While the first critical element in Montana's emergence was having a father who took an interest in his athletic development and endeavored to nurture it, this investment of time and focus also required a delicate balancing act. Under different circumstances, it all could have gone very badly. All that pressure could have yielded burnout, alienation, hatred. It could have produced some steel-country version of Southern California phenom Todd Marinovich, the can't-miss creation of uber-paternal athletic engineering who flamed out with the Los Angeles Raiders just as Joe Montana was nearing the end of a brilliant career with the San Francisco 49ers. But the elder Montana avoided many of the pitfalls associated with so many sports fathers, managing to push the son toward achievement without causing rebellion or resentment—without pushing him away. In the end, it probably worked because the father was driving the son to reach for something the son truly wanted.

"You can push a kid and when they see what you're trying to do, and their head's screwed on right, they'll take it, they'll appreciate it," Crawley said. "And Joey's head was screwed on right."

Sports cemented a deep bond between the two, a connection that proved strong enough to withstand the usual adolescent tensions and the complexities of raising a young man of such obvious athletic potential without allowing him to become spoiled, disrespectful, or arrogant. From the boy's childhood, there always seemed to be a duality to their relationship. "Joe and Mr. Montana were best friends who happened to be father and son," said college friend Steve Orsini. In time, obedience gave way to trust.

The fact that Theresa supported Joe Sr.'s efforts cannot be overlooked as a significant factor in Montana's development. A loving mother who delighted in cooking traditional Italian dishes—including Joey's favorite, ravioli—she was not the sort to nag her husband about pushing their son. She was not the type to ridicule Joey's athletic aspirations. By all accounts, the mother completely bought into her husband's belief that their son could someday play professional sports. She could see how much her boy loved competing, the way it lit him up, the way it fostered in him a sense of self and possibility. Her enthusiastic encouragement contributed to a solid domestic foundation bereft of conflict. At the same time, Theresa was usually the one who made sure Joey did his homework, providing the necessary balance to his life. Although he was a reasonably good student, he later conceded, "I was really concentrating on sports."

One of the reasons the dynamic between father and son worked so well was the eventual transition to organized sports that handed off much of the coaching to others, including Crawley, a beer salesman with a discerning eye who volunteered his time as head coach of the Little Wildcats.

"Joey had a lot of speed, and I noticed right away that he could roll out and throw equally well, with good accuracy, to his left or his right, which was very unusual for a right-handed kid," said Crawley, a stout, gregarious man with a raspy voice.

Once a star lineman and fullback at California University of Pennsylvania, a small liberal arts and teachers college, Crawley had earned tryouts with the Philadelphia Eagles and the Pittsburgh Steelers, where he survived until the final cut of training camp. He wound up playing several years of semipro ball and eventually spent two decades as a college football official, refereeing games all across the country, including the Rose Bowl, while climbing the corporate ladder at Jones Brewing Company, owned by the actress Shirley Jones, where he became vice president of sales and marketing. Crawley knew the game and had a knack for interacting with young boys. His coaching provided a critical bridge between the father's backyard instruction and the more complex high school days to come.

When Crawley saw Montana loafing during wind sprints—even though he was beating his teammates by several steps—the man with the whistle gruffly urged him to reach for something more, introducing a concrete example of how to strive not just for victory but for his own potential. When he cracked his helmet after colliding with a tackler—a jarring experience that left him momentarily dazed—it was with a measure of pride that Crawley and the other coaches watched him race to the sideline and demand another, presaging the tenacity that would propel him forward in the years ahead. The once-timid player shattered an important psychological barrier by destroying his headgear. "I think that was a turning point," said assistant coach Clem Uram. Never again would anyone wonder about Montana's ability to take the punishment required to play the game.

Beyond his obvious skills, Crawley was struck by his maturity level. "He was a very intelligent ballplayer, a heady ballplayer, like a coach on the field," he said. "You could talk to him like an adult. He was a quick learner, and he made good choices."

At an age when many of his teammates were still trying to master snap counts and the fundamentals of blocking and tackling, Montana soaked up Crawley's careful instruction about the nuances of the game. "I put in plays where the quarterback had to make a decision, and from that, he learned," he said. "Bit by bit, I taught him how to play the game . . . how to play the game by thinking through all the choices and possibilities." When to dump it off short. When to tuck and run. Confronted with each predatory defensive act, he learned how to react in a way that gave him the best chance to move the chains, taking the first tentative steps toward his life in the pocket. It was a fitful process for a young boy still growing and maturing and trying to learn his multiplication tables and his spelling words, but his combination of instinct and applied knowledge frequently put a knowing smile on Crawley's face.

The beer salesman was the first man outside the Montana household to glimpse the future, quietly predicting, when the boy was ten, "This kid is going to be an All-American."

Such heady talk served only to validate the father's already high expectations.

The revolution began downriver, with a burst of fire and a billow of smoke. The year was 1875. On a tract of land just west of the Monongahela River, eight miles north of Pittsburgh in the village of Braddock, Scottish-born industrialist Andrew Carnegie opened his first steel mill. A new age dawned, on the same field where, more than a century earlier, in a decisive battle of the French and Indian War, forces led by British general Edward Braddock had been routed. The wilderness had finally been tamed, not just by military might but also by the consolidating force of the industrial revolution. Carnegie was not the first American to employ the still-new Bessemer process, which produced larger quantities of the still-precious metal more efficiently. But by harnessing the cutting-edge technology on a mass scale and embracing business practices that would one day be called "vertical integration"—just as the demands of an emerging continental infrastructure began to surge—Carnegie gave birth to an industry that made possible, or at least practical, many others. Cheap steel transformed America, nowhere more profoundly than Pittsburgh, where the Ohio, Allegheny, and Monongahela rivers converged like nautical superhighways, and the surrounding Monongahela Valley. By the end of the nineteenth century, once-sleepy western Pennsylvania was producing nearly half of the world's steel, as well as abundant supplies of coal, iron ore, and kerosene-yielding petroleum (first discovered on American soil at Titusville, north of Pittsburgh, in 1859), much of it shipped to customers via the Monongahela, which became one of the busiest waterways in the western hemisphere.

As the industrial age gathered steam, the region became a magnet for immigrants seeking a better life, especially central and southern Europeans with little or no formal education, hearty souls undeterred by the prospect of demanding, often dangerous manual labor. The rapid influx of first-generation Americans gave rise to dozens of melting-pot communities that depended, directly or indirectly, on the steady demand for steel and coal.

The town of Monongahela, a horseshoe-shaped municipality located on a western bank of the river about twenty miles south of Pittsburgh, traces its roots to 1769. During the Whiskey Rebellion, an antitax insurrection that threatened the new republic during George Washington's presidency, a group of Pennsylvania rebels conducted a meeting that was credited with peacefully ending the revolt. It happened on a bluff near the present-day intersection of Main Street and Park Avenue, three blocks from Montana's boyhood residence. Like many communities in the valley,

Monongahela exploded from little more than a settlement to a vibrant town in the early years of the industrial surge, crossing 5,000 by 1900 and peaking at 8,922 residents in 1950.

During Montana's formative years in the 1960s and early '70s, with the steel and coal economy still going strong, the so-called Mon City resembled hundreds of ethnically diverse, blue-collar towns scattered across the American industrial heartland. Unemployment and crime were low. Seven new car dealers vied for business in a town with eighteen churches and eighteen taverns. A large percentage of the men in town commuted to work in mills and mines in neighboring towns, traversing the steep, circuitous two-lane roads up and around the river. Shoppers converged on the locally owned stores on Main Street for nearly every conceivable need, from hardware to prescription drugs. Most mothers stayed home to raise their children. Front doors routinely remained unlocked. But it was also a time of mounting unease, especially if you happened to be an eighteen-year-old boy with a low lottery number.

"Vietnam cast a shadow across our generation," recalled Don Devore, one of Montana's high school teammates. "The thought of having to go to Vietnam was always in the back of your mind."

After a merger of school districts, predominantly white Monongahela High School consolidated with predominantly black Donora High School, located in the steel town of Donora eight miles south. As the new Ringgold High spread classes across two campuses, the tension associated with throwing two rival communities together led to riots and unrest, some along racial lines. After a bloody stabbing incident at Monongahela, security guards patrolled the halls and a menacing vibe permeated the place.

For decades, educators in Monongahela and elsewhere had maintained a rather rigid schoolhouse discipline by cultivating a certain amount of fear. Students entered the system conditioned by their parents to respect authority figures. Those who stepped out of line were paddled, and many were destined to be punished more severely at home. "The thinking of the day was, the fear would give [the teachers] some amount of control," recalled former Ringgold teacher Steve Russell. But the students were starting to change. Many were experimenting with illicit drugs. And fear was losing its power.

Like every corner of America, Ringgold was forced to deal with a new generation of students who had been influenced by the televised civil resistance of the era, young people who felt no obligation to sit down and shut up. They had seen their contemporaries stand up for racial justice and against the Vietnam War, and they had been moved by the horror of Kent State. But at Ringgold as in other parts of the country, petulance sometimes masqueraded as legitimate protest. When the senior class learned their senior trip had been canceled, due to the rowdy behavior of the previous graduating class, a large group skipped the morning classes and began a noisy outdoor protest. The crowd eventually burst through the front doors and began running through the halls. One teacher who made the unfortunate decision to try to stop the procession, a small man who wore horn-rimmed glasses, was knocked down by a student, beaten, and stuffed in a garbage can.

In their own way, teachers were also starting to challenge authority. Organized labor had been a force in the valley for decades, winning significant wage and benefit hikes for the rank-and-file workers while fomenting an increasingly adversarial relationship with industrial management. When a union movement swept through the various autonomous school districts in the early 1970s, at a time of mounting inflation, modestly paid, newly empowered teachers all across the valley began demanding raises and other concessions. Cash-strapped school districts resisted and a wave of teacher strikes roiled the area, dividing communities and contributing to an increasingly dark civic mood.

"If you were a teacher at that time, you were really torn," said former administrator and teacher Tom Caudill. "You hated to go out on strike because you were there to make a difference for the kids. But so many teachers felt like they had to take a stand in order to negotiate a decent contract."

Even the mills and mines were prone to cyclical layoffs and occasional strikes, and the number of jobs had already peaked in the halcyon days of the postwar boom. But output and demand remained high, despite the knowledge that foreign competitors were starting to eat into the American manufacturers' business. Conditioned by the abundance of opportunity represented by the familiar red glow in the distance and by the increasingly generous contracts negotiated by the unions, relatively few students planned to continue their studies in college. "The caliber of students you had here, many of them struggled academically," said Steve Russell, who later became the principal at Ringgold. Few young people of the day talked about escaping the blue-collar life to pursue white-collar professions. Each year, large numbers of students graduated from high school and immediately went to work at a steel mill. It was easy to believe those jobs would last forever.

As the son and grandson of a steelworker, Ulice Payne understood the benefits of such a life. "For most people the steel mill was a pretty good option. Good pay. Good benefits." Some jobs were easier than others, and like many of his contemporaries, Payne learned the pecking order, from the finishing mills, where steel was cut and rolled, to the blast furnaces, which required significant intolerance to intense heat and therefore paid the most. "The problem was, beyond the mills or the military, there weren't many other good options," he said. A good student who became president of the Ringgold student body, Payne aspired to go to college, a door that would have been closed to him if he had not also been a talented basketball player. "Basketball for me was a way out, so I took it pretty seriously," said Payne, who earned an athletic scholarship to Marquette, where he played on the 1977 NCAA championship team before embarking on a successful business career.

For a generation, a steady procession of western Pennsylvania high school stars had escaped the magnetic pull of the soot and smoke by earning athletic scholarships and, in many cases, playing professional sports. The list began with two quarterbacks who, each in their own way, loomed over the landscape in the sixties: Joe Namath, who learned to throw the bomb in Beaver Falls before moving on to the University of Alabama and the New York Jets; and Johnny Unitas, a Pittsburgh native who put his buzz cut and his icy veins to work for the Baltimore Colts after matriculating at the University of Louisville. In time, sportswriters would begin referring to the area as "the cradle of quarterbacks," an appropriate description for an area that has produced a long line of nationally acclaimed signal-callers, including Johnny Lujack, George Blanda, and Babe Parilli (and, in the years after Montana, Jim Kelly, Dan Marino, and Rich Gannon).

Before becoming an all-star center fielder for the Cincinnati Reds and New York Yankees, Ken Griffey Sr. was a standout running back and wide receiver for the Donora Dragons in the late 1960s, playing on the same field where Montana would later elude tacklers. The school also produced St. Louis Cardinals slugger Stan Musial, the son of a steelworker who played baseball and basketball but not football. Minnesota Vikings kicker Fred Cox, a veteran of four Super Bowls, played four sports at Monongahela.

"You grew up hearing about all those great athletes, with an understanding that there was something pretty special about this area," said Don Devore, one of Montana's high school teammates, whose father owned Devore Hardware on Main Street.

Monongahela boys grew up wanting to be part of something that was important in their town, a closely watched institution that unified the community and reflected their values. Even when the football team was poor, it gave many fathers and mothers a chance to stand tall, secure in the knowledge that their boy had worked hard and paid the price to represent their little corner of the world in those autumn showdowns with neighboring towns. From the perspective of an unlettered man who worked his tail off all week, hard enough to feel it in every fiber of his body, and looked at the world through the prism of someone who often felt like an easily replaceable cog in a mighty engine, never to be patted on the back, the experience was not merely entertainment. It was validation.

The creation of Ringgold complicated the matter of the local sports teams, with two longtime rivals suddenly joining forces as the unified Ringgold Rams, who played their football games at Donora's Legion Field. Several times during Friday-night games, fights broke out in the stands, prompting the school board to reschedule games on Saturday afternoons, when, in the light of day, tempers cooled.

The Ringgold teams managed to avoid the strife. A small number of athletes fell into what Ulice Payne called the "militant camp," players who were increasingly vocal about matters political and social—away from the team. But it never touched the varsity programs, which remained color-blind zones. "When you run wind sprints with a guy long enough, and you get cursed out by your coach together, that binds you," Payne said. Writing about the situation years later, Montana said, "The players on the teams got along fine. Race was no big deal to us."

For many of the working-class athletes who wound up going out for football at Ringgold, seeking an outlet for their aggression and their ambition, the road to controlled violence on a chalked field began with daily fistfights, one young punk challenging another over some grudge or simply the desire to prove who was tougher. "I got in a fight every day, 'cause in our neighborhood, that's what you did," said Paul Timko, who was one year older than Montana. The first time he got beat up by a bigger kid, Timko ran home crying and instead of consolation, he was confronted with his parents' indifference. "One of these days," his father said, mocking his son's tears, "you'll be toughened up." The need to prove one's guts could be seen in the nervous young boys who were coaxed by friends and older brothers to confront their fears by playing hockey on frozen parts of the river, their ears attuned to the ominous sound of cracking ice. By the time the sturdy sons of steelworkers and coal miners pulled on numbered jerseys and helmets for the first time, they were already conditioned to the thrill and the pain by furious games of tackle contested in cramped backyards and vacant lots. "If you drove through town in those days, you always saw groups of boys outside, one neighborhood bunch playing another," said Don Devore. The sight was like a steady heartbeat of that time and place, because in a culture imbued with the hard-edged ethos of men who worked with their hands and needed to scrub up at night, football was more than a game. "Your parents expected you to be tough, and playing football was a big part of that," said Timko, who became Montana's first football rival.

Montana was not the sort of kid to go looking for fights but by lining up against all those boys who measured themselves through a lens that valued physical and mental toughness, he learned something he could never fully absorb from his father: how to compete.

After suffering through consecutive losing football seasons—including a winless campaign in 1970, the second year of the merger—the Ringgold administration made a change at the top in 1971. Chuck Abramski was not the sort to tolerate losing.

By the time he arrived in Monongahela, Abramski had already developed a winning reputation at several western Pennsylvania public schools. But his passion for the game often pushed him near the edge. He coached for several years at Brownsville, part of the Big Ten Conference that included Ringgold. In the days leading up to a Ringgold game against Brownsville in 1969, the Rams' coaches were convened in the office, watching opposition film, when suddenly the clicking sprockets yielded a rather amusing sight: Abramski, clearly upset, ran up to a rubber yard-line marker and kicked it so hard it landed in the stands.

Long before he coached a game at Ringgold, the players and staff knew he was different. "Chuck was a good football coach but he was also nuts," said assistant coach Alan Veliky.

By the summer of '71, the high caliber of high school football played in the western part of the state was widely acknowledged across the country. Much as the rise of the steel industry could be traced to the abundance of the essential elements required to produce the metal—iron ore, limestone, and coal—football thrived in the area at least in part because several key ingredients conspired to make the sport such a force: the ethnic diversity of the steelworkers and coal miners who flooded the region and began mingling their bloodlines; their suitability to the sort of exertion required by the game and the resulting societal emphasis on physical strength and toughness; and the influences of harsh geography and decentralized population trends that tended to produce small communities located only a few miles apart, which promoted a civic chain of independence, pride, and rivalry. All this, and the sons of steelworkers really liked to hit.

Like many other aspects of Ringgold, the football program was accustomed to a certain austerity that approached neglect. When Abramski arrived, he discovered a shopping cart full of beat-up old shoes with missing cleats, the mud still caked on from the previous season. Some of the uniforms didn't match. Some of the shoulder pads were falling apart. They were still using the old-style suspension helmets, the ones with very little insulation between head and plastic. After linebacker Rich Goldberg suffered a concussion, his father bought him a modern helmet with inflatable padding—the kind many prosperous schools across the country had been wearing for several years. His teammates treated the helmet like a technological marvel. One night, in a spurt of surging team pride, some of the players gathered at the gym and spray-painted their old headgear, adorning each with a ram's horn, drawn by hand. Some horns wound up bigger than others.

Meeting with parents and players, Abramski pushed an optimistic line, determined to build a winning foundation on a winning attitude. Frequently he reminded all who would listen, "Losing can be a habit; so can winning."

Soon after taking over, he announced a summer weight-lifting program to get his players into shape before preseason practice. But this exposed a problem: The school didn't have a weight room. After years of resisting the influence of free weights, many football coaches across the country were just starting to embrace the idea, and Abramski was determined to ride the wave. Without a budget to tap, he worked with a group of players and their parents to build weights—some of which were assembled out of spare parts in the basement of Devore Hardware.

To conduct his weight-training program, Abramski commandeered the cramped basement of a nearby grammar school, crowding the equipment alongside an ancient coal-fired furnace, which had recently been abandoned. The night when they moved in, the room was covered in soot. The ceiling was so low, many of the players had to duck. In the heat of the day, with no air-conditioning, it felt like a sweatbox.

"It was like a dungeon," Carl Crawley recalled with a chuckle.

"We didn't know anything about weights," said offensive lineman Don Devore. "But we knew we wanted to get better, and that summer we all worked hard in that weight room to get stronger . . . which brought us closer as a team."

Not everyone showed up.

The same activity that promoted unity also created dissension.

By the time he graduated from Finleyville Junior High and entered Ringgold in '71, Montana was well established as a three-sport athlete. At Finleyville, he had started as a seventh-grader on the ninth-grade basketball team. "A real money player even then," in the words of head coach Tom Caudill. Instead of playing on the junior high football team, he had continued with the Monongahela Wildcats, growing stronger and more confident with each passing year. About the time his new football teammates at Ringgold were sweating in the weight room, Montana was busy playing summer baseball, in which he alternately pitched and played shortstop. Montana could bring the heat. He pitched three perfect games in the youth leagues and would become a powerful force on the mound for Ringgold as well, but his zeal to win sometimes caused him to press too hard, especially if the fastball hurler was two or three runs down and needed a strikeout. "Joe could be very emotional out there," said junior high competitor and high school teammate Ulice Payne. "If he was in trouble, you had to stay light on your feet in the batter's box. He really needed to win."

Abramski was not impressed with Montana's versatility. He saw the young man's absence as a direct challenge to his authority and proof that he was not sufficiently committed to football.

"Chuck took it personally," said quarterbacks coach Jeff Petrucci. "He had no compassion for kids playing other sports. He wasn't one of those guys who wanted to share his athletes."

The first preseason camp under Abramski was intense. After moving out of their homes and into the Monongahela gymnasium, where they slept on army cots, the Rams practiced three times a day in the blistering August sun as the new coach ran around the field jerking helmets, yelling obscenities, filling the space with his manic sense of purpose.

"All of us had heard about Coach Abramski from his previous job down at Brownsville, and then, that first day, we learned what a maniac he was," said quarterback Paul Timko. "His idea was to treat us like a drill sergeant, to make it so rough on all of us that we'd bond together."

The players grew accustomed to a familiar refrain, usually delivered after an especially heated drill.

"Son, I'm bustin' your fucking ass 'cause I love you!

"When I stop bustin' your fucking ass, you'll know I don't care!"

But just as the general student population was starting to openly resist authority, athletes in 1971 were no longer so easy to dominate.

When only about half the team returned to the practice field after lunch on the first day, an agitated Abramski sent one of his assistants to the cafeteria to fetch the rest of the squad. Several minutes later, he trotted back onto the field alone. "They're all gone."

"Piss on 'em," Abramski thundered. "We don't need 'em."

Among those who quit were several returning starters, including a linebacker who happened to be one of the best athletes on the team. In the days ahead, Abramski kept pushing, believing, like Woody Hayes and Bear Bryant, that the hard-line tactics would separate the wheat from the chaff.

Like many others, Devore experienced the sort of pain he had never felt in his life—deep in the pit of his churning stomach and deep in his cramping legs. Lying on his cot at night, as he heard some of his teammates fighting back tears, his own eyes welled up. He considered quitting. But at this moment of weakness, his thoughts turned to his mother and father, who had not wanted him to play football. "I couldn't figure out what I would say to them . . . how they would react," he said.

The ones who stayed demonstrated their commitment to building a winning football program at Ringgold, including a sophomore quarterback named Montana, who earned his way onto the varsity roster. Like other coaches before him, Abramski could see Montana's talent but, for reasons that had less to do with performance than his absence during the off-season program, the coach kept him on the bench while Timko took most of the snaps. One year after a winless campaign, the Rams finished a vastly improved 4–6, demonstrating to one and all that Abramski was leading the program in the right direction.

The first hint of trouble arrived by telephone.

Carl Crawley's home phone rang around midmorning, before he started his daily beer rounds.

"Carl, I think you need to get over here. . . ."

Concerned after a brief conversation with a friend at the Monongahela campus of Ringgold, Crawley got in his car on that August day in
1972 and made the short drive to the school. When he arrived, Joe Montana Sr., his good friend and hunting buddy, was in the midst of a heated
conversation with Abramski. Upset with the way the coach was treating
his son, the father was threatening to transfer the boy to nearby Butler
High, where he had a friend on the coaching staff.

Years after he began encouraging his son to make the most of his athletic skill, the senior Montana remained a constant presence in Joey's sporting life, watching intently from the bleachers, filling the air with the
whiff of great expectations. The father was always in the son's head,
reminding him to be precise in his mechanics and motivating him with
the glorious possibilities within his reach, if only he played up to his potential. In time, the world would come to see Montana as an extension
of Bill Walsh, but it was the pushing and prodding by Joe Senior which
made that Montana possible, exerting a deep influence that set his son on
the road to greatness.

Up to this point, according to those who were around at the time, the
father had always deferred to his son's coaches and never interfered with
their decisions. "Joe's father never bothered me as a coach," said Tom
Caudill, his junior high basketball coach. "Yes, he would come to practice, practically every night. But he never came up to me [saying], why
aren't you doing this or that? Joe's dad wasn't like that."

But by refusing to give Montana a chance to win the starting quarterback job heading into his junior season, Abramski had crossed a line with
the father, who felt compelled to stick up for his boy.

Standing in the breezeway between the two buildings, Crawley and
another family friend attempted to defuse the situation. "I tried to calm
Joe down," he said. At that point, Crawley wasn't interested in diving into
the issue of whether Joe should be playing quarterback. "I just didn't want
to see him move his kid on a whim . . . do something he might regret . . .
because I felt like the situation would work itself out."

News of the confrontation reached the players, and when Montana returned to practice, some of his teammates were not very happy to see him. Especially among Timko's friends, Montana's failure to participate in the off-season workouts created a certain amount of bad blood that would not soon dissipate. Amid the whispers about closed-door meetings, they were left wondering how the father's intervention would affect their team and the quarterback competition.

During a scrimmage, Montana faded into the pocket and was immediately crushed by Timko, who was playing both ways, and fellow defensive end Chuck Smith.

"I heard the crack," said Devore, the left tackle. "One of the hardest hits I've ever heard. You could almost hear the air going out of Joe as he hit the ground."

Timko delivered his lick with such force, Smith tumbled to the ground alongside the quarterback. "I took more of a blow than Joe did," Smith recalled with a laugh many years later. "Paul just crushed the both of us."

As the quarterback crawled off the ground, Abramski got in the face of every offensive lineman, apparently believing that they were not blocking for Montana.

"They go full speed all the time!" Abramski yelled, pointing toward the defense.

"You go full speed all the time!" he thundered toward the offense.

Soon all the linemen were running laps.

The experience of facing off against his rival every day in such a direct way toughened Montana, but also left him increasingly weary. "Every day he just beat the hell out of me," remembered Montana, who didn't play defense and therefore never got the chance to hit back.

In the season opener against the Elizabeth Forward Warriors, Timko started and was shaky. At the half, after he had tossed two interceptions and Ringgold trailed 14–0, Abramski grabbed him by the face mask and flashed a nasty look. "One more and I'm putting Montana in!"

When he was picked off again, on the second play of the second half, a mistake that led to yet another Warriors touchdown, the coach inserted Montana, who performed reasonably well but could not manage to affect the devastating 34–6 loss.

Confronted with a simmering quarterback controversy that divided the community and the team, Abramski still resisted starting Montana, which provoked a nasty shouting match with quarterbacks coach Jeff Petrucci.

"Because Joe hadn't come to the off-season lifting program, Chuck didn't want to play him," Petrucci said. "He was wrong and I told him he was wrong. It got pretty heated . . . Joe did nothing wrong. Absolutely nothing . . . Chuck just couldn't deal with the fact that [Montana] wasn't a one hundred percent football player. It was all Chuck's ego."

Like many other coaches across the country, Abramski could not feel the cultural winds shifting. He lived in a world where the football coach was a demigod, able to impose his will on the field and off, mashing all those disparate personalities into one powerful organism, squeezing so hard that the individual eventually disappeared. Montana was probably the first football player Abramski ever encountered who wasn't completely committed to football. By asserting his right to play basketball and baseball—and therein challenging the head coach's definition of commitment—he was saying he didn't want Joe Montana to disappear.

Abramski's zealous coaching played a significant role in Montana's development, but Petrucci, who doubled as a driver's education teacher, proved to be a much greater influence in his evolution as a passer. A former record-setting quarterback at California University of Pennsylvania, he was the first to work with Joe to throw the ball at precise points on the field, helping him hone a skill that would become crucial in the years to come.

Watching the way Abramski treated Montana left a profound impact on Petrucci. When he became a high school and college head coach, he was determined to strike a different chord. "I wanted kids to play other sports, and was a big proponent that kids need to hear from other coaches and be around other players," he said.

Like many others around the program, Petrucci believed Montana was the better quarterback and deserved the chance to start. During the closed-door argument with his boss, he pushed an idea he had already floated with the rest of the staff: They should start Montana at quarterback and move Timko to tight end, where the Rams had just lost a player to a season-ending injury. Abramski believed Timko was the better player and rejected the idea at first, yelling about the need to reward an athlete who had paid the off-season price. By attaching such meaning to the weight program, Abramski was questioning Montana's toughness while promoting an idea that undermined him with the other players: How could he ever be really good if football didn't mean everything to him? Such thoughts never completely vacated the coach's mind, but under the circumstances, Petrucci's argument proved to be too compelling.

When the next game on the schedule was canceled because the rival's schoolteachers went on strike—a common occurrence in those days, as the newly assertive unions tried to maximize their leverage during football season—administrators hastily arranged a scrimmage against Churchill. Montana looked impressive running the offense, and Abramski agreed to start him the following week against powerful Monessen.

A good athlete with a strong arm, powerful legs, and a linebacker's manner, somewhat in the mold of future Pittsburgh Steelers quarterback Ben Roethlisberger, Timko lacked one quality that would define and empower Montana. The pressure—and the lingering residue of his mistakes—often overwhelmed him. For a quarterback, this can be a debilitating weakness. Trotting back onto the field against Elizabeth Forward, he was still consumed by Abramski's warning, still bothered by his last interception, which clouded his judgment and his focus.

"I had a hard time letting stuff go," he said. "Joe wasn't like that. He had a real quarterback mentality. Nothing seemed to bother him."

The way Montana battled for the position earned Timko's respect, but the muscular young man who had been forged by all those neighborhood fights, by all those years of absorbing and administering powerful licks in the youth leagues that constituted a feeder system for Ringgold, struggled to compartmentalize his own surging fury. "We were too competitive to be friends," he said. "Can you ever be friends with someone you're competing with? . . . Somebody who's trying to take your job?"

By Montana's junior year, when he was driving to school in a little sports car, teachers and administrators at Ringgold were whispering among themselves what they were hearing from the athletic coaching staff: This Montana kid has the makings of something special.

For all the inherent danger in the way his father pushed him, it was clear that Montana had absorbed all the teaching and the single-mindedness without gaining an inflated sense of his own importance.

He didn't strut. He didn't mouth off. He didn't cause any trouble. Still skinny, growing toward six foot two, with long hair, he cast an introverted air that disarmed those who were inclined to be sensitive to the flowering of athletic entitlement.

Throughout his life, Montana's family, friends, and teammates were struck by the dichotomy in his personality. "Once he walked on the field, you look at him and can tell, that's the guy in charge," said 49ers receiver Dwight Clark. "He was the five-star general who had this aura about him. You wanted to follow that guy into battle." But the same man who commanded a huddle with a quiet but firm presence, able to approach the most desperate situation on a football field with ice water in his veins, repeatedly seizing the moment with confidence and a clear head as millions watched, was rather shy in real life. He did not like to be the center of attention. Too much focus on him made him uncomfortable, and he was the sort of man who battled nerves if he had to speak in front of a crowd. In most instances, whether he was fifteen or thirty-five, he happily faded into the wallpaper, which once led 49ers running back Wendell Tyler to remark, "If you didn't know Joe, you wouldn't know he was Joe Montana."

In homeroom at Ringgold, teacher Steve Russell sometimes needed to remind him to keep his hands off the girls.

"Oh, Mr. Russell," he would respond apologetically, while sheepishly lowering his head.

"I almost felt guilty for saying anything, Joe was so nice, so self-effacing."

Some nights, Montana stopped by the filling station where Russell pumped gas to make a little extra money, shooting the breeze while his teacher earned eighty-five cents per hour.

Around his teammates, he developed a reputation as a practical joker who enjoyed pulling silly gags, such as filling one guy's underwear with shaving cream or hiding another's shoes. "We learned if something was going on . . . if something was missing . . . Joe was probably behind it," said basketball teammate Ulice Payne.

This sort of behavior would become a fixture of his competitive life. As the undisputed leader of the San Francisco 49ers, he often went to great lengths to mess with his teammates. He was always hiding Roger Craig's keys. Once, after practice, he stole Freddie Solomon's clothes, making one of his favorite targets . . . one of his favorite targets. During a 49ers training camp, several members of the team walked out of the dining hall to find their bicycles dangling from the lofty branches of a nearby tree—wondering how the culprit managed to climb so high with such a payload. "If something happened, you could put your money on Joe," explained teammate Guy McIntyre. "He was almost always the person behind the prank."

Such mischief was his way of keeping things light, reflecting the only child's way of treating his teammates like the brothers he never had. He loved being one of the guys, until it was time for him to take the field and morph into that other Joe Montana.

"Joe was a nice kid," Timko said. "I don't think he got in a lot of fights growing up."

Even after he overcame the timidity that coaches saw early in his youth football career, Montana approached the contact inherent in the game as a means to an end. He did not need to hit somebody to feel better about himself. To him, football was never about rage. The driving force behind his competitiveness was an unmistakable joy of playing the game—and finding a way to win.

"Joe is not an aggressive human being," Petrucci said. "Now, you put him in a position to compete, then you'll see aggression."

On a memorable Saturday, the last day of September 1972, the Ringgold players put on their uniforms and helmets, loaded onto a yellow school bus, and made the short drive to Monessen. It was common in those days for teams in the area to dress at home, for two principal reasons: The schools were so closely situated, and most of the visiting dressing rooms were cramped or nonexistent. At Monessen, the visitors congregated before the game and at halftime in the woodshop classroom at the adjoining trade school. The players also understood the need to keep their helmets on at all times, because opposing fans sometimes threw bottles and rocks.

One of the powerhouse programs in the WPIL (Western Pennsylvania Interscholastic League), the Monessen Greyhounds, who had allowed just six points in three games, were favored to capture the Big Ten Conference championship—and wipe the field with the struggling Ringgold Rams. A large crowd of perhaps 6,000 packed into the stadium, which the newspapers referred to as "The Hounds Lair," to see well-established stars such as Monessen running back Bubby Holmes, headed to Minnesota, and Ringgold linebacker Chuck Smith, who later played for West Virginia. Many fans weren't sure who Ringgold's number 13 was when the game started. Soon they would all learn his name.

"We all learned that night what we had in Joe," said teammate Chuck Smith. "He was a natural and Monessen didn't know how to deal with him."

Trailing 7–0 early in the first quarter, Montana faded into the pocket from his own 21 yard line and hit Timko for a 19-yard completion. Montana to Timko. It was a combination that would be seen and heard all night long—totaling eight receptions and three touchdowns—as a new age dawned between old rivals. "The combination," wrote local sportswriter Ed Gray, "was just too much for the Hounds to cope with."

As the teams battled to a 34–34 tie that Gray proclaimed "a moral victory" for Ringgold, Montana completely vindicated Petrucci and others who had been pushing for him to take the job. Completing 13 of 24 passes for 256 yards and four touchdowns—including the first of many to his friend Mike Brantley—he looked like a quarterback who was going somewhere.

"That game put Joe on the map," Petrucci said. "It was a real defining moment."

That night and in many others to come, teammates often were struck by Montana's calm demeanor, the way he never got too excited, too high or too low.

An example of his unflappability could be seen during a game against Laurel Highlands. Following a Ringgold touchdown, fullback Craig Garry trotted onto the field to relay the two-point conversion play from the head coach. In the excitement, Garry forgot the play. "I just went blank," Garry recalled. Many quarterbacks faced with such a situation would have called a time-out and jogged to the sideline. Not Joe Cool. "Joe didn't miss a beat," Garry said. "He just calmly called a play—a 36 slant pass—to me, threw it perfectly, I caught it, and we had our two points."

In a preview of coming attractions, Ringgold claimed a 14–12 victory over Belle Vernon Area when Montana rallied the Rams for the winning touchdown with 1:29 left, finding receiver Don Miller in the end zone.

Ironically, no player benefited from Montana's ascendance more directly than the man he had supplanted. Timko thrived at tight end, attracting attention from recruiters all over the country before signing with the University of Maryland. He didn't realize it until the switch was made, but he also felt more at ease as a receiver, removed from the mental burden of being a quarterback. "It was nice to have all the pressure off, the pressure of winning and losing on your shoulders," he said. But at the same time, he struggled to let go of the one that got away. It bothered him, the way things worked out. He replayed it over and over again in his mind, wondering what might have been.

Before the first bell, Montana often could be found in the Monongahela gym playing basketball. Plenty of regular students and even teachers showed up to take part in the pickup affairs, and anyone who wound up with the short straw of having to guard Montana was in for a sweaty first period.

Endowed with an impressive vertical leap for a man who was still growing to six foot two, Montana was Ringgold's designated jump ball specialist, even though the team's center, Ulice Payne, was six foot six and headed for the Final Four. Often, as the teams approached center court for the opening tip-off, the sight of Montana drew snickers—until he outleaped his much taller competitor to control the ball. Frank LaMendola, the Rams' head coach, moved him into the starting lineup as a sophomore. "Joe was very coachable and led by example on the court rather than by words," recalled LeMendola, who called him "very unselfish." Working at both forward and guard—and even, after Payne's graduation, at center—Montana could can it from long range and he could drive powerfully to the hoop. He was a vigorous defender. His ability to quickly flick an outlet pass to half court was instrumental in Ringgold's fast-break offense.

Nearly a decade before he would be called upon to master the quick reads of the West Coast Offense, Montana displayed an uncanny ability to find the open man with what could best be described as an intuitive touch. Long before Jerry Rice, Roger Craig, and John Taylor entered his field of vision, he practiced the art of just-in-time delivery on the basketball court, hitting Ringgold players including Payne, Mike Brantley, and Melvin Boyd at the precise instant they became open—and sometimes even an instant before.

"Our coaches would get really pissed off because Joe would try passes that a lot of guys couldn't pull off," Payne said. "But he had a knack. His timing was something. His eyes were always up and he was always looking to pass."

His passing ability became a powerful weapon for the Rams, especially when opponents tried to press. "Nobody could press us [effectively], because Joe could throw it anywhere," recalled assistant coach Alan Veliky.

During Montana's junior year, he was part of the greatest basketball team in Ringgold history, featuring five starters who earned Division I college scholarships. The 27–2 Rams strung together sixteen straight victories and finished third in the state tournament, losing in the semifinals to a General Braddock team they had already beaten twice.

On an electric night at the Civic Arena in Pittsburgh, 8,900 fans showed up to watch the Rams knock off General Braddock, 54–47, to capture the WPIL championship. The Falcons pressed nearly the entire game, and Montana proved to be the key man in consistently breaking the defense, demonstrating the poise that would define his athletic career.

"I thought that was Joe's finest hour," Payne said. "The only way we were going to win was if we could break the press. When it really counted, Joe never got flustered."

This defining trait carried over to the football field.

Beneath the surface, Abramski never let go of the grudge concerning his most famous pupil. He had a big mouth and a big ego and it was only a matter of time before his hurt feelings overwhelmed his judgment. But as the 1973 football season arrived, he could see Montana was the key to his team. Abramski built the Rams' offense around Montana, calling him "the next Joe Namath."

"Let's put it this way," he told a reporter from *The Pittsburgh Post-Gazette.* "Montana is taller than Namath and [former Notre Dame star Terry] Hanratty, can run faster, has as strong an arm . . . and is a better basketball player."

Prior to the season opener against Ringgold, Thomas Jefferson head coach Bap Manzini said, "We have to stop Montana. He's an excellent passer."

Employing a menacing rush, the Jaguars found a way to neutralize the senior quarterback, claiming a hard-fought 8–6 victory that turned on a failed two-point pass in the closing minutes. But it proved to be the only blemish in a breakthrough 8–1 regular season, as Montana finished his high school career with 20 touchdown passes. After leading the Rams to a share of the school's first Big Ten championship, spoiled by a first-round playoff loss, Montana earned Parade All-America honors and emerged as one of the year's most-prized recruits, fielding scholarship offers from a long list of major programs, including Georgia, Michigan State, Notre Dame, and Purdue.

Johnny Majors, who had recently taken over the long-suffering University of Pittsburgh program, tried to convince him to stay close to home. Majors was on his way to the 1976 national championship with a powerful team built around Heisman Trophy–winner Tony Dorsett. One cold and wet day at Pitt, Abramski and Petrucci were watching practice when Majors walked away from a scrimmage to visit with the two high school coaches.

"How's my boy?" the gravelly voiced Majors wanted to know.

After several minutes of small talk, much of it about Montana, Majors walked away, reached the hash mark and suddenly turned back to face the men from Ringgold.

"Make sure to tell Joe I said hello."

Abramski liked the attention Montana brought him, especially from high-profile coaches such as Majors, who accorded him a new level of respect in the wooing process, and he desperately wanted to affect his pupil's choice. Through the years, the fiery coach went out of his way to help a long list of his players earn scholarships. But he exerted little influence on Montana's college destination.

By the middle of his senior year, Montana was a young man facing two decisions. Some scouts believed he was an even better basketball player, and several major basketball schools offered him scholarships, including North Carolina State, which captured the NCAA championship that winter behind Player of the Year David Thompson. But football appeared to be his stronger option. Once he made the decision to play football, none of the other schools had a real chance. He was headed to Notre Dame.

For as long as he could remember, Montana had dreamed of playing football for the Fighting Irish, just like his boyhood idol Terry Hanratty. Now it was there for the taking. All he had to do was sign on the dotted line. He could fulfill his boyhood fantasy and make his father happy, too. Yet there was also a practical reason football and South Bend ultimately prevailed. Like his father, Montana believed, given his relatively modest stature, that he had a much better chance of playing professional football than professional basketball. Even before he departed Monongahela, he was focused on a distant end zone.

# CHAPTER TWO

# Green Jerseys

As THE INDIANA COUNTRYSIDE UNFOLDED like a picture postcard through the windshield of Ulice Payne's 1967 Chrysler New Yorker, he could tell his friend was troubled. It was the autumn of 1974, and as Payne steered the big gas-guzzler along an easterly course, headed home to Pennsylvania's Mon Valley, Joe Montana was opening up about his disappointing freshman season with the Notre Dame football team. With Tom Clements firmly established as the starting quarterback and a long list of contenders ahead of him, he had been relegated to running the scout team for the defending national champions. He was restless. He was lost in a crowd.

"He was getting a little discouraged, a little impatient," recalled Payne, who had driven through South Bend to pick up Montana on his way home from Milwaukee, where he was a sophomore at Marquette. "Suddenly he was surrounded by all these other talented athletes and they're all competing for playing time. He was looking forward to spring ball, so he could show what he could do."

Soon the conversation between young men turned to young women. Notre Dame had recently become a coeducational institution—the first women were admitted in 1972—and the student body remained overwhelmingly male (although St. Mary's College, a female-only school, was located down the street).

"What's it like going to a place with so few girls?" Payne wanted to know as the big Chrysler thundered along toward steel country.

Not long after this trip, Montana imported his own girl from back home. Kim Moses was a pretty young woman who had grown up just down the street from Payne in Donora. She was Montana's first real girlfriend, at a time when the consuming focus on his athletic ambitions allowed little time for anything else. Montana's parents tried to convince their son to wait. They were both so young. But the quarterback knew what he wanted. Eighteen-year-old Joe and nineteen-year-old Kim said their vows at South Bend's Sacred Heart Catholic Church on January 4, 1975. Kim landed a job as a secretary in the sports information office and they moved into a small apartment in the nearby town of Mishawaka.

The origins of Notre Dame football can be traced to 1887, when the sport spread from the pioneering schools of the Northeast into the Midwest, but it was a trip to the towering cliffs of the Hudson River in 1913 that put the small Catholic school on the map. When the unheralded Fighting Irish traveled by train to take on the powerful Black Knights from the United States Military Academy at West Point, quarterback Gus Dorais and end Knute Rockne unleashed the football equivalent of an ambush. At a time when the forward pass remained an obscure weapon, used only in desperation, Dorais shocked the cadets with his aerial aggressiveness and mastery, completing 13 of 17 for 243 yards, including a 40-yard touchdown bomb to Rockne. The 35–13 rout established the power of the forward pass and turned the giant killer into a giant.

Under the direction of the astute and innovative Rockne, who was hired as the school's head coach in 1918, Notre Dame became the most iconic program in college football. In a remarkable thirteen-year run, the Fighting Irish posted five perfect seasons and won 88 percent of their games, featuring a string of All-Americans including tragic hero George Gipp, who was later immortalized by a young Ronald Reagan in the Hollywood tearjerker *Knute Rockne All-American*. When Rockne, on his way to California to star in an instructional film, died in a plane crash, fans across the land felt a profound sense of loss.

For Catholics across America, Notre Dame football emerged as a source of tremendous affinity and pride. At a time when religious intolerance still flowered in various parts of the country, the excellence embodied by the Fighting Irish united parishioners in a secular pursuit deeply engrained in the national character. "It made us all stand a little taller," remarked Edmund P. Joyce, a onetime altar boy who became the university's longtime executive vice president.

Fawning coverage by prominent sportswriters in New York and elsewhere—especially the influential Grantland Rice, who introduced the world to the fabled "Four Horsemen" in the 1920s—reinforced Notre Dame's unusual place in the sporting culture. Aggressive use of radio in the early years of the medium helped cement the program's continental constituency, eventually paving the way for a short-lived network television contract in the early 1950s that reflected the power of the Fighting Irish as a commercial draw—and ultimately, caused a backlash among peer colleges that prompted the majority to unite behind a system that severely restricted TV coverage. Many officials simply feared competing with the Fighting Irish, and the resulting bureaucracy their majority will forever empowered—the National Collegiate Athletic Association—sprang to life as a heavy-handed attempt to moderate the free-market forces embodied by the school's widely envied subway alumni. By midcentury, the combination of competitive success, media favoritism, and just plain jealousy earned Notre Dame a unique distinction: At once, it was the most beloved and most despised college football program in America.

After Rockne's premature death, Notre Dame remained a dominant force under Frank Leahy, who won four national championships in seven years behind Heisman Trophy–winners Angelo Bertelli, Johnny Lujack, and Leon Hart.

By the early 1960s, however, the program was imploding. The slide began soon after Leahy's premature exit in 1954 and accelerated under Joe Kuharich, a onetime Irish guard who arrived in South Bend after largely unsuccessful stints with the National Football League's Chicago Cardinals and Washington Redskins. In the spring of 1963, when Kuharich abruptly left Notre Dame to take a position at the NFL headquarters, the Irish football program was thrown into the sort of turmoil that only slightly exceeded his just-completed tenure as head coach: 5–5, 2–8, 5–5, and 5–5, a steaming pot of mediocrity that inspired near rebellion among the alumni and plummeting confidence among the players. Despite continuing support from the administration, Kuharich abandoned the school at the worst possible time in the football cycle, when finding a suitable replacement for the coming season would prove extremely difficult. Feeling the need to stabilize the situation while providing the time to search for a permanent coach, the Notre Dame president, Father Theodore Hesburgh, one of the most influential religious figures in America, and his right-hand man, Father Joyce, who oversaw the athletic department, promoted career assistant Hugh Devore to run the program in 1963. Under Devore, the bleeding of a once-proud institution intensified. After the Irish finished 2–7, Devore was thanked for his service and shown the door. One and done.

By the time the British Invasion of American popular music took the country by storm in 1964, Notre Dame had suffered through five straight nonwinning seasons. It took an intense Presbyterian named Ara Parseghian to wake up the echoes. At Northwestern, a small private school surrounded by the giant land-grant institutions of the Big Ten, the son of Armenian immigrants had won more than he had lost, including four straight victories over fast-fading Notre Dame. In South Bend, his impact was immediate. Quickly restoring Notre Dame to national prominence with a 9–1 season in '64, Parseghian soon emerged as one of the sport's leading coaches, capturing the first of two national championships two years later, despite a controversial 10–10 tie with Michigan State, when he was widely mocked for running out the clock.

By the end of the sixties, one aspect of the Notre Dame program seemed increasingly anachronistic. For forty-five years, the administration routinely declined all bowl invitations, determined to avoid the sort of academic disruptions caused by the team's trip to the 1925 Rose Bowl. Of all the battles Parseghian won on behalf of Notre Dame football, perhaps the most important and far-reaching was his leading role in convincing the university administration to overturn the postseason ban. "After all those years, the resistance was still very significant," Parseghian said. "But I felt very strongly that we needed to be playing in bowl games. It was an important step to take for our program." It also helped that university officials saw the significant fees paid to participating teams as a way to fund academic scholarships. When Notre Dame returned to the bowl scene on January 1, 1970, losing to national champion Texas 24–11 in the Cotton Bowl, the bowl system was transformed. The change would profoundly shape the ensuing years of Notre Dame football, including the fast-approaching career of a quarterback from Monongahela, making possible a moment that would define him for the ages.

As Montana moved from high school to college, the sport was transitioning from one era to the next, still grappling for definition. The last of the nation's major teams had finally integrated, closing an unfortunate chapter that once reflected the cultural stain of segregation. Starting in 1972, the NCAA had begun allowing freshmen to play in varsity games, a revolutionary change destined to profoundly affect the sport. The increasingly activist governing body was moving aggressively to limit the number of scholarships a team could award, which would promote a new age of parity. The NCAA still maintained firm control over the sport's presence on national television, restricting even the most prominent programs, including Notre Dame's, to no more than two appearances in a single year, an artificial limit that many schools were beginning to question. (The Sunday replay of the Irish games was not subject to the ban.) Fans across the country could watch just one live game each Saturday on the ABC television network, an exclusivity that gave every contest the feel of a big event.

On the last Saturday of November in 1973, millions of fans from coast to coast tuned in to see Bo Schembechler's undefeated Michigan Wolverines battle Woody Hayes's undefeated Ohio State Buckeyes to a hard-fought 10–10 tie. This intense rivalry game reflected college football at its best—and worst. Regional spheres of influence still promoted a certain amount of athletic provincialism, and the Big Ten remained trapped in a bygone age. While 10–0–1 Ohio State, by virtue of a Big Ten vote, would go on to represent the conference in the Rose Bowl, 10–0–1 Michigan was forced to stay home for the holidays because the league prevented its teams from playing in other postseason games. Maddening as this arcane rule was to Michigan and its fans, the resulting controversy eventually spurred the Big Ten and Pac-8, its Rose Bowl partner, to change course and allow their teams to fully participate in the postseason, bringing big-time college football a bit closer to a game the next generation would recognize.

Four years into the new age of bowling, on December 31, 1973, Parseghian took what may have been his best team to face Alabama in the Sugar Bowl at Tulane Stadium in New Orleans. The Crimson Tide, coached by the towering Paul "Bear" Bryant, was a juggernaut that had already been proclaimed the national champion by United Press International, the poll of coaches that traditionally selected its titlist before the bowl games. (This too would soon change.) The Associated Press media trophy remained up for grabs, and the epic battle of unbeaten college football brand names—meeting for the first time—lived up to the considerable hype. With about two minutes remaining, backed up to his own three-yard line, Notre Dame quarterback Tom Clements converted one of the greatest third-and-eights in college football history. Needing a first down to maintain possession and prevent a possible winning score by the Crimson Tide, Clements retreated into the end zone, eluded the rush, and fired a pass toward a secondary receiver, tight end Robin Weber, who caught the ball cleanly at the 38. Game over. Notre Dame ran out the clock on a dramatic 24–23 victory, securing Parseghian's second national championship and launching Ara and his era toward the lofty realm forever occupied by Rockne and Leahy.

Eight months later, Montana arrived in South Bend as part of a large freshman class featuring many of the best high school players in America. Even as he started making friends, struggled to keep up with the sometimes rigorous demands of his classwork, and began to negotiate the first tentative steps of independence, it did not take him long to begin feeling invisible and insignificant on the football team. His goal to "play varsity as a freshman" proved unrealistic.

Like most major schools, Notre Dame fielded a junior varsity team that played a limited schedule to give younger athletes a chance to prove themselves. But even on the JV team, Montana was overlooked as fellow freshmen Gary Forystek, Kerry Moriarty, and Mike Falash took most of the snaps. In three games, he threw a grand total of six passes, completing just one.

"No one cared about how I was performing," he recalled. "Psychologically, things were really tough for me . . . I had to walk into a stadium full of people and couldn't even dress for the [varsity] game."

In practice, he spent most of his time mimicking the opposing quarterback, giving the first team a good look, fighting to be noticed.

"I knew Joe had great potential, and we had very high hopes for him, but he was behind some pretty good quarterbacks," Parseghian said. "The first thing you noticed right away was he had good escapability. He could evade a rush and he could stand in the pocket on third-and-eight and make something happen."

After guiding the Fighting Irish to a 9–2 mark, Parseghian shocked the college football establishment by announcing his resignation, telling the press, "I am emotionally and physically exhausted." The decision transformed the Orange Bowl rematch two weeks later against first-ranked Alabama into a sentimental farewell. Parseghian's exit—after a 13–11 victory over Bama—unwittingly altered the trajectory of Montana's career.

"I must be some kind of genius," he quipped many years later. "I recruit Joe Montana and retire the next year."

In the closing days of 1963, when the deal with Parseghian nearly fell apart after news of it prematurely leaked to the press, Father Joyce was prepared to offer the job to Missouri's Dan Devine, one of the hottest young coaches in the game. A decade later, his enthusiasm for Devine had not cooled. At the time of Parseghian's retirement, the man who had won two Big Eight championships in Columbia was rapidly being chased out of the state of Wisconsin. After four years as head coach of the Green Bay Packers, where Vince Lombardi's ghost shadowed him at every turn,

Devine appeared to be on the fast track to the unemployment line. When Joyce approached him once again, this time to take over a program firmly established alongside Nebraska, Alabama, Ohio State, Southern Cal, and several others in the sport's upper echelon, he was eager to return to the college game and escape the stench of his own failure, even if it meant succeeding such a popular and dynamic coach.

Disappointed by the departure of the man who had recruited him, Montana nevertheless hoped the new guy would recognize his talent. Devine quickly became troubled by his practice habits, which was understandable because the sixth team quarterback was not a player who enjoyed practice or looked particularly impressive on the practice field. Much as he found it difficult to get excited about his accounting classes, Montana struggled to see the connection between football preparation and performance, and this created a wedge between the player and his head coach. When Devine called him in to his office and demanded to know why he was not displaying a better command of the offense, Montana told him he had been shooting pool the night before, instead of studying his playbook. "I was pretty rough on him," Devine said. "Probably too rough. But I wanted him to realize that he had to improve."

Like most coaches, Devine believed practice reflected readiness—that a player inevitably played on Saturday the way he had rehearsed during the week. He also viewed playing time as a reward earned by practicing well. "Ninety-nine percent of the time, that philosophy is probably right," said fullback Steve Orsini, another Pennsylvania product who watched the unfolding drama. "I know it was in my case. I got better as I worked harder. But Joe wasn't that way. Some of Joe's best qualities didn't kick in until you started to keep score . . . and Coach Devine couldn't see that."

The first hint of this deeper truth came into view during the 1975 spring game when Montana completed 7 of 12 passes for 131 yards and three touchdowns, an impressive performance that brought him out of the shadows and into direct competition with junior Rick Slager, who opened the season as the starter. The issue remained unsettled throughout the fall, as the indecisive Devine appeared incapable of making a choice and sticking with it. At times, Montana played poorly and gave Devine reason to doubt him, including a 10–3 home loss to Michigan State, his first career start. But the mythical rise of Montana as a Notre Dame folk hero began with two memorable games that October.

On a steamy afternoon in Chapel Hill, prohibitive favorite Notre Dame trailed the North Carolina Tar Heels, 14–6. After watching the struggling Slager throw three straight incompletions, Devine benched him. When Montana ran onto the field, the clock showed 6:04 remaining.

"None of us knew we were witnessing the birth of something," recalled Ken MacAfee, the three-time All-America tight end. "All we knew is we were in a pretty desperate situation."

One of the attributes Devine could not see in practice was Montana's innate competitiveness when the scoreboard glowed. In live action—especially when the situation appeared dire—he suddenly became a different person, driven by a combination of instinct, experience, and adrenaline to harness some deeper force. Everything in his life seemed to be a contest: He wanted to be first out of the shower after practice so he could be first in line at the chow hall. If he was shooting pool and the loser bought the beer, he was pushing with every fiber of his being to win the prize. If you challenged him to throw stones at a sign, he treated the experience like the Super Bowl. "Joe's competitiveness was just off the charts," said Steve Orsini.

The other quality that escaped Devine was the way Montana seemed oblivious to the pressure of a tense situation, projecting a radiating confidence, filling the huddle with a sense of urgency but also an unmistakable calm.

"In situations like that, you just felt comfortable with Joe," said Notre Dame tailback Vagas Ferguson, who arrived on the scene in 1976. "Regardless of down-and-distance. Regardless of the yard line. It was his presence. He just put us all at ease."

It took Montana just five plays to march the Irish 73 yards. Al Hunter's two-yard run and Montana's two-point pass to Doug Buth tied the score, 14–14.

After North Carolina drove nearly the length of the field before missing a short field goal, Montana took over at his own 20 yard line with 1:19 remaining. A field goal would win it, and as he broke the huddle and a deafening roar engulfed Kenan Stadium, the call was a draw play up the middle. Devine wanted a quick first down. But as he looked out across the defense, Montana watched the cornerback take two steps back. Click. There it was. He knew exactly what the movement represented: the vulnerability it created for the defense and the opportunity it offered for the offense. When he pulled back from center, he saw receiver Ted Burgmeier wide open, in the seam created by the cornerback's adjustment, running a seven-yard out. As the rush approached, he rifled a pass into the distance. It landed cleanly and the pursuit began.

"I saw that the cornerback had overrun the play," said Burgmeier, who had previously been among Montana's quarterback rivals. "I just wanted to get what I could, then run out of bounds . . ."

After a heady fake toward the open field, Burgmeier pivoted and raced upfield, outrunning the defense for an 80-yard touchdown to give Notre Dame a stunning 21–14 victory.

In six plays, the backup quarterback had completely altered the game's complexion, turning a likely defeat into a triumph so dramatic that Devine called it "my biggest victory ever."

Still, he kept Montana on the bench.

Seven days later, as a quarterback controversy swirled, Notre Dame fell into a mighty hole on the road against Air Force. Once again, Slager started. Once again, he needed to be bailed out.

When Montana entered the game just before the half, Air Force led by a touchdown. He started the second half and, under his direction, the offense sputtered as the Falcons padded their lead, reaching a 30–10 blowout with 13:30 remaining.

"Then Joe Montana kicked in . . . like somebody flipped a switch," Orsini said.

The first drive took seven plays, culminated by the quarterback's one-yard plunge and the first of three Dave Reeve extra points, which narrowed the margin to 30–17 with 10:26 left.

Feeling the effects of Colorado Springs' 6,035-foot altitude, the Notre Dame offensive players began running off the field directly to an oxygen tank stationed near the bench, filling up for another mad dash to the end zone. "We knew we'd better get replenished, because we felt very strongly that the defense was gonna hold and Montana was gonna take us down-field again," Orsini recalled.

The second drive took three plays, including a 66-yard strike to Mark McLane, who might have gone all the way if he had not been shoved out of bounds at the seven. On the next snap, Montana hit a wide-open Mac-Afee in the back of the end zone, making it 30–24 with 5:29 remaining.

"Joe's leadership during that rally was outstanding," MacAfee said. "It showed what he was capable of. When we had Joe in there, we were never truly out of a game."

All across America, fathers and sons drenched in the lore of the Fight-ing Irish sat beside static-popping AM radios, sharing a moment energized with the feel of historic significance, consumed by the elaborate mental pictures painted by Al Wester and Pat Sheridan on the two hundred–plus station Mutual Broadcasting System network. Only two Notre Dame games were televised live that season—Boston College and Southern Cal—and so one of the greatest comebacks in Irish history demanded not passive eyeballs focused on a color screen, but active brains and ears en-gaged in the constantly changing calculus of down-and-distance, im-mersed in the tension of the unsaid, invested in the pounding drama of careful play-by-play mingled with vivid imagination.

The climax came after another stout defensive stand and a short punt, which put Notre Dame in business at the Air Force 45. Even after all those fireworks, the clock still showed 3:29 remaining when tailback Jerome Heavens squeezed in from the one, sealing a remarkable 31–30 Irish victory.

As fans across the blue-and-gold nation beamed with pride about the quarterback many were starting to call the Comeback Kid, Devine went out of his way to minimize Montana's efforts, telling reporters, "I'd hate to single out Joe as being the one responsible" for the victory.

Indeed, it was a team victory and Montana was quick to share the credit with his offense and a determined defense that kept slamming the door and forcing punts. But Devine's muted reaction to the quarterback's decisive turn at the helm seemed odd to many of his players, especially those who had seen up close the power of his leadership.

Asked whether he should be starting, Montana struck a diplomatic tone with reporters. "Sure, I'd like to start," he said. "But it's hard to explain. Maybe I can do better coming in [off the bench]."

Then the Comeback Kid vanished.

As Montana fought for playing time, a young man who would one day be a Notre Dame legend in his own right was still confined to the shadows, holding tightly to a seemingly impossible dream.

No single person has ever reflected the power of the Notre Dame mystique quite like Daniel "Rudy" Ruettiger. Growing up in the steel town of Joliet, Illinois, Ruettiger was seduced by the magnetic force of Rockne, Leahy, Parseghian, the Four Horsemen, Paul Hornung, et al . . . by an institution that symbolized excellence. Despite his unimposing five-foot-six, 185-pound frame, his modest athletic skills, and his marginal high school grades, Ruettiger dreamed of playing football for the Fighting Irish. To many of his friends and family, it seemed like a ridiculous quest, such an ordinary young man playing alongside all those great athletes. But he was undeterred by their doubts. After serving a hitch in the U.S. Navy, Ruettiger was motivated into action by the sudden death of a close friend who had encouraged him. He moved to South Bend and began working toward his dream. Finally, on his fourth try, he was admitted to Notre Dame as a twenty-five-year-old junior in the fall of 1974, which allowed him to walk on to the football team just as Montana was arriving as a freshman.

"I wasn't going to live my life in regret," he said. "That's why I worked my butt off. I didn't want to look back and regret not trying to do something that was important to me: contributing in some way to that football team and getting the chance to run out of that tunnel, just once."

For two years, as an anonymous member of the scout team, the physically overmatched Ruettiger survived the grueling experience of daily workouts while pushing the elite scholarship athletes, overcoming various hardships while proving something—to his doubters and to himself. Some players liked him. Some didn't, especially when Devine stopped practice to acknowledge the little squirt who played with such heart while helping prepare the first teamers for brutal Saturdays. *Why can't you be more like Ruettiger?* In such instances, Ruettiger always juggled two emotions: pride for the recognition and a certain gathering fear. "I wanted to say, 'Cool it, coach, these guys are a lot bigger than me and they can whip my ass,'" he recalled many years later.

Like most of the scholarship players, Montana didn't know him personally and probably couldn't call his real name on a twenty-dollar bet. But he knew him as a competitor, a tenacious little bulldog who stared out from behind his face mask with a steely resolve and fought hard on every down. "Montana was one of the ones who always showed me respect . . . encouraged me," Ruettiger said. "He understood what it meant to struggle."

After working for years to convince the right people in Hollywood to translate his story to the big screen, Ruettiger achieved yet another dream when *Rudy,* the 1993 motion picture starring Sean Astin, transformed him into Notre Dame royalty. Just like that, Rudy became as synonymous with the Fighting Irish as Knute Rockne, the Four Horsemen, and the Comeback Kid. To cross the cinematic goal line, he allowed the filmmakers to take a certain creative license with some aspects of his journey, including the decision to make Devine the heavy. All parties, including the coach, agreed such tension was needed to create sufficient narrative drama. In this, the Notre Dame mystique melded with Hollywood myth. In reality, Devine was very supportive of Ruettiger throughout his time at Notre Dame. Heading into the final home game of the 1975 season against Georgia Tech, Devine, unbeknownst to Ruettiger, planned to dress him, aided by at least two players who voluntarily offered their place on the roster. However, the bulk of the film was accurate, including the depiction of the fans chanting his name—albeit for reasons not fully explained: the notoriety he had gained as a campus boxer.

As the real-life Ruettiger made it into the game for three snaps and sacked the Georgia Tech quarterback on the final play—culminating a remarkable journey transformed by Hollywood into a universal story about one underdog's aspiration, struggle, and eventual triumph—another young man dressed in blue was feeling increasingly frustrated. In Montana's unfolding drama, Devine was fast becoming a real-life villain.

Unlike the affable, often fiery Parseghian, who closely managed every aspect of the program, infusing it with an unmistakable passion that mirrored his own, Devine was a distant, stoic figure who delegated significant authority to his assistants. To his players he could seem aloof and uninspiring. "He looks like a parish priest from Bridgeport [who] should be making sick calls someplace," *Los Angeles Times* columnist Jim Murray once wrote. Lacking Parseghian's polish and charm, he often spoke to his players in incomplete sentences containing unfinished thoughts. The manner in which he managed the operation fomented a certain amount of sniping behind his back, especially with regard to the high-profile quarterback situation. The way he handled Montana created significant locker room dissent.

"It didn't take us long to figure out Joe was the guy who should be starting," Ken MacAfee said. "We could tell he had something special. But Devine didn't care for him and Joe was pretty resentful of the way he was treated. It didn't make any sense."

In hushed tones, receiver Kris Haines often discussed the situation with his teammates. "Everybody on the team kept wondering, why doesn't [Devine] like this guy?" he recalled. "Everybody questioned what Devine had against him."

Like many others within the Notre Dame family, Parseghian, settling into retirement, was puzzled. "Dan was down on him for some reason," he said. "I have never understood exactly why. Joe felt like he was being mistreated. It was difficult for many of us to understand why Joe wasn't playing . . . why [Devine] was saving the guy until he was in trouble."

Injuries played a role. After being hampered by a broken index finger toward the end of 1975, Montana entered the final scrimmage of the 1976 preseason as the number-two quarterback on the depth chart, behind starter Rick Slager. While directing the number-two offense against the number-one defense, Montana turned to flee a fast-approaching Ross Browner and was crushed from the opposite direction by Willie Fry—a devastating lick that separated his right shoulder. "I feel bad for Joe," Devine said. "He was just starting to come along again."

After Montana worked diligently to rehabilitate the shoulder, he was cleared to play at midseason. But Devine refused to use him, casting the entire 1976 season in a fog of bitterness. He entered 1977 as the third quarterback on the depth chart, causing him to contemplate quitting the team. Imagine the impact on football history.

The way Montana responded to the situation offered a window into his personality. He bitched and moaned behind Devine's back, but never confronted him directly on the issue, never demanded a private sit-down to aggressively plead his case. This reflected two central characteristics: First, he was the sort of young man who tended to avoid confrontation. Second, he was taught to respect authority figures, even if the lip-biting came as his stomach churned with bile.

Years later, Devine struggled to try to combat the notion that he had mishandled Montana, telling one reporter, "At the time, I did things I had to do, and I tried to explain them to him, and I know it must have been hard for a kid to understand."

Wondering if he would ever get another chance to play football, Montana stoked his competitive juices during the 1977 off-season by playing on a basketball team that won a closely watched intramural tournament. Even this victory was bittersweet: It caused him to wonder if he had made the wrong decision, choosing football over basketball.

On the heels of disappointing seasons of 8–3 and 9–3 in 1975–76, Devine approached his third year with a veteran team—including eleven returning starters on defense—that was expected to contend for the national championship. After a decisive 19–9 road victory over defending national champion Pittsburgh, third-ranked Notre Dame traveled to oppressively hot Jackson, Mississippi, and suffered a shocking 20–13 loss to a mediocre Ole Miss team headed for a 5–6 finish. Montana didn't play a minute in either game.

"We weren't prepared for that Mississippi heat," recalled tailback

Vagas Ferguson, who went down with a hamstring injury against the Rebels. "Oh, man, was it hot. The fatigue factor was very high. When we got tired, it was over."

Notre Dame was an independent, without a conference championship to play for, so Irish athletes routinely focused only on the ultimate goal, which seemed to be slipping away after the disastrous trip to Mississippi. Two days later, the seniors convened a meeting without Devine's involvement. It was contentious. Several of the veterans took turns trying to light a fire. "It's gut-check time," Orsini lectured his teammates. "We're better than what we've been showing."

Lack of offensive production was one of the team's biggest problems, and Montana's frustration intensified during a road game in week three against Purdue. When starter Rusty Lisch struggled and the Irish fell behind, Devine inserted backup Gary Forystek. Chased out of the pocket, Forystek turned his head, starting to cut to the right, and was blindsided by Purdue's Fred Arrington, who staggered him with a powerful blow. "Just an unbelievable hit," said Orsini, who watched helplessly as his teammate tumbled to the ground, unconscious. Trainers immediately rushed onto the field, acting quickly to prevent him from swallowing his tongue.

Watching the disturbing scene from the sideline, Montana felt for his teammate, who was rushed to nearby St. Elizabeth's Hospital with a concussion and a fractured clavicle. (Later in the game, word arrived from the doctors that he would recover completely, but he was lost for the rest of the season.) Now Montana expected to get the call. Surely now he would get his chance. Now. But no. When Devine put Lisch back in, unwilling to give his third-string quarterback a shot even under dire circumstances, Montana privately seethed as the Irish fell further behind. He wondered what the hell Devine was thinking. He wondered why the man didn't believe in him. Purdue quarterback Mark Herrmann, a freshman playing in just his third college game, was repeatedly torching the Irish secondary, showing the kind of touch that would make him the NCAA's all-time passing leader by the time he graduated to the NFL. From the sideline, as Montana watched Herrmann's impressive performance with a combination of irritation and admiration, 1975 seemed like ancient history.

Finally, early in the fourth quarter, with the unranked Boilermakers leading 24–14, smelling the sort of upset that could deal Devine and his program a devastating blow, the Notre Dame coach turned to Montana.

"I'm sure in Coach Devine's mind, he was thinking: Damn! I'm down to Montana," Orsini said.

Montana stepped onto the field as an underdog with something to prove.

In this moment more than ever before, he, too, was a Rudy.

On first down from his own 20, Montana faded into the pocket and scanned the field, gripping a football in a real game for the first time in nearly two years. As the Purdue rush converged on him, the quarterback released the ball, which wobbled through the air and landed several feet short of its intended target, tight end Ken MacAfee's reaching hands.

"It was the ugliest wounded duck you've ever seen," MacAfee said. "Joe hadn't played in such a long time, he was rusty and nervous."

Trudging back to the huddle, MacAfee collared Montana. "Look, just settle down and play your game."

Soon the nerves dissipated and Montana found his touch, connecting on three of his next four passes and leading the Irish close enough for Dave Reeve's 32-yard field goal, which cut the margin to seven. Thus began a very familiar script. After a Luther Bradley interception, Montana needed just two plays to find the end zone, hitting MacAfee with a 13-yard, game-tying touchdown. After trading punts, Notre Dame got the ball back and Montana led a six-play, 58-yard march to clinch the 31–24 victory, culminated by David Mitchell's five-yard run.

As the Fighting Irish started partying like it was 1975, sportswriters converged on the locker belonging to the game's rather composed hero, who completed 9 of 14 passes for 154 yards in the final quarter, which earned him Midwest Back of the Week honors from UPI. Engaged in a philosophical discussion about the merits of starting versus subbing, Montana said, "When you come off the bench, things probably aren't going like they should be. There's no time for pressure."

The question of whether Montana was more effective as the football equivalent of a relief pitcher had been debated since the North Carolina comeback. But with the quarterback's shoulder completely healed, fans whipped into a frenzy by his latest heroics, and the head coach's job security increasingly a topic of discussion wherever Notre Dame fans gathered in those pre-Internet, pre–talk radio days, Devine moved swiftly to name him the starter for the home opener against Michigan State.

"Finally it came down to Devine not having any choice in the matter," MacAfee said. "He played Joe out of desperation."

When he heard his buddy was finally starting a game, Ulice Payne called him up and began making his travel plans. This he had to see in person. Six months after helping the Marquette Warriors storm to the NCAA basketball championship, Payne was headed toward his senior basketball season while making plans for law school. He packed up the Chrysler and plotted a course for South Bend.

"You have to stay with us," Montana insisted.

Joe and Kim were heading toward their third anniversary, one of the power couples of Notre Dame football, but still very young. "They seemed very happy," Payne recalled. While Joe battled for his starting position, his wife handled a variety of secretarial chores in the sports information office, headed by Roger Valdiserri, the widely respected publicity man who once convinced quarterback Joe Theismann to alter the pronunciation of his family name—to rhyme with Heisman—in an unsuccessful attempt to snag college football's most-prized individual award.

When Payne showed up at the apartment where Kim and Joe lived on the first Friday of October, he had a difficult time opening the front door. It would only go back so far, as if something was blocking it from behind. So he squeezed his muscular, six-foot-six frame through the narrow opening with his suitcase in tow and slammed the door shut. That's when he noticed all the recliners.

"You could hardly walk in that [living] room, because they had five or six La-Z-Boy chairs," Payne said. "For some reason, I thought that was really funny."

The Comeback Kid later explained that the chairs were trophies earned for his various player-of-the-game performances.

The next day, when he drove over to Notre Dame Stadium with

Montana's parents, Payne noticed a steady stream of cars featuring "Dump Devine" bumper stickers. Unsatisfied with back-to-back three-loss seasons and unnerved by the upset by lowly Ole Miss, one fan spray-painted over Devine's name on the parking place outside his office, proclaiming it "5 minute parking." "Notre Dame football was going through a real struggle . . . a funky situation," he recalled. "The people I talked to, most of them didn't like Dan Devine . . . They wanted to win but not for Devine."

Feasting on steak sandwiches in the parking lot, Payne, Joe Sr., and Theresa mingled with Irish fans as a sellout crowd of 59,075 converged on the house that Rockne built. The father was a bundle of nerves, well aware of the game's importance.

While tailgating and later in the stands, Payne struck up conversations with random fans, talking up his boy, filling the air with stories about Monongahela and Ringgold and a little man waiting impatiently for his father on the front steps.

*You know Joe?*

*What's he really like?*

*Who are you again?*

At some point, as the pregame festivities continued around him, it hit Payne. He was an adult now, a man of the world, and one of his childhood friends was walking onto a big stage. For one of the first times in his life, he felt genuine pride for one of his friends. Not merely happiness or excitement. Pride. The sort of pride that comes from sharing someone's joys and heartbreaks. The sort of pride that comes from brotherhood. He had witnessed the struggle and now he was watching the ascendance out of the muck. It was a very adult moment. The feeling overwhelmed him as he watched Montana and his teammates run onto the field, overlooked by Touchdown Jesus, the sound of the Notre Dame fight song pulsating the crisp fall air.

In the first of twenty-one straight starts, Montana led Notre Dame to a 16–6 victory over Michigan State. He proved steady at the controls even though his numbers were poor: just 8 of 23 through the air for 105 yards with three interceptions. The Irish relied heavily on a defense that came up with big plays when they were needed—including four turnovers and eight sacks—as well as the powerful outside running of Jerome Heavens, who returned from a 1976 knee injury by rushing for 136 yards. Late in the first quarter of a scoreless game, Montana hit Heavens right on the numbers, wide-open with clear sailing to the end zone. But he let the ball slip right through his fingers, later telling reporters, "I'll be dreaming about that one the rest of my life."

Two days after improving to 4–1 with a 24–0 victory over Army, Devine called the four captains—Willie Fry, Ross Browner, Steve Orsini, and Terry Eurick—into his wood-paneled office on the first floor of the Athletic and Convocation Center for their regular early-week meeting. The coach liked to take the temperature of the squad in such sessions, private informal encounters in which the team leaders could personally interact with a man who wasn't big on personal interaction.

With the upcoming rivalry game against fifth-ranked Southern Cal scheduled for national television, Devine discussed several aspects of the team's preparation and then, nonchalantly, reached behind his desk and pulled out a jersey. "What do you think of this?"

It was not blue.

It was not white.

It was not gold.

It was green.

At first, the players were puzzled because Notre Dame's colors have always been blue and gold. "We thought maybe he was getting our input for shifting to green [jerseys] the next year," Orsini recalled.

Then a smile rose across Devine's face.

"This is a secret," he said. "You can't tell your roommate. Your can't tell your girlfriend. Your can't tell your parents. You can't tell anybody. We're going to wear green jerseys just like this Saturday against USC."

Browner, a two-time All-American and winner of the 1976 Outland Trophy as the nation's outstanding interior lineman, immediately grasped the significance of the switch. "Coach Devine was trying to supply us with a spark," he said. "To maximize the impact of the spark, he wanted us to keep it to ourselves until he could spring it on the rest of the team."

As the captains departed Devine's office, sealing the clandestine maneuver in a circle of trust, one thought rattled around in Orsini's head: How could such a secret possibly hold until kickoff?

Since the days of Rockne, Southern Cal versus Notre Dame has been recognized as the premier intersectional rivalry in college football. At a time of small athletic budgets, when travel costs loomed large and teams tended to play nearly all of their games relatively close to home, the clash of the Midwest and West Coast powers immediately assumed enormous national significance. Historians credit a passenger train encounter between the Notre Dame coach and the USC athletic director for launching the rivalry, sealed by Mrs. Rockne's desire to visit sunny Southern California every two years. The series began in Los Angeles in 1926, with the Fighting Irish earning a tight 13–12 victory. The following year, more than 100,000 delirious fans packed into Chicago's Soldier Field to watch the Irish edge the Trojans, 7–6. It's been a measuring stick, a culture clash, and a cross-country feud ever since. Through the years, the game has proved decisive several times in the annual national championship wars, including USC's 20–17 upset of first-ranked Notre Dame in 1964, which denied the Irish a title in Parseghian's first year. Once the rivalry became a television fixture in the fifties, it quickly emerged as one of the small number of games that defined the sport in the nation's consciousness.

By the time the ABC crew descended on South Bend on October 22, 1977, Southern Cal owned three consecutive victories in the yardstick series. Devine's two losses had been close (seven points in '75 and four points in '76) but among the Notre Dame upperclassmen, the sting of 1974 was still fresh and vivid. That year, after rolling up a 24–0 lead before a big crowd at Los Angeles Memorial Coliseum, the Irish surrendered 55 unanswered points. It was a stunning thing to watch, a tale of two routs. Anthony Davis opened the second half with an electrifying 102-yard kickoff return, igniting one of the most memorable turnarounds in college history.

"As a Notre Dame football player, you understood the history with

Southern Cal, the significance of the game," said tight end Ken MacAfee. "You really didn't need any extra motivation to get up for that game."

As the players began arriving in the locker room to dress for warm-ups, Devine's secret plan remained a well-kept secret. Several players noticed that they had been issued white socks with a green stripe, rather than the traditional white socks with a blue stripe. Who wears green stripes with blue jerseys? Instead of being tipped off, the athletes assumed it was a careless mistake. A quick-thinking manager, who knew the truth, took the blame for his crew. He lied and lied well. (The decision to provide the new socks and risk the players' suspicion had been made intentionally because many athletes were taped over their socks; they would not have had enough time to re-tape the new socks later.) Some players started complaining to the captains about how ridiculous they were going to look on national television wearing their conventional blue jerseys, gold pants, and white socks with green stripes. Damn Devine. Can't he do anything right? Then they all headed out to the field and started getting loose as the stadium slowly filled to capacity.

At the appointed time, as kickoff approached, the players ran off the field and back into the tunnel, and headed to the locker room for their pregame rituals. Receiver Kris Haines was one of the last players to head up the tunnel, and just as he started up the steep stairway, he could hear the sound of whooping and hollering in the distance. "I didn't know what was going on until I got [into the locker room]," he said. "It was a madhouse in there."

While the players were on the field, the managerial staff had hung a green jersey in front of every locker. By the time Haines walked through the door, his teammates were furiously ripping off the blue jerseys and pulling on the green ones, no longer complaining about the mismatched socks. "There was this massive adrenaline flow in the room," Browner recalled. "You could feel it." The jerseys produced "a great psychological lift," in the words of running back Jay Case. All-America cornerback Luther Bradley, one of the team's hardest-hitting defenders, called it a "stroke of genius" that empowered the Irish to "go and kick some butt on the field."

Because football is a game so dependent on emotion, coaches throughout the game's history have employed a variety of methods to inspire their athletes, trying to ensure that they take the field mentally juiced to lay it all on the line. At the time of Devine's intervention, a bronze plaque hung on his locker room wall, commemorating Rockne's famous "Win one for the Gipper" plea when the Fighting Irish trailed Army at the half in 1928. While the story about former Notre Dame star George Gipp's dying request may have been apocryphal—Rockne was not above stretching the truth or inventing it out of whole cloth—the speech itself testified to the power of carefully crafted sentiment in motivating young men to give their all . . . and the eternal search for a game day edge.

More often, successful coaches with less oratorical flare have learned how to lift their players through more nuanced methods. Enter Dan Devine, who moved Saint Patrick's Day to October to put the fight in his Irish. Despite his failings as an inspirational leader, the taciturn Devine understood the power that could be harnessed from something as subtle as a color change, especially when the color in question was so closely associated with Irish Catholic culture, pride, prejudice, the Black and Tan rebellions, St. Paddy and his snakes. (On Friday, to stoke the fire, Devine had arranged for Notre Dame tennis coach Tom Fallon to stop by the football locker room to sing several Irish ballads, including the stirring "The Wearing of the Green," which includes the haunting line, "They're hangin' men and women for the wearin' of the green.")

The green jersey gambit was a brilliant stroke, and it lit a fire under Notre Dame at precisely the right time.

"Coming out of that tunnel, we were at an all-time high emotionally," Orsini said. "There wasn't a man out there who wasn't ready to run through a wall to get to Southern Cal."

Notre Dame crushed the Trojans, 49–19. Like his defensive teammates, who forced four turnovers and managed to contain future Heisman Trophy–winner Charles White when it counted, Montana played an inspired game. He ran for two touchdowns and threw for two more—both to MacAfee—while hitting 13 of 24 passes for 167 yards. Time after time, he converted critical third downs in playing his best game yet, prompting ABC to name him Chevrolet Offensive Player of the Game. It was the first time many non–Notre Dame fans across the country became aware of the lanky number 3 as he rolled left, rolled right, stepped into his throws, and withstood the punishment from USC defenders, including Mario Celotto.

Catapulted back into the national championship race, Notre Dame jumped from tenth in the AP and eleventh in the UPI to fifth in both polls. The team was starting to jell, and Montana was leading the way. In routs of Navy (43–10) and Georgia Tech (69–14) he passed for 260 and 273 yards, respectively.

In a road trip to Gator Bowl–bound Clemson, just then rising under new coach Charley Pell, he rallied the Irish from a 10-point fourth quarter deficit, running for two late touchdowns to cap a 21–17 victory. Afterward, tailback Vagas Ferguson was surprised by his quarterback's reaction.

"We're all jumping around hollering [in the locker room], excited about this big win," recalled Ferguson, who helped set up the winning touchdown by gaining 36 yards on a screen pass. "But not Joe. You wouldn't have known we had even won the game. He was happy and all that but you could see he wasn't the kind of guy who was going to get too excited . . . even after he brought us back."

Like many others, Ferguson was beginning to appreciate a quality that set Montana apart: his ability to maintain that emotional even keel—never too high, never too low.

Ross Browner called him "The General."

"Okay, General," he would often yell toward him when the defense ran off the field. "Let's go."

It was a bittersweet time for Montana. He and Kim were starting to have problems and it was just a matter of time before the marriage ended in divorce, prompting Kim to leave her job in the sports information office. "We were a high-profile couple," Kim said many years later. "It was awkward." Looking back on the breakup years later, Joe said he realized they had "rushed into" the marriage because they "needed each other." "In reality," he said, "we had different perspectives on life." Soon Kim would depart South Bend for good and land the first of a series of jobs in television, eventually becoming a prominent producer.

After lopsided victories over Air Force (49–0) and Miami (48–10), the 10–1 Fighting Irish earned an invitation to play undefeated, first-ranked Texas in the Cotton Bowl. Despite the nine straight wins, Notre Dame headed to Dallas as an underdog to the best Longhorns team of the decade.

As 1978 approached, the Big Four bowl games were at the height of their historical importance, reflecting the power of tradition and NCAA-enforced order. Pasadena's Rose Bowl, first and richest among equals, annually pitted the champions of the Big Ten and Pac-8. The other three games found stability and a measure of commercial and competitive liberty in agreements that provided a single host team but allowed them to lure the best available opponent. The Sugar Bowl, played at the still-new Superdome in New Orleans, featured the Southeastern Conference champion. The winner of the Southwest Conference qualified for the Cotton Bowl in Dallas. The Big Eight champion headed to Miami to play in the Orange Bowl. No other bowls were played on New Year's Day, or, in the case of 1978, the day after New Year's Day, because when the first solar revolution of the new calendar fell on a Sunday, the organizers always agreed to bump the action to Monday.

For many years, the bowls and polls lived in separate orbits as the wire services frequently crowned champions who proceeded to lose in bowl games and one prominent team proved it could stay home and collect trophies. But those days were long gone as 1978 dawned. Both wire services now waited until after the big games to crown their champion, due in no small measure to Notre Dame's influence. Twice since returning to postseason play, the Irish had knocked off undefeated top-ranked teams: Texas in the 1971 Cotton Bowl and Alabama in the 1973 Sugar Bowl. Not long after Tom Clements found Robin Weber, plunging a dagger into the hearts of Crimson Tide fans everywhere, the UPI coaches poll finally threw in the towel, conceding what every eight-year-old boy in Birmingham instinctively knew: Bowl games count.

Texas, the nation's only undefeated, untied team in 1977, entered the Cotton Bowl bidding for the program's fourth national championship since 1963 against fifth-ranked Notre Dame. The other contenders—

second-ranked Oklahoma, third-ranked Alabama, fourth-ranked Michigan, and sixth-ranked Arkansas—found themselves engaged in an activity that seemed almost unnatural: pulling for the Fighting Irish.

By game time, the Notre Dame players were tired of hearing how elusive Heisman Trophy–winning tailback Earl Campbell was. (One of the best of all time, the tough-to-topple Campbell rushed for 1,744 yards as a senior, most of those after sustaining at least one hit.) They were tired of hearing how menacing Outland Trophy–winner Brad Shearer was. They were tired of being reminded that not even Big Eight champion Oklahoma nor Southwest Conference runner-up Arkansas had managed to score a touchdown against the vaunted Longhorns defense. They were tired of being confronted, every time some reporter shoved a microphone or a notebook in their faces, with the consensus opinion that they could not possibly, under any circumstances known to man, beat Texas.

"Being an underdog can really help you get ready to play, especially when it feels like a home game for the other team," said Browner, who arrived in Dallas as the winner of the Lombardi and Maxwell awards.

As a capacity crowd of 76,701 filled the Cotton Bowl on a sunny, relatively mild day, most expecting a coronation of Fred Akers's Longhorns, Browner and his defensive teammates focused on job one: neutralizing Earl Campbell. Utilizing a game plan that Irish defensive coordinator Joe Yonto called "corralling," Notre Dame wanted to force Campbell inside, where he would find the yards tougher while facing the strength of the defense. "Coach Yonto told us, 'If anybody hits [Campbell], hold him up for another couple of guys to hit him, so we can break his spirit,'" recalled Browner. Central to this strategy was "stuffing the middle" and disrupting quarterback Randy McEachern's ability to pitch wide to his money back.

Two minutes into the game, McEachern gathered the snap from center, turned right down the line, and immediately came face mask to face mask with Browner, who very nearly caught the pitch in midair. The ball tumbled just out of Browner's grasp, but he chased it down, giving Notre Dame a first down at the Texas 32—and setting the tone for the day. Four plays later, Dave Reeve's 47-yard field goal gave the Irish a 3–0 lead.

On a day when the Notre Dame defense forced six Texas turnovers and held the best running back in college football to four yards per carry—well below his 6.5 average, requiring a Cotton Bowl–record 29 attempts, for 116 yards—Montana methodically marched the Fighting Irish up and down the field, turning five of the turnovers into Notre Dame points. Relying heavily on the powerful one-two running punch of Jerome Heavens and Vagas Ferguson, who ran for 101 and 100 yards, respectively, and a dominating performance by the offensive line, Notre Dame controlled the game from start to finish. The quarterback made several clutch passes, completing 10 of 25 for 111 yards. By the time he hit a streaking Ferguson with a 17-yard touchdown strike to make it 24–3 in the second quarter, the game was over.

"Everything just went perfect for us," said linebacker Doug Becker, whose interception set up the touchdown to Ferguson. "We just kept attacking them, and attacking them, and attacking them."

Early in the fourth quarter of Notre Dame's 38–10 rout, Devine started emptying his bench. As Montana joined the rest of the first-team offense on the sidelines, Rusty Lisch took his place behind center. What a difference a few weeks had made in the lives of these two men. The player who had opened the season as the starting quarterback was now reduced to mop-up duty, his presence offering a subtle reminder of how one seized opportunity can ripple through a life . . . and the life of a team.

While Irish eyes were focused on Dallas, Notre Dame's upset was just one piece of an unusual day of college football culmination unfolding across the country. Favored Alabama crushed Ohio State in the Sugar Bowl, 35–6, but Washington upset Michigan in the Rose Bowl, 27–20, and Arkansas shocked Oklahoma in the Orange Bowl, 31–6.

With the top two teams going down to defeat and three 11–1 teams surviving the melee who could reasonably make a case for the big prize, voters in both the AP and UPI polls awarded the national championship to the Fighting Irish, who leapfrogged from fifth to first, over third-ranked Alabama, who finished second. Arkansas wound up third. It was a result tinged with controversy, especially in Alabama, where many Crimson Tide fans felt victimized by the Notre Dame mystique.

When news spread of the title sweep, which also included the Football Writers Association's Grantland Rice Trophy as well as the Mac-Arthur Bowl, presented by the National Football Foundation, Devine's reserved demeanor was temporarily sidelined. "I usually try to hold my emotions in, but I'm kind of quivering all over right now," he told reporters.

Before kicking off against Texas, someone in the Notre Dame organization had scrawled a message on a locker room blackboard: "It's not how you start, it's how you finish."

Like all championship teams, the 1977 Fighting Irish benefited from strong leadership, including First Team All-Americans Ross Browner, Ken MacAfee, and Luther Bradley, as well as center Dave Huffman, linebacker Bob Golic, defensive lineman Willie Fry, and fullback Steve Orsini. The team owed a tremendous debt to Dan Devine's green-jersey spark. But the catalyst was Joe Montana. If Montana doesn't storm off the bench to rally the troops to beat Purdue, the title slips away into the West Lafayette mist. It all goes back to Purdue and the switch that enabled everything that followed. Although he failed to receive any significant individual recognition—save the honorable mention All-America honor from the Associated Press—the quarterback who ultimately was empowered not just by his own talent and drive and calm but also by Devine's desperation, earned the enduring respect of his teammates, who understood his profound impact.

"The truth is, we felt like we won the national championship in spite of Dan Devine," MacAfee said. "No way we win it without Joe. He was the difference."

# CHAPTER THREE

# Chicken Soup

As the scoreboard clock dipped below the eight-minute mark in the 1979 Cotton Bowl, Joe Montana stood on the Notre Dame sideline, giving teammate Kris Haines an earful.

"Kris! What the hell were you thinking?"

With every syllable out of his mouth, a trail of white vapor flowed from his unbuckled gold helmet into the frigid Dallas air.

On the previous series, Haines, a senior receiver for the Fighting Irish, had collided with a defender and been flagged with a costly personal foul penalty, causing yet another Notre Dame drive to stall.

The Fighting Irish trailed the Houston Cougars, 34–12, and millions of football fans across the country had already changed the channel from CBS to ABC, where number-one Penn State and number-two Alabama were locked in a classic Sugar Bowl duel. The national championship would be decided in New Orleans and in Pasadena, where number-three Southern Cal kicked off against number-five Michigan later in the afternoon. The stakes in Dallas were somewhat lower. The winner would go home with a very nice-looking trophy, and as the minutes dwindled, the hardware seemed a lock for Houston, where the trophy case still had plenty of room.

Montana felt like hell. He was shivering. His head was pounding. But the Comeback Kid was conceding nothing. He was running out of time and he was irritated because Haines's mental error had helped force him off the field empty-handed. It was not the first time.

After capturing the 1977 national championship, Notre Dame entered the 1978 season ranked fifth and was considered a serious contender to repeat. Despite the loss of several key starters, the Fighting Irish returned a veteran team led by Montana, a fifth-year senior who was firmly established as the starting quarterback.

The season opened against unranked Missouri on an unusually hot early September day in South Bend. Notre Dame amassed 324 yards of total offense but was repeatedly stymied by a stubborn Missouri defense. In the first quarter, Montana drove the Irish inside the Tigers' 20 and fumbled. Twice in the second quarter, he tossed interceptions deep in enemy territory. In the third quarter, the Irish were turned away in two stabs from the Missouri one—first Montana and then Vagas Ferguson.

By late in the third quarter of a scoreless game, Montana still had not thrown to Haines, and the speedster from Sydney, Ohio, was especially anxious to make a big catch. Even before kickoff, the defensive back who spent the day shadowing him started running his mouth. Haines gave it right back to him. All day long they were yapping insults up and down the field and Haines kept waiting for a ball to be thrown his way. He wanted to burn the guy so bad, he could taste it.

After turning down the chance to play on the defensive side of the ball for Woody Hayes at Ohio State and Bo Schembechler at Michigan, Haines chose Notre Dame because the coaches thought he could play receiver. The adjustment to college ball was not easy. Soon after arriving in South Bend, he found himself scrimmaging with Montana, when the quarterback was still working his way up the depth chart. The post corner route proved especially difficult, because Montana kept hitting him in the back of the head. "He was so accurate, and his timing was so good . . . and I couldn't get my head turned back around to catch it in time," Haines said. He soon grew tired of getting thumped in the back of the helmet, so he learned to run the route with precision, which helped him crack the starting lineup as a true freshman in 1975.

When Montana sent Haines downfield on a post corner in the third quarter against Missouri three years later, he ran the route perfectly, faking toward the post before breaking sharply toward the front corner of the end zone, heading for the left pylon. The defender bit on the fake, leaving him wide open as Montana fired a bullet in his direction. Haines snagged the ball for a 34-yard gain before being shoved out of bounds at the Missouri three. Then he lost his cool.

"I had a temper. I was fiery. And I made a big mistake," he said.

Charging over to the defender, he began taunting the Missouri man, running his mouth about his big catch. One thing led to another and Haines reached out and slapped him on the helmet. "I gave him a good whack," he said. "His head went sideways." Then came the flags. The blatant personal foul drew a 15-yard penalty.

"I've thought this through so many times," said Haines, who wound up playing three seasons for the Chicago Bears. "If I had a chance to do it over again, I would've tried to dive over the pylon and it never would have happened. But I was emotionally charged up. I was fed up with this guy, who was the weakest DB they had . . . and wouldn't shut up. I lost control of my temper. Big, big mistake."

Instead of working from first-and-goal at the three, Notre Dame was pushed back to the 18, where the defense stiffened. Devine sent Joe Unis in to attempt a field goal but the snap was bobbled and the kick never took flight. Another opportunity lost. Notre Dame never got so close again. On the strength of Jeff Brockhaus's 33-yard field goal with 13:10 remaining in the game, Missouri upset Notre Dame, 3–0, handing the Irish their first shutout at home since 1960.

The next Saturday, when fifth-ranked Michigan came to South Bend and beat Notre Dame 28–14 as Montana tossed two more interceptions, giving the Irish their first 0–2 start since 1963, the season started to unravel.

Four months later, as Montana stood on the Cotton Bowl turf chiding his receiver for drawing another personal foul penalty, left unsaid was the lingering memory of the first and how one immature act had impacted a devastating loss. As Houston lined up for a punt, Haines knew his quarterback was right to get in his face, even though the quarterback was having a lousy day, too.

"Nobody had to remind me that I messed up in the Missouri game and the loss was kinda my fault," he said. "I wasn't going to let myself forget that. It was the start of a pretty difficult year."

As the quarterback and his receiver prepared to head back into the game and try to get something going on offense, they watched freshman Tony Belden burst through the Houston line to block the punt. Steve Cichy caught the ball in midair, broke two tackles, and raced 33 yards for a touchdown, narrowing Houston's lead to 34–18 with 7:25 left in the game. It was time for Montana and Haines to stop bickering and go back to work, because the most improbable comeback in bowl history had just begun.

On December 31, 1978, a blast of arctic air descended across a large swath of the United States, dumping massive amounts of snow and ice and causing widespread power outages. For usually mild North Texas, the storm proved especially devastating, making the Sunbelt metropolis of Dallas feel more like Cleveland or Buffalo. Local meteorologists were calling it the worst winter storm in thirty years, creating the climate for one of the coldest, windiest, most miserable bowl games ever played. In Dallas County alone, 75,000 homes were without power as the new year dawned, a figure that soon escalated. "If you are living near tall trees," said a Dallas Power and Light official, "you are either without electric power or soon will be." The temperature dipped to 20 degrees and the persistent wind, gusting up to thirty miles per hour, pushed the wind chill toward 10 below zero.

The slow bus ride from the team hotels to the Cotton Bowl was treacherous and surreal. Ice-heavy trees slumped over roadways and abandoned cars occupied ditches. As the glistening glass and steel towers of downtown Dallas loomed in the distance—a familiar sight to all who were caught up in the new nighttime soap opera of the same name, turning the fast-money culture of Texas oil barons into a pop-culture cliché—the players looked out to see almost completely vacant streets. "It was like a ghost town," said Notre Dame tailback Vagas Ferguson. "It was spooky."

Like many major stadiums around the country, the Cotton Bowl converted to artificial turf not long after it became available, in 1970, riding the wave of the future. By the late '70s, the Dallas carpet was aging fast and players and coaches across the country were starting to complain that such surfaces allowed too little give and therefore contributed to certain injuries. The fake stuff also froze easily, so long before the Houston and Notre Dame players arrived, the grounds crew scraped at least an inch of ice from the field and covered it with the sort of ice-melting salt being applied to the city's slick streets and highways. "The problem was, the pellets stayed there," Haines said. "When you got hit or you slid on the ground, you had to deal with those pellets."

Officially, the game was a sellout, because bowl organizers had moved roughly 72,000 tickets, about the same as the previous January, when Notre Dame spoiled Texas' national championship coronation on a clear, mild day with all the usual pomp and pageantry. But even at kickoff, media estimates of 30,000, less than one half of capacity, struck many as incredibly generous. "If there were 30,000 people there a lot of 'em must have been invisible," said Notre Dame offensive tackle Bob Crable. Those fans brave enough to weather the conditions, including Haines's father, who made the trip down from Ohio, were forced to scrape at least an inch of ice from their seats. They bundled up in heavy coats and blankets and drank liberally from thermoses and hip flasks. When Houston started blowing out Notre Dame, the crowd dwindled to perhaps 10,000, significantly smaller than what many Texas high schools attracted on a routine Friday night.

For Notre Dame, the trip to Dallas was awash in disappointment. At the start of the year, an optimistic Devine told reporters, "We are defending our national championship and they'll have to take it away from us on the field." The defense quickly crumbled. After losing to Michigan, the Irish tumbled out of the top twenty and Devine once more began to feel the heat. Making it back to the Cotton Bowl was an achievement, after such a poor start, but finishing 8–3 was not cause for celebration in South Bend under any circumstances.

Like his teammates, Montana felt the sting of what might have been. In his only full year as the Notre Dame starter, he became only the third Irish quarterback to throw for more than 2,000 yards in a season (completing 54 percent of his attempts for 2,010 yards, with 10 touchdowns and nine interceptions), ranking twentieth in the NCAA passing statistics and also running for another six touchdowns. In a 38–21 victory over Georgia Tech, he tied a school record by completing 10 straight passes.

The Comeback Kid also directed two more heart-pounding rallies. Against ninth-ranked Pittsburgh in the fifth game of the season, the Irish trailed 17–7 with 13:46 left; he completed seven straight passes—two for touchdowns—to key a 26–17 win. The offensive line, which had struggled in September, was beginning to jell and it made the difference. "I needed to have the time to throw and I got it," Montana said. Like many others, Pitt head coach Jackie Sherrill was impressed with his ability to locate the open man. "You give a passer like Montana time and he'll find someone to throw to," Sherrill said.

In the regular season finale against eventual UPI national champion Southern Cal, Montana played perhaps the greatest game of his college career. Ineffective in the first half as the Trojans built a 17–3 lead, he wound up completing 20 of 41 passes for 358 yards and two touchdowns—including 17 of 26 for 296 yards and both touchdowns in the second half.

"We might have been too geared up to stop the run that we were vulnerable to Montana's passing," USC head coach John Robinson said. "I told everybody he is a great passer, and he proved it. Once he got going."

Trailing 24–6 early in the fourth quarter, Montana led a furious rally, seizing a 25–24 lead on a 12-yard pass to Pete Holohan with forty-six seconds left. But in one of the greatest finishes ever seen in the series, USC quarterback Paul McDonald out-Montanaed Montana, completing a 35-yard pass to Cal Sweeney to set up Frank Jordan's 37-yard game-winning field goal with no time remaining. USC 27, Notre Dame 25.

"It was a remarkable comeback," Devine told reporters. "The one thing

I asked our kids was not to quit. And they didn't. There was no doubt we were a different team in the second half."

Despite the heroics, Montana, who graduated in December with a degree in business and marketing, was overshadowed by several other quarterbacks who turned in better years, including four who finished among the top ten in the Heisman Trophy balloting: Penn State's Chuck Fusina, Michigan's Rick Leach, Clemson's Steve Fuller, and Washington State's Jack Thompson. Playing quarterback at Notre Dame imbued him with a certain cachet, but even so, when he arrived in Dallas to cap his college career, Montana remained a relatively obscure figure on the national stage.

For Houston, playing in the Cotton Bowl was a big deal. After many years as an independent, and therefore, a second-class program in the pecking order of Texas football, the university negotiated a milestone in 1976 by joining the Southwest Conference, one of the five premier leagues in college football at the time. By then, longtime head coach Bill Yeoman had already made a name for himself and his Cougars by inventing and perfecting the veer offense, an option-based scheme that became popular across the country. Unranked in the preseason, Houston stormed out of the shadows to tie for the conference crown in its first year of eligibility. Two years later, Yeoman proved 1976 was no fluke. Once again, the wire service voters and various media organizations completely ignored the Cougars before the 1978 season, picking perennial powerhouses Texas and Arkansas as the SWC favorites. But Houston finished 9–2, scoring victories over both the Longhorns and the Razorbacks to win a second title and earn a trip to Dallas to face Notre Dame.

In the days leading up to the game, Yeoman made one thing perfectly clear: he did not believe in leprechauns. Across the decades, the power of the Notre Dame mystique was often debated, especially in the aftermath of yet another miracle finish, especially when opposing teams allowed themselves to be intimidated by the accumulated weight of all that glittering Golden Dome history. Psychologically, the mere possibility that the Notre Dame mystique somehow translated into what happened on the field was enough to mess with opposing players' minds. This is why Yeoman felt the need to push back when talking to reporters heading into the Cotton Bowl. He understood how to deal with blitzing linebackers and scrambling quarterbacks and wily coaches. He did not know how to defend against something he could not see. This business of the Notre Dame mystique, he said, is "garbage."

A nasty strain of the flu began working through the Notre Dame team in the days leading up to the game. Haines missed two days of practice with a high fever. Among the bug's victims was Montana, who felt increasingly weak as kickoff time arrived. Like many of his teammates, the quarterback found it hard to get fired up about a meaningless bowl game to conclude a disappointing season. He just wanted to get it over with and go home.

After winning the coin toss, Notre Dame elected to defend the north end zone, which would prove to be a critical decision, giving the Irish the wind in the first and fourth quarters. The tone of the day was established on the third play from scrimmage, when Houston's Emmett King fumbled into the arms of Irish defender Jay Case. Montana went to work, hitting Jerome Heavens for 27 and Dean Masztak for 26. On the ninth play of the 66-yard drive, the quarterback ran it in from three yards, giving Notre Dame a 6–0 lead after a missed extra point. On the ensuing kickoff, the slippery ball rolled off Terry Elson's fingers and Bob Crable fell on it at the Houston 25. Vagas Ferguson caught a nine-yard screen pass from Montana and rambled another eight on a sweep. Pete Buchanan scored on a one-yard run, making it 12–0 after Montana's two-point pass fell incomplete.

Then Notre Dame started beating itself. With just over a minute remaining in the first quarter, Houston was forced to punt from deep in its own territory but got the ball back when Notre Dame fumbled. Three plays later, quarterback Danny Davis, the veer master who was known more for his skill in running the option than his arm (he passed for 1,053 yards and rushed for 349 in '79), hit Willie Adams all alone in the end zone for a 15-yard touchdown pass. The Notre Dame man defending him slipped on the treacherous turf, underscoring how difficult it could be to simply remain vertical, much less make a play.

"It was a crazy atmosphere to play in," Ferguson recalled. "It was so unbelievably cold. We were all miserable."

In the second quarter, with the wind suddenly at his back, Davis took control, exploiting a Montana fumble, after a bad exchange with All-America center Dave Huffman, and two Montana interceptions to lead the Cougars to another touchdown and two Ken Hatfield field goals, giving Houston a 20–12 halftime lead.

What started so well quickly turned into one of the worst halves of Montana's college career. Not only was he dealing with incredibly difficult field conditions, especially an oppressive wind that repeatedly veered his second-quarter passes off course, but he was also beginning to feel sicker and sicker. When the Notre Dame team walked into the locker room, the quarterback was immediately examined by a very concerned training and medical staff. He was trembling. He was nauseated. "I felt like I was sitting in a bucket of ice," he recalled.

After discovering that his core temperature had plunged to 96 degrees, the team doctor, Les Bodnar, diagnosed him with hypothermia and began administering treatment to try to warm him up. They bundled him in blankets and fed him bowl after bowl of chicken soup.

"I remember seeing Joe in the trainer's room," Haines said. "He looked really bad. I'm thinking to myself, 'We're toast.'"

In the press box, a telephone rang. It was New York calling.

Douglas S. Looney was a familiar face around big-time college football. He had covered the game for several years, including the last four for *Sports Illustrated*. He spent significant time in South Bend writing about Notre Dame and was one of Dan Devine's closest friends.

Over cocktails the men often discussed the quarterback situation, and Looney was as puzzled as many others by Devine's reticence to play Montana, until circumstances in 1977 essentially forced his hand. "I can't say I fully understood why Dan didn't think he was the right guy, but for the longest time, he didn't," Looney said. "Somehow, looking through Dan's prism . . . Joe didn't look like a quarterback who was going to take them to the national championship . . . He underestimated Joe like a lot of people underestimated Joe."

Like the participating teams, Looney understood the Cotton Bowl was not the big game of the day and that it would not warrant the cover story in the following week's magazine. After taking a measure of the situation at halftime, his editor called to say they would need his story right after the game ended, which meant that Looney would not be able to go to the locker room to talk with players or attend the postgame news conference with the coaches. Unlike his daily newspaper competitors, who would have several hours to write (or, in the case of the still numerous afternoon papers located around the country, until early the next morning), Looney would be forced to write his story while the game was still being played. For this he was always prepared. In the days leading up to the game, he had conducted interviews with various players and coaches, giving him the voices he needed to enliven his game story under several different possible scenarios. Aware of the deadline pressure he was likely to face for this particular game, he began writing the guts of two different stories: one reflecting a Notre Dame victory; another for a Houston win.

The 1979 Cotton Bowl was not Looney's first business trip to the Dallas–Fort Worth Metroplex. Four years earlier, in one of his earliest reporting assignments for *SI*, Looney covered a championship rodeo in Fort Worth, a trip that required him to jump through various logistical hoops. Job one upon arriving in town was finding a Western Union facility that could send his article back to the magazine in what amounted to one long telegram. This was the preferred method for traveling sportswriters to file their stories in those days, unless you happened to have access to the latest technological marvel, the telecopier, forerunner of the fax machine, which most football press boxes offered for a fee. When he learned that the only Western Union vendor in town would be closed on Sunday, the day he needed to transmit, he politely explained his predicament to the clerk, a rather cranky middle-aged woman. She was not impressed with *Sports Illustrated* or the least bit interested in solving the customer's problem.

"We're closed Sunday, just like the sign says!"

Thinking on his feet, Looney offered the woman fifty dollars for her solemn pledge that she would open the store at eight o'clock on Sunday morning and promised her another one hundred bucks when she transmitted the story. "Let me see the money," she said with a scowl. Then they shook on the deal.

After covering the rodeo and writing all night at his nearby hotel, Looney drove through a driving rainstorm to the Western Union office. When he approached the front door and saw the lights on and the woman inside, his heart skipped a beat. "I was just so happy because if she hadn't been there, I was really going to be in trouble," he said. Standing in the pouring rain, getting drenched from head to toe, he knocked on the door. The woman saw him and pointed at the clock on the wall, which showed 7:57.

"Eight o'clock!" she yelled, and turned away.

Resisting the urge to shatter the glass or throw a fit, Looney waited in the rain for another three minutes, carefully shielding several sheets of typing paper under his coat. When the woman finally let him in and transmitted the story, he paid her the agreed fee and went on his way with a feeling of enormous relief.

Four years later, Looney arrived in Dallas no longer needing the services of Western Union. Like a growing number of sportswriters, he had parked his typewriter and started writing and transmitting his stories using one of the first portable computers. The bulky Teleram weighed about fifty pounds and featured a tiny screen but it represented a revolution in the news business, allowing direct communication with the home office through a modem, connected to a telephone through an acoustic coupler.

When the teams returned to the field for the second half, they could see many of the spectators had headed for home or hotels, seeking heat and the possibility of a more interesting game on television. The exodus soon accelerated.

With Montana still in the dressing room, presumed finished for the day, backup Tim Koegel proved ineffective. Like Montana, he struggled with the unpredictable wind. On the first drive of the second half, Koegel sent Haines on a go route but he severely underthrew the ball and it was intercepted. "It was kind of embarrassing," Haines said. "I knew we were in deep trouble then." Eight plays later, Davis scored on a four-yard run. About two minutes later, Bobby Harrison blocked an Irish punt to set up another Davis touchdown, this time from the one. By the middle of the third quarter, Houston led 34–12 and Looney started to write his story.

"Because it looked like Houston was on its way to a big victory, I took the draft of that version and started shaping it into a full story, analyzing the game and writing about what this big win meant to Bill Yeoman's program," Looney said.

Toward the end of the third quarter, when Notre Dame's number 3 emerged from the dressing room, Looney was too busy typing to notice.

Bolstered by the chicken soup and the blankets, which helped raise his temperature back to normal, Montana began lobbying the doctors to clear him to play. Beyond the physical effects of all the medical attention, something started to stir inside him. He still felt awful, and the game appeared to be lost, but the Comeback Kid was too competitive to sit in the locker room and listen to the debacle on the radio. He could feel his college career slipping away, and he didn't like the thought of it ending like this. Not if he could make a difference. "I wanted to get back in the game, if it was humanly possible," Montana explained later.

When he slipped off his blue jacket and started tossing a football to a teammate on the sideline, warming up in preparation for reentering the game, Montana could feel his fingers going numb. But at least he was no longer shaking uncontrollably.

During his absence, the sports information staff had explained to reporters that he was suffering from "extreme chilling," without further explanation. Only later would the full measure of his gritty performance be completely understood. When the doctors released him and he returned to the field near the end of the third quarter, even his teammates remained unaware of the severity of his condition.

"If ever anybody had an excuse to not play, it was Joe," Ferguson said. "He was sick and it was cold and he was getting hit. Their defense was really lighting us up. But he wasn't gonna let us down like that."

On his first possession, with the Irish trailing 34–12, Montana quickly tossed another interception. The man who had pulled out so many miracle finishes kept pushing Notre Dame deeper into a dark hole.

When the fourth quarter began, Houston's victory seemed all but assured. The personal foul penalty on Haines and a failed fourth-down pass by Montana gave the Cougars another chance, but the Irish defense slammed the door, prompting the punt that was blocked by Cichy and returned by Belden. Pulled away from his discussion with his hotheaded receiver, Montana hit Ferguson for a two-point pass, cutting Houston's margin to 34–20 with 7:25 to play.

Like the Notre Dame mystique, Montana's reputation as a rally master was a source of psychological strength for his teammates, even on a day when he had already turned the ball over four times and the unpredictable wind so often sucked his throws toward an unintended trajectory. When the defense held Houston and the Irish started moving the ball for the first time since the first half, even as the minutes ticked away, a jolt of adrenaline began to spread through the team. "Right then our whole bench started to bubble," said Cichy, who scored on the blocked punt. Perhaps they could still win. Perhaps Montana could do it one more time.

"Joe inspired confidence in people," said two-time All-American offensive tackle Bob Crable, then a freshman. "Once you demonstrate that you can bring a team back over and over again, [teammates] start to believe in your ability to get the job done, even when the situation appears desperate. There's a power to that and Joe had that power."

Over the remaining minutes, this power would be put to a test and so would Montana's ailing body.

After completing two clutch passes, a 17-yarder to Dean Masztak, and a 30-yarder to Jerome Heavens, and benefiting from a pass interference flag near the goal line, Montana called his own number from the three. Then he hit Haines in the end zone for a two-pointer, cutting Houston's lead to 34–28 with 4:15 remaining.

"I think that's when I started to believe," Haines said.

In the CBS television booth, Lindsey Nelson and Paul Hornung watched the rally with a sense of gathering déjà vu. In their roles as play-by-play man and color analyst, respectively, for the syndicated Notre Dame television network, the two men had seen this movie before. North Carolina. Air Force. Purdue. Clemson. Pittsburgh. USC. Like the Notre Dame players and fans, the two television veterans had learned to appreciate Montana's ability to reverse deficits.

"There are guys who are just game players, who lay it all on the line and somehow make something good happen," said Hornung, the former Notre Dame quarterback who won the 1956 Heisman Trophy. "Joe was one of those guys. He was able to make the play at the time when he needed to make the play. We started to see during those days how truly great he was."

Long established as a sports broadcasting icon, the colorful Nelson was closely associated with the Cotton Bowl for more than thirty years. Well recognized for his folksy Tennessee twang and his fondness for loud sports jackets, Nelson had already called the action for two of the most memorable college football games of all time. In the 1954 Cotton Bowl, while working with the legendary Red Grange on NBC, he watched with a sense of disbelief as Alabama's Tommy Lewis raced off the sideline and tackled Rice's Dicky Maegle, temporarily preventing a touchdown but earning a lifetime of infamy. During the 1963 Army-Navy game on CBS, when director Tony Verna gave him the cue that forever changed sports television, he explained to viewers, "Ladies and gentlemen, what you are seeing is a tape of Army's touchdown. This is not live, but is something new. . . ." Thus the age of instant replay was born. Fifteen years later, the Cotton Bowl provided him with yet another historic stage.

"The conditions were so bad and neither team played very well," Nelson recalled. "We certainly didn't think it was going to be remembered as a classic at the start of the fourth quarter."

Statistically, the Notre Dame defense turned in a mediocre performance, allowing 288 total yards and giving up several big plays. But in the fourth quarter, when it counted, the battered unit, led by Jay Case,

Mike Calhoun, and Steve Heimkreiter, repeatedly stopped Houston and put the ball back in Montana's hands.

After another punt, Montana and his teammates began driving once more toward the goal line. With 1:50 to play, he scrambled out of the pocket and raced into the open. Five. Ten. Fifteen. Sixteen yards. Then came disaster for Notre Dame. Cougars linebacker David Hodge, the Defensive Player of the Game who recorded a team-leading 15 tackles, clobbered Montana from behind near the Houston 20, knocking the ball loose. When Houston's Tommy Ebner recovered, all appeared lost for the Irish. All that remained was for Houston to run out the clock.

"I remember being so deflated coming off the field," Haines said. "I thought for sure it was over."

On the sideline, reduced once more to a spectator, Montana felt the sting of his fumble but tried to keep his head in the game.

In the open-air press box, Looney was still furiously typing his story about the landmark victory for the Houston program. As soon as the game ended, he would be ready to hook up the acoustic couplers and push the Send button to make his deadline. Every so often, he pulled his fingers away from the keyboard and rubbed his hands together, to get a little circulation going in his freezing digits.

On the field below, Houston was having a hard time running out the clock from deep in its own territory. Devine used his last two time-outs to stop the ticking, on first and third downs. With forty-six seconds left, the Cougars lined up in a punt formation but a Notre Dame player jumped offsides. Only in retrospect would this penalty prove to be a turning point. With fourth-and-six suddenly reduced to fourth-and-one, Bill Yeoman was determined to avoid another blocked punt or another wind-addled shank; the Cougars were averaging just 25 yards per punt, one yard shorter than Notre Dame. Yeoman chose to go for it, which proved to be a gigantic miscalculation. The handoff went to the bullish Emmett King, a powerful runner who was averaging 3.6 yards per rush against the Irish. On his twenty-first carry, however, King lunged left and was stopped cold, first by freshman defensive tackle Joe Gramke and then by senior linebacker Mike Calhoun. No gain. Notre Dame ball.

"I didn't have second thoughts about going for it," Davis insisted.

Time seemed to be on Houston's side, unless you happened to believe in leprechauns.

When the Irish offense ran back onto the field, the aging stadium felt incredibly empty, like the site of some meaningless scrimmage. Cotton Bowl officials cringed at the picture of their tradition-rich game being shown to the rest of the country by the CBS cameras. Along the sidelines, nearest the field, entire rows had been abandoned or never used; the end zone sections were completely vacant. The prevailing background color in most shots was not Irish blue nor Cougar red but metallic silver, the shade of the mostly empty stadium seats. The only place where a crowd formed was along the perimeter of the end zone, where bundled-up newspaper photographers and television cameramen competed for elbow room with sportswriters who had abandoned the press box for a closer view of unfolding history.

Twenty-eight seconds remained when Montana took over at the Houston 29. With no time-outs remaining, he had no way to stop the clock except by making a first down, getting out of bounds, or throwing an incomplete pass.

Around the country, the various Notre Dame fans prayed for another miracle finish, including recently graduated fullback Steve Orsini, who had moved to New York City to begin his career working for a major accounting firm. When the game got out of hand, Orsini and his friends contemplated turning it off. It was painful to see his old team getting socked so badly. But something made him keep watching. "I just had a feeling," Orsini said. "I knew what Joe was capable of."

Three years removed from his triumphant ride off the field, still-unknown Rudy Ruettiger watched with the perspective of an outsider who had stormed the gates and now felt imbued with special knowledge. On those final three plays against Georgia Tech, the intense noise of the house that Rockne built had faded away in his mind, fortifying him with a clarifying calm, allowing him to focus intently on his assignment.

Suddenly he understood what all those players had been trying to explain to him. As he watched Montana break the huddle in Dallas, facing yet another desperate situation, Ruettiger knew the quarterback had clicked a switch and gone to a special place most fans could never truly comprehend.

With the game coming down to one decisive play, Montana was not concerned about the cold, his ailing body, his various frustrations with Devine, or the emotion associated with his last college game. He was able to focus on the task at hand: putting the ball in the end zone. Of such situations, he once said, "You get in a certain mode on the field and everything else is blocked out . . . I guess you can call it living in the moment."

"It was so freaking cold the whole day," Haines said, "but you know what? On that last series, I don't remember the cold."

Haines initially planned to wear gloves but was overruled prior to kick-off by Devine, who told him, "The Green Bay receivers don't wear gloves."

Benefiting from apparent confusion by the Cougars defense, Montana scampered around right end for an 11-yard gain, giving the Irish a first down at the Houston 18, which temporarily stopped the clock. Rushing to the line of scrimmage, he hit Haines for another first down, and the receiver stepped out of bounds at the eight with six seconds left. Houston called its final time-out to brace for the final assault as millions of football fans—including many who had wandered back over from the Sugar Bowl—struggled to process the shocking reversal.

"So it all comes down to this," Lindsey Nelson told his CBS audience, explaining to viewers how Montana had returned after "becoming chilled and . . . running a slight temperature" to "spark the surge of Notre Dame here in the closing moments."

On the sideline, Montana held a towel to his face with his right hand and gestured with his left as he conferred with Devine and offensive coordinator Merv Johnson, who asked the head coach, "Do you want to get in two quick plays or one for sure?"

"Two."

Like the rest of the coaching staff, Devine was dressed in several layers, including a hooded blue jacket stitched with NOTRE DAME on the back. His head was covered in a green wool toboggan topped in yellow. His socks and shoes were still soggy from a pregame inspection of the field, and he was still feeling the effects of bumping into one of the ice-clearing machines.

"Joe, let's run a ninety-one. If it's not there, get rid of it right away."

As Montana headed off the field, Devine gave him one final instruction. "If your first pass is incomplete, you call whatever is most comfortable for you."

As their time together drew to a close, the Notre Dame coach had grown to appreciate Montana's unique qualities, traits that had escaped him in the early days, when the young man's practice performance struck him as inadequate and less impressive than his rivals. By granting him the freedom to rely on his own judgment in such a critical situation, he was validating the young man's rise from frustrated scout teamer to the undisputed leader of a football team that fed off his confidence, found strength in his tenacity, and implicitly trusted in his ability to somehow find a way to win.

Despite bringing home the 1977 national championship, Devine's six-year tenure proved otherwise unacceptable by South Bend standards (53–16–1) and he was never fully embraced by the Notre Dame fans. His name would never be uttered in the same breath as Rockne, Leahy, and Parseghian, although Gerry Faust, the Cincinnati high school coach who replaced him after the 1980 season, would preside over a much paler shade of mediocrity (30–26–1). To many who sported the "Dump Devine" bumper stickers, the way Devine squandered Montana was emblematic of his failings as a leader.

Like many other Notre Dame players of the era, Haines would always view his coach through a conflicted lens. "Coach Devine had a lot of faith in me when I wasn't doing great," Haines said. "He stuck by me, and I'll always remember that."

Like Montana, Haines was an intensely competitive man who desperately wanted to win his last college game. But in the shadow of the Missouri game, he was also a man seeking redemption. When the quarterback returned to the huddle, the receiver who was well known for his hot temper wanted the ball. "I can beat that guy, Joe," he insisted. "I can beat him."

The call, known in the playbook as "91 out," was a quick pass, thrown after a three-step drop and intended to be drilled toward Haines with a low trajectory, so he could make a diving catch and the defender would have a very difficult time making a play. As the secondary receiver, Ferguson ran a clear-out route about ten feet away from Haines, the same one that had produced the two-point conversion as the rally began.

Montana fired the pass to Haines but it was too low and fell incomplete as the clock stopped with two seconds remaining.

On his way back to the huddle, Montana looked to the sideline for guidance, trading hand signals with the coaches before turning back to his huddle. The game was his to win or lose now, and with one play left, he trained his eyes on Haines.

"Can you beat him again?"

"Yeah. Let's go."

Montana called the same play but, while moving his finger across the wet ground, like some sandlot dreamer, he instructed Haines to run a slightly deeper route. Ferguson's job was to run right up the seam and force the defense to cover him, drawing a linebacker away from Haines.

When he pulled back from the snap, Montana could see a linebacker rushing toward him, so he rolled right, effectively turning the 91 into something closer to the very similar 63. The Houston cornerback was playing soft, toward the back of the end zone, and as the clock ticked to zero and Montana fired a bullet, low and away, the cornerback converged toward Haines and so did a nearby linebacker.

"There's no way that play should've worked, as slippery as it was," Haines said.

The pass was a perfect strike—too low to be picked off and just high enough for Haines to make a diving catch with both feet inbounds, tying the game 34–34 on the last play.

"I went to the short side of the field and Kris kept fighting the coverage and got free," explained Montana, who completed just 13 of 34 passes for 163 yards and three interceptions. "He made a super catch, but he does that all the time."

"Joe had to throw that ball just right, and he threw it just right," recalled Ferguson, who was perched about ten feet away from Haines as the clock ticked to zero.

Four months after the devastating loss to Missouri, half an hour in real time after he had been scolded by his quarterback for making another mental mistake, Haines achieved not merely redemption but historic veneration, forever linked with Montana on the play that capped the unlikeliest of all comebacks.

When the official signaled touchdown, Montana leaped into the arms of the nearest offensive lineman, thrust his right arm into the air, and sprinted off the field. But the drama was not quite over. Joe Unis, a walk-on from Dallas, kicked the extra point through the uprights . . . but Notre Dame was flagged for a procedure penalty, pushing the pause button on the Irish celebration—and preventing, for another minute, the players' hasty retreat from the bitter cold. Backed up 15 yards, Unis booted it through again, sealing a remarkable 35–34 Notre Dame victory. "Every kicker fantasizes about winning games like this," Unis told reporters when he and his teammates started to thaw out.

"These players have done it for four years," said Devine, who called the rally "the greatest" of his coaching career, a superlative he kept reassessing during Montana years. "It's amazing the number of comebacks they've had."

In the illustrious annals of Notre Dame football, forever animated by a long line of improbable comebacks—including the Army shocker in 1928 made famous by Rockne's "Win one for the Gipper" speech, and the Montana-led surge past Air Force in 1975—the 1979 Cotton Bowl occupies a special place of honor. Certainly it would have mattered more if the game had decided a national championship, but the fact that it was a rather meaningless affair, viewed in person by a tiny crowd of dedicated fans, did not diminish the verity it represented: No other victory in Irish history so profoundly demonstrated the transformative power of perseverance. And no one persevered in the face of all that adversity quite like Joe Montana.

Only afterward would Montana's teammates learn that their quarterback had suffered from hypothermia before leading the most dramatic reversal in bowl history. "At the time," the hero later revealed, "I had no idea how serious it was. They didn't tell me you can die pretty quick from that." The condition was not mentioned in newspaper accounts the next day. Like many others, *The New York Times* reported only in passing that he had been "suffering a cold and touch of flu all week." Montana's heroics earned plenty of column inches in papers large and small across the country, but the full context was not immediately available. Nor was any mention made of the apparent healing power of all those bowls of chicken soup.

As the full picture began to emerge, the contest soon to be known in Notre Dame lore as the Chicken Soup Game became one of the defining moments of Montana's football career, forcefully demonstrating his ability to summon an intense competitiveness even under significant mental, physical, and climactic distress. The performance revealed many of the traits that made him such an effective quarterback. Even after playing horribly, he did not lose his confidence. Even after his team appeared beaten, he refused to give up. Even with his body weakened, he was propelled by a strong desire to lead his team out of a deep hole. By displaying a remarkable ability to perform under the worst possible conditions while conjuring a burning desire to win, Montana offered an object lesson about the surging electric force of the various intangibles that would be so closely associated with him in the years ahead.

In the television booth, after the climactic ending, Hornung, the once and forever Golden Boy, could not contain his emotion.

"Unbelievable! Unbelievable finish!"

In the other end of the press box, Looney was experiencing a different sort of reaction. The game was over and he was supposed to be pushing his button any minute now. But, like Houston, he had a problem. Shoving his computer over one seat, Looney asked his colleague Neil Amdur from *The New York Times* to take a look at the first paragraph of his story and "see if anything won't do." When Amdur started reading the typically well-crafted story by one of *SI*'s most eloquent writers, which proclaimed one of the biggest victories in Houston Cougars history, he immediately started laughing.

"I was probably the only one at the game who didn't see all of Montana's comeback . . . because I had my head down writing," Looney said.

When his phone rang and the editor wanted to know the whereabouts of his story, Looney explained, "I'm going to need some more time."

# CHAPTER FOUR

# Number Eighty-Two

SEVERAL WEEKS BEFORE THE Cotton Bowl, in early December of 1978, Joe Montana's future began to unfold at a table for three inside an Italian restaurant off Columbus Street in San Francisco. His name was never mentioned, but the meal would prove to be a prerequisite event in the flowering of the Montana legend. Over dinner and drinks with two friends, Edward DeBartolo Jr., the brash young owner of the San Francisco 49ers, candidly discussed his frustrations about his struggling team. As the talk inevitably turned to the subject of a new head coach, DeBartolo insisted, "I want Chuck Noll or Don Shula!"

Without question, the Pittsburgh Steelers' Noll and the Miami Dolphins' Shula ranked among the finest coaches in the National Football League, but because he was still new to the NFL, DeBartolo was not aware that attempting to hire either man would place him at risk of a tampering charge. After explaining this inconvenient truth, KRON-TV sportscaster Ron Barr tossed his own candidate into the conversation. "If you hire Bill Walsh, I promise you three Super Bowls!"

Bill Walsh?

In time, this bold prediction would make Barr look like a seer, but around the NFL in 1978, Walsh was tainted with a toxic aura.

Once Walsh had been a rising star with the Cincinnati Bengals, wielding his significant intellect to become the mastermind of a potent offense under the direction of Paul Brown, one of the most influential figures in the history of professional football. Long before he launched the expansion Bengals, Brown had built a towering reputation as head coach of the Cleveland Browns from 1946–62, introducing a long list of innovations and capturing seven league championships while helping guide professional football into a new age. When the Bengals' offense began to generate buzz, most of the credit flowed to the aging Brown, who also owned the team, but in fact, he delegated almost complete offensive authority to Walsh, who began to look very much like a head coach in waiting. Operating under the assumption that he would be named to replace Brown when his boss decided to move to the front office, Walsh happily planted his flag in Cincinnati. But something happened, and the legend abruptly turned on his protégé. Some close to the situation believed it was Brown's ego, bristling at the rising profile of an assistant coach who was starting to garner attention for his offensive creativity. Whatever the cause, the circumstances of the break proved especially painful for Walsh, who was informed, during a telephone call from a reporter on New Year's Eve in 1975, that offensive line coach Bill Johnson would be taking over as head coach of the Bengals.

Several days later, when a devastated Walsh confronted Brown and re-signed his position, Brown refused to give him a recommendation. At least two NFL teams approached him about head coaching vacancies, but their interest soon cooled when one of the giant figures in football history began bad-mouthing his former assistant, culminating their eight-year relationship with a series of vindictive acts that left Walsh emotionally and professionally wounded.

"What happened in Cincinnati [was] shattering to me and it took me a long time to get over it," he told biographer David Harris. "It was an excruciating experience, the worst of my professional life."

After spending a season as offensive coordinator of the San Diego Chargers, where he worked with the gifted young quarterback Dan Fouts, the forty-five-year-old Walsh was hired as Stanford's head coach in 1977. A native of Los Angeles, Walsh had played football at San Jose State and started his coaching career at Washington Union High School in the East Bay town of Centerville. He later served as an assistant at the University of California in Berkeley and Stanford in Palo Alto before spending a year under Al Davis with the Oakland Raiders. Geographically and spiritually, returning to the Bay Area represented a homecoming.

At Stanford, an academically rigorous underdog amid football powers, his offense immediately took the Pacific-10 Conference by storm. Riding the arms of quarterbacks Guy Benjamin and Steve Dils—who led the NCAA in passing in '77 and '78, respectively—Walsh's Cardinal compiled a two-year mark of 17–7 and earned consecutive bowl bids.

"What Bill accomplished during those two years was quite significant," said John Ralston, the former Stanford coach who led the Cardinal to back-to-back Rose Bowls. "He showed what he could do under difficult conditions."

Soon after arriving in Palo Alto, Walsh was introduced to Ron Barr, a gregarious young man with a booming voice who had recently arrived in San Francisco after several years as a sportscaster in Seattle. In addition to his high-profile position as the lead sports anchor at Channel 4, Barr handled the play-by-play duties for the Stanford radio network and also hosted the coach's weekly replay television program. The two men quickly became close, setting in motion the unlikely chain of events that led him to the 49ers.

Two months after Walsh took over at Stanford, the DeBartolo family purchased controlling interest in the 49ers for $17.5 million. In one of his first assignments for Channel 4, Barr traveled to the annual NFL owners meetings in Palm Springs, where he snagged an exclusive interview with thirty-one-year-old Edward DeBartolo Jr. One thing led to another and the owner and the sportscaster became close friends. In those early years, the man known as Eddie D. or Mr. D or simply Eddie needed all the friends he could get.

His father, Edward DeBartolo Sr., grew up dirt poor in Youngstown, Ohio, and clawed his way to the top, becoming one of the most successful shopping center developers in America and eventually diversifying into banks, hotels, and racetracks. By the late seventies, he had amassed a fortune estimated at more than $400 million. A stern figure who always dressed impeccably, usually in a dark suit, he bristled at the whispered innuendo that he had underworld connections.

Eddie, who followed in his father's footsteps by earning a degree from Notre Dame, was a back-slapping, smart-ass extrovert who loved to party, drink, and gamble, always accompanied by a bodyguard who carried a loaded pistol. After spending several years learning various aspects of the family business, he arrived in San Francisco full of ambition and impatience to make his mark in football—and make his father proud.

The franchise he purchased had never won a championship but its very existence had blazed a trail. In 1942, when the National Football League (and, for that matter, Major League Baseball) remained confined to the cities of the East Coast and Midwest, lumberyard owner Tony Morabito began lobbying the NFL for a San Francisco franchise. He was repeatedly rebuffed. For various reasons, the NFL, still a rather cautious enterprise with a difficult business model, was hesitant to expand, especially to the distant West Coast. Exploiting the demand for franchises and the postwar boom, a rival league emerged in 1946: the eight-team All-America Football Conference, featuring Morabito's San Francisco 49ers, the first major professional sports team in the Bay Area. The same year, the NFL's Rams fled Cleveland, where they faced intense competition from the AAFC's most powerful team, Paul Brown's Cleveland Browns, and migrated to Los Angeles, where they shared Los Angeles Memorial Coliseum with the AAFC's struggling Dons. It would take baseball another twelve years to finally shatter the continental divide.

Led by quarterback Frankie Albert, a left-handed former Stanford star, the 49ers finished second in the western division for four straight seasons, advancing to the league championship game in 1949 as the poorly financed AAFC crumbled. The 21–7 loss to the Browns—who won all four of the fledgling league's titles—was the first major disappointment in 49ers history. It would not be the last.

When the league folded, three teams were accepted into an expanded NFL: the 49ers as well as the Browns and the first incarnation of the Baltimore Colts.

In the NFL, the San Francisco franchise fell into a pattern of dependable mediocrity, posting a record of 120 wins, 128 losses, and 10 ties (.484) in its first twenty seasons.

Like many professional teams of the era, the 49ers played their games at a facility that was never intended for such significance. Kezar Stadium was built for high school football, and through the years it also hosted motorcycle racing and track-and-field competitions. Located in Golden Gate Park in the heart of the city, it was surrounded by various working-class taverns, which provided ample opportunity for football fans to work up a good buzz before heading to the game. Kezar could be a rowdy place, especially when the 49ers were losing, and many fans grew accustomed to the sound of one whiskey bottle after another rolling underneath the wooden benches toward an eventual crash, littering the pathway below with broken glass.

The troubled heart of San Francisco fans was forever shaped by two memorable games against the Detroit Lions at Kezar in 1957. First came the day of the Alley-Oop pass. Toward the end of the regular season, with the Niners trailing by three, R. C. Owens squeezed between two defenders in the end zone and leaped toward the clouds to bring down a game-winning touchdown from Y. A. Tittle, the tenacious Texan who, with the Giants, would one day lose three straight championship games. "I knew I had to lay it in the end zone, high, and I just reared back and threw as hard as I could," Tittle explained. The leaping catch became a signature move for Owens, foreshadowing a similar maneuver a quarter-century later. While the Alley-Oop tantalized San Francisco fans with the whiff of greatness, what happened one month later brought their hopes crashing to earth. In a playoff to decide the western conference bid to the NFL Championship Game, San Francisco squandered a commanding 27–7 third-quarter lead against the Lions, losing 31–27 after quarterback Tobin Rote led a furious rally.

By the time Dick Nolan directed the 49ers to three straight western division titles from 1970–72—culminated with three consecutive playoff losses to the Dallas Cowboys, including two in the NFC Championship Game, one step from the Super Bowl—the narrative was firmly established in the minds of San Francisco fans: The Niners could not win the big game.

After suffering through three straight losing seasons, the Morabito family fired Nolan and replaced him with Monte Clark, a well-regarded coach and general manager who finished a surprising 8–6 in 1976, narrowly missing the playoffs. When DeBartolo arrived, the team appeared to be headed in the right direction. Then he put his faith in the wrong man.

Joe Thomas was a gifted evaluator of football talent. All you had to do was ask him. As the player personnel director of the Minnesota Vikings and the Miami Dolphins, he was deeply involved in building two franchises that would rise to power in the early '70s. But by the time he became general manager of the Baltimore Colts in 1972, his penchant for arrogance and bizarre decision-making was well known across the league. Under the often incoherent leadership of Thomas and owner Robert Irsay, who had briefly owned the Rams before trading the franchise for the Colts, Baltimore quickly slid from Super Bowl contender to the cellar, finishing 5–9, 4–10, and 2–12. "Joe Thomas was in way over his head," recalled Howard Schnellenberger, one of two head coaches he fired. In time, despite Thomas's ineptitude and Irsay's meddling—he once demanded, in the middle of a game, that Schnellenberger change quarterbacks—the Colts began to ascend under head coach Ted Marchibroda. When Thomas tried to fire Marchibroda—despite two straight playoff seasons—Irsay showed his general manager the door instead. His NFL career appeared to be over.

Because they were new to the league, the DeBartolos entered the millionaires' club ignorant of the disdain with which most knowledgeable football people viewed Thomas. When Thomas, an old friend with Ohio roots, contacted the family patriarch and helped set the purchase of the franchise in motion—a deal for which Oakland Raiders owner Al Davis would receive a finder's fee—the old man insisted that the former Colts executive become their new general manager. The reasoning, on the surface, made perfect sense: He knew the business, and they didn't.

Unaware that Clark, a widely sought coach, had negotiated a contract giving him complete authority over football operations, Eddie DeBartolo was quickly pulled into an ugly turf war between the head coach he inherited and the general manager his father had installed. When DeBartolo sided with Thomas, who dismissed Clark, the new owner looked clueless. The newspapers lambasted him as a Midwestern rube out of his element in sophisticated San Francisco and the fans dismissed him as a rich brat who didn't understand the game. This was an impression he would struggle to overcome as the franchise quickly descended into chaos. In an act loaded with symbolism, soon after taking over, Thomas instructed a staffer to throw away vast amounts of the team's records, photographs, and archives, including priceless game films.

"Joe Thomas went about wrecking everything," recalled Art Spander, the longtime columnist for the *San Francisco Examiner*. "He was a disaster."

The trashing of the franchise included his decision to waive quarterback Jim Plunkett, the underachieving former Stanford star who would one day lead the Raiders to the Super Bowl, and acquire Buffalo Bills running back O. J. Simpson, the 1968 Heisman Trophy winner who became the league's first 2,000-yard rusher in 1973. Not only was the Juice over the hill—he rushed for just 593 yards and a single touchdown in 1978—but the high price paid to bring him to San Francisco—five draft picks, including a first-rounder, and the trading of leading rusher Delvin Williams—would severely hamper the team well in to the future.

A domineering force who was widely mocked by the fans and the media who covered him, Thomas hired and fired three more head coaches in the next two years—three men who had never been NFL head coaches and would never get another opportunity. No one doubted who was in charge. Under the direction of career assistant Ken Meyer, Joe Namath's onetime position coach with the University of Alabama and the New York Jets, the 49ers tumbled to 5–9 in 1977, including five straight losses to start the season. In 1978, San Francisco slid into the cellar with a miserable 2–14 finish, the worst in franchise history. Pete McCulley was dumped by Thomas nine weeks into the season, after a 1–8 start, and replaced by Fred O'Connor, who presided over an equally woeful 1–6 run to end the year.

The 49ers finished dead last in the league in points scored (13.7) and twenty-third out of twenty-eight in points allowed (21.9).

No wonder DeBartolo was frustrated as the pasta and wine flowed with Ron Barr.

Several days after Barr passionately pushed Bill Walsh as the savior of the 49ers, the sportscaster was invited to a team luncheon in a ballroom at the Fairmont Hotel, the majestic landmark that served as DeBartolo's home away from home when he was in from Youngstown. Shortly after arriving, Barr discreetly pulled him aside.

"Eddie, I've got somebody I want you to meet," he said. "Let me have the key to your room. Then come up in fifteen minutes."

When the owner arrived in his suite, Barr introduced him to Bill Walsh and then excused himself, leaving the two men to get better acquainted.

Discussing his advocacy for Walsh many years later, Barr said, "Having worked with Bill . . . I sensed greatness in him."

Soon DeBartolo felt the same way. By the time Stanford arrived at Houston's Astrodome to play Georgia in the Bluebonnet Bowl on New Year's Eve 1978, the framework of a deal was in the works, though it remained a closely guarded secret. Then Georgia enhanced the drama, at least among the small circle who knew. After the Bulldogs jumped out to a 22–0 lead early in the third quarter, causing channels across America to click away from the syndicated Mizzlou telecast in search of Dick Clark's countdown, Stanford came roaring back. After Walsh made some key adjustments, Steve Dils—who had completed an astounding 63.2 percent of his passes that season—led one of the greatest rallies in bowl history, passing for three touchdowns and driving the Cardinal close enough for Ken Naber's 24-yard field goal in the closing minutes, which gave Stanford a shocking 25–22 victory.

More than an hour after the game ended, while walking across the deserted field with Walsh, Barr needed to know something.

"What the hell went through your mind when you saw Georgia go up 22–0?"

Walsh didn't hesitate.

"I looked up at the scoreboard," he said, "and I knew Eddie was at home with his friends in Youngstown, having a party. And he probably had a little hat on his head and a horn in his mouth, saying, 'This is the offensive genius I want to hire?'"

After a few moments of well-timed silence, Walsh said, "The second thing I thought of, I looked at the scoreboard and all I could see were dollar signs flying out the window!"

When the school's charter jet was stranded in Chicago by a severe winter storm—the same climactic event that played havoc with Montana's New Year's Day in Dallas—the Stanford crew wound up staying an extra night in Houston. (Like many others across the country, he caught a few minutes of Notre Dame's rally against Houston, marveling at Montana's performance and unable to imagine the way their lines would soon connect.) Over dinner and drinks, a relaxed Walsh laughed along as a Channel 4 producer mocked him with a spot-on imitation of Howard Cosell, drawing the attention of the entire dining room.

"Bill, you're nothing but a white-haired old man! You have no future in professional football!"

Even as sportswriters in the Bay Area and elsewhere began reporting that Thomas was on his way out and Walsh would become the new San Francisco head coach, the final negotiations dragged on for several days into the new year. Determined to keep a lid on his personal involvement in the deal, while protecting his scoop, Barr stopped by Walsh's house and conducted a live interview with the Stanford coach for the early evening newscast. Barr asked him about the rumors and Walsh smiled and spoke in general terms about the 49ers and the NFL, without saying much of anything.

After pitching back to the studio, Barr turned back to his buddy as soon as he knew they were off the air. "Okay, Bill, let's go into your office and tape an interview for when you take the job."

Believing the deal was a fait accompli, Barr shot the interview as if Walsh had just been hired, went back to the studio and cut the package and arranged with his producer to have it ready to go—when Bill gave him the word. When the negotiations hit a snag two days later, the sportscaster took both men out to dinner, where copious amounts of wine were consumed before Barr returned to the station to read the eleven o'clock sportscast. Concerned that the deal could fall apart, Barr leaned over to DeBartolo and whispered, "If you fuck this up, I'm gonna go on the air and rip your ass from end to end!" DeBartolo couldn't be sure Barr was bluffing, but he was determined to seal the deal.

Two days later, when the 49ers informed reporters of a news conference scheduled for several hours later to announce their new leader—hired for the princely sum of $160,000 annually—someone at Channel 4 pushed a button to air Barr's exclusive first interview with the man of the hour. The tape began playing before many local reporters were even aware of the pending media event, leaving some of Channel 4's competitors bewildered.

Soon after Walsh was introduced to the media as the new head coach and general manager of the San Francisco 49ers, fundamentally altering the history of professional football—and the life of Joe Montana—*Chronicle* sportswriter Ray Ratto started to put two and two together. He walked up to Barr, who was leaning against a wall at the back of the Hyatt House hotel ballroom, and complimented him on his scoop. But he had one question. "Ron, why was Bill wearing the same clothes on Friday for your live shot that he was wearing today?"

After the Cotton Bowl, Montana packed his bags and moved to Manhattan Beach, soaking up the Southern California sun while working out and awaiting the NFL draft. To finance the relocation, he signed with a management agency, which helped him procure a small loan.

It was an age before the combines, which would soon reduce every prospect to a series of widely shared digits, and it was an age before the draft was televised, which meant it was a time before talking heads forever searching for something to say about every possible pick, filling the air not just with information but noise. Like many other aspects of American culture in 1979, the draft still retained an element of mystery that would be lost in the years ahead.

Even in this less sophisticated climate, the buzz on Montana was not good. In the complex calculus of professional football, several aspects of his profile caused coaches and personnel gurus to view him skeptically. Most important, his arm was no rocket launcher. Stacked up against the other quarterbacks coming out of college that year, Montana was unlikely to win any distance contests. Plus, at six foot two and 185 pounds, he seemed rather small for a quarterback, which suggested he might be too fragile to survive in the rough-and-tumble world where linebackers thrived on violently slamming quarterbacks to the ground. Furthermore, while developing a reputation as the Comeback Kid at Notre Dame, he had also proven to be inconsistent, prone to moments when he was cold as well as hot.

Representatives from several teams showed up in Los Angeles to put Montana through a workout, including Zeke Bratkowski, who coached quarterbacks for Bart Starr's Green Bay Packers. Bratkowski liked what he saw and urged Starr to draft him, especially when it looked as though he would still be available in the third round, where gambles can more easily be justified. "The more you looked at the whole package, it seemed to us that Joe was being underrated," Bratkowski said. Starr initially agreed but, with a long list of holes to fill on a struggling team, he eventually catered to his defensive coaches and took a lineman with his third-round pick, which the former quarterback, winner of five league championships, would long regret.

The most prized quarterback in the draft, Washington State's Jack Thompson, could stand in the pocket and throw it a mile. He looked like a future superstar. Thompson, known as the Throwin' Samoan, was also bigger, and presumably more durable. The marquee attraction for a weak team, he amassed an NCAA-record 7,818 career yards in Pullman at a time when the vast majority of college teams relied heavily on the run. When Cincinnati selected Thompson as the third pick overall, the expectations swirling around him included comparisons to Roger Staubach. But he turned out to be a bust for the Bengals and was eventually traded to Tampa Bay, where his career ended before his twenty-seventh birthday.

With the seventh pick, the New York Giants chose Phil Simms. When

NFL Commissioner Pete Rozelle called his name from the podium at New York's Marriott Marquis, dozens of Giants fans in attendance filled the room with boos. Phil who? The drafting of an obscure quarterback from Kentucky's tiny Morehead State struck many New York supporters as yet another misstep by the hapless Giants, who had not earned a playoff bid since the Kennedy administration. One of the founding franchises of the NFL, New York owned four league championships but was a dreadful 72–136–4 since 1964. Seven months before the draft, the psyche of Giants fans had been battered by one of the most memorable gaffes in league history: With New York on its way to an apparent victory over Philadelphia in the final seconds, quarterback Joe Pisarcik inexplicably fumbled a risky handoff, instead of taking a knee. When the Eagles recovered and scored a game-winning touchdown, the play became a powerful symbol of the team's futility. Around this time, a group of especially frustrated fans conceived and funded a banner that was flown over Giants Stadium, the team's new home in East Rutherford, New Jersey, during another painful Sunday: 15 YEARS OF LOUSY FOOTBALL, WE'VE HAD ENOUGH. Recalling the furor about Simms, Giants general manager George Young said, "It wasn't like Phil was an unknown. He was to the fans. But not to us or anyone else around the league."

Indeed, despite completing less than 50 percent of his passes, Simms had also attracted the attention of the new head coach of the San Francisco 49ers. Like recently hired Giants head coach Ray Perkins, Walsh was impressed by Simms's arm, and seriously considered drafting him. However, when it looked as though Simms would go in the first round, Walsh, without a first-round pick, kept looking. For the Giants, selecting Simms proved to be a very astute move, as he became one of the cornerstones of a resurgent New York franchise destined to challenge the 49ers in the coming decade.

The third and final quarterback to go in the first round, Clemson's Steve Fuller, also worked out for Walsh but he came away unimpressed. Fuller was selected twenty-third overall by Kansas City and was headed for several years as a backup with the Chiefs, Rams, and Bears.

Because of the still-lingering residue of the Joe Thomas nightmare,

Walsh approached his first draft without a first-round pick. (The deal proved a bust for all concerned: Because San Francisco had posted the worst record in the league in 1978, the Bills wound up with the first over-all pick in the draft, which they wasted on Ohio State linebacker Tom Cousineau, who wound up signing a three-year, $1 million deal with the Montreal Alouettes of the Canadian Football League.) After sizing up the poor hand he had been dealt, well aware it would take several years of drafting and trading to assemble the sort of team he wanted—if he could survive so long—Walsh identified his second- and third-round priorities: a wide receiver and a quarterback.

Steve DeBerg, the only quarterback on the roster, remained a question mark in Walsh's mind. In 1978, operating behind a weak offensive line, he had ranked near the bottom of the league's passing statistics. The question was, what could he be in Walsh's system?

The search for another quarterback to push DeBerg or perhaps one day take his place also included strong consideration of his own former pupil Steve Dils, who wound up lasting until the fourth round, the ninety-seventh overall selection by Minnesota.

But all roads eventually led to Montana, who had also caught the at-tention of former 49ers quarterback John Brodie. When Sam Wyche, the Niners' quarterbacks coach, flew down to Los Angeles with the primary assignment of taking a close look at UCLA wide receiver James Owens, he also called Joe, who was living nearby, and asked him to take part in the workout. Recalling the scene, Montana said, "Most of the stuff we did was for the benefit of James . . . But as the workout progressed, Sam started testing my arm to see if I could throw certain types of passes."

When he returned to San Francisco about two weeks before the draft, Wyche presented a good report about Owens, whom the Niners wound up taking with their first selection, the first pick of the second round. But he was much more impressed with Montana and insisted the boss return to L.A. to see him in action. Watching him throwing various passes with pinpoint accuracy—passes that required a delicate touch, passes that re-quired a fast release—Walsh was immediately drawn to his footwork, which reminded him of Joe Namath. "He was quick, agile, and fluid in his movements, almost like a ballet dancer," Walsh said.

While other teams overlooked Montana because he did not fit their mold of what a successful NFL quarterback looked like, Walsh took a measure of the player's tools and saw a good fit with the very different picture animating his fertile imagination.

"I knew of his inconsistency," he later explained. "I also knew of his competitiveness. If he could be great for one game, why not two, why not repetition? . . . I was anxious to zero in on this guy."

Walsh saw Montana not as he was but what he could be.

With the last pick of the third round, the eighty-second overall, the 49ers drafted Montana. It is worth noting that his name was called only after a long list of long-forgotten players, including George Andrews, Jon Giesler, Rick Sanford, and Greg Roberts. If San Francisco had not taken him, he might have lasted until the sixth round, according to 49ers intelligence.

The quarterback learned the news in a telephone call. He had spent several hours camped out at a diner in Manhattan Beach, nervously guzzling coffee with his new agent, Larry Muno, while waiting for news. Neither of them understood it just yet, but the call that finally came was the first critical step in breaking the mold.

As Montana headed for San Francisco, professional football was transitioning from one era to the next.

Since completing its merger with the American Football League in 1970, the NFL had consolidated its hold as the country's most popular sport, adding franchises in Seattle and Tampa Bay to grow to twenty-eight teams. With ABC, CBS, and NBC paying a combined $144 million for annual television rights, each team now generated more from TV than ticket sales, validating Commissioner Pete Rozelle's vision and providing the owners with a measure of once-unimagined financial security.

The symbiotic relationship was reflected in the immense popularity of

ABC's *Monday Night Football*, which fused journalism and showbiz like no program in television history. What started out as a widely debated proposition among network executives—that football could succeed in prime time—quickly exploded into a cultural phenomenon embraced by 50 million viewers who relished experiencing the sport through the filtered lens of three men who somehow elevated game coverage to an art form: the acerbic blowhard Howard Cosell; his jock foil, "Dandy" Don Meredith; and straight man Frank Gifford.

At a time when most fans could access just two games on a given Sunday, and technological roadblocks and network programming decisions made widespread same-day game highlights impractical, millions of fans stayed tuned to *MNF,* even if the game was a blowout, to watch the halftime clips package narrated by Cosell. The feature offered a widely anticipated glimpse at the broader league picture. "We all lived for that," recalled future ESPN sportscaster Chris Berman. "It was appointment viewing because we were all so hungry for more."

The NFL was booming, but storm clouds loomed on the horizon. As revenue and salaries skyrocketed, the once-impotent NFL Players Association was starting to become more assertive. At least one owner was beginning to question the compact that tied a franchise to a particular city. Several wealthy fans were starting to think through the process of expanding the football calendar.

The Pittsburgh Steelers of the American Football Conference were approaching their fourth Super Bowl championship in six years, the most dominant run since Vince Lombardi's Green Bay Packers captured five league titles in a seven-year period ending in 1967. Two of those titles had been won against the Dallas Cowboys, who made five appearances in the decade, with two victories, staking an undisputed claim as the most powerful National Football Conference franchise. Both teams were nearing the end of their run at the top.

Led by quarterbacks Terry Bradshaw and Roger Staubach, respectively, the Steelers and Cowboys reflected the conventional offensive thinking of the day: dominate the line of scrimmage. Establish the run. Keep the defense honest with a deep passing threat—but avoid the risks that can result from passing too often and in certain down-and-distance situations.

Three unrelated but converging events challenged this conventional thinking starting in the late 1970s.

The first was the intervention of the NFL's competition committee during the off-season of 1978. Several officials, led by Cowboys general manager Tex Schramm, became concerned by the increasingly forceful complaints they were hearing: The game was getting boring. Such criticism was impossible to empirically demonstrate, but after the scoring average dipped to 17.2 in 1977—the lowest since 1942—the league moved aggressively to tilt the game toward greater offensive production. Defenders were limited to one hit on a receiver, permissible only within five yards of the line of scrimmage, until a pass arrived. "This was a big advantage for the offense," recalled former St. Louis Cardinals safety Benny Perrin, noting, "It wasn't quite so easy to make those receivers pay such a high price." At the same time, pass-blocking rules were liberalized to allow offensive linemen to extend their arms in certain defined ways without drawing a holding penalty.

Next came the hiring of Don Coryell as head coach of the San Diego Chargers in September 1978, ushering in the age of Air Coryell.

The third critical event was the arrival of Bill Walsh as an NFL head coach. His philosophy was already established before the rules changes took effect, but the coincidental timing certainly played to his advantage.

By the time he took over the 49ers, the cerebral Walsh was forty-seven, prematurely gray, and imbued with a professorial air, like a mad scientist plotting some complicated formula. "There was this misconception about Bill," said his longtime friend, former UCLA head coach Terry Donahue. "Because he came across as this professor type, a lot of people didn't understand what a fierce, hard-nosed competitor he was."

The roots of his offensive philosophy could be traced to former San Diego Chargers and San Diego State head coach Sid Gillman, the father of the modern passing game. Gillman passed on his voluminous playbook and his meticulous method of teaching to his assistant Al Davis, who became the conduit between the Gillman ethos and Walsh during Walsh's brief stay in Oakland. Of the experience, Walsh later said, "I learned more football in one year with the Raiders than in any ten years I spent elsewhere."

Like many great innovations, the genesis of Walsh's offense was fueled by a combination of practicality and desperation. In his second year with the Bengals, when quarterback Greg Cook went down with a season-ending injury and the team acquired journeyman Virgil Carter, he was confronted with a rather sobering reality: Carter did not have a very powerful arm. Determined to solve the problem, Walsh devised a short passing game to accentuate Carter's skills. The system emphasized quick throws—many from three-step drops—and carefully timed routes. To the surprise of many, the sum of all those short passes added up to something powerful as Carter finished third in the AFC in passing and Cincinnati won its division. This was the beginning of what would one day be called the West Coast Offense. The scheme proved even more effective in the hands of the more talented Ken Anderson, especially after the Bengals began to acquire more gifted receivers.

The history of professional football might have unfolded differently if Stanford had not pursued Walsh following his one season with the San Diego Chargers—and if he had not been so desperate to be a head coach. The transformation of strong-armed Dan Fouts into a Hall of Fame quarterback began under Walsh, who initiated his teaching by flipping on the projector to reveal the fruits of his Cincinnati experiment. "It was just so different, so counterintuitive, and so effective," recalled Fouts.

By the time Walsh took over the 49ers, San Diego's Coryell was leading Fouts in a different direction. Air Coryell became the antithesis of Walsh's scheme—going for the jugular vertically instead of trying to string together first downs horizontally. "Not only were we going to attack on every play, we were going to attack every inch of the field . . . put the defense back on their heels," Fouts said.

Both offenses descended from Gillman, different interpretations of the same revolutionary idea: The pass could be more than a tactic. It could be a strategy.

On his first day at the rookie minicamp several weeks after the draft, Montana walked into a Howard Johnson's restaurant in Redwood City, just down the road from the 49ers' practice facility. He was on a lunch break, just like the guy at the counter.

"Are you with the 49ers?"

"Yeah."

"I'm Dwight Clark."

"I'm Joe Montana."

Clark was stunned. He thought for sure the scrawny-looking guy must be a punter.

When Walsh had traveled to Clemson, South Carolina, to size up quarterback Steve Fuller in preparation for the draft, Fuller's roommate answered his phone call. His roommate just happened to be Dwight Clark. At Walsh's invitation, the former Tigers receiver came along to shag some balls—and wound up stealing the audition. Impressed by Clark's abilities, especially his long stride, Walsh drafted him on a hunch, in the tenth round, the 249th player overall.

After their memorable meeting, Montana and Clark quickly bonded, spending much of their free time together playing video games and drinking beer, unaware of the historic moment just over the horizon.

After some tense negotiations that lasted into late summer, Montana signed a four-year, $500,000 contract—including a $50,000 signing bonus—and devoted himself to learning Walsh's offense.

He was obsessed with becoming a winning quarterback. Seven games into his rookie season in 1979, when the winless 49ers traveled to the New Jersey Meadowlands to face the New York Giants, the quarterback provided some tickets for his old friend Steve Orsini, who sat with his parents. San Francisco turned the ball over three times, surrendered 377 yards, and was crushed by the Giants, 32–16. It was another ugly day in another woeful season for the 49ers. Except for his placement-holding duties, Montana didn't play a snap.

Not needing to shower, he quickly changed and emerged from the locker room to visit with his former Notre Dame teammate. "No one came up to him," Orsini recalled. "I mean no one. He was just another player. It was like he was invisible."

The small talk eventually turned to big talk, and Montana's frustration that he was not playing more.

"But Joe, you're just a rookie!" Orsini told his friend, trying to encourage him. "You're lucky to even be on this team. This is a tough league."

Orsini soon headed for home, struck by his friend's surging competitiveness and privately wondering if the Comeback Kid would ever get the chance to prove himself in the NFL.

As he watched Montana begin to soak up the offense, Walsh felt increasingly validated in his selection. He liked the way the young man was able to pick up the nuances of the system, later telling his biographer, "Joe was wonderful to coach. He could do everything you asked . . . It was just a question of adjusting him to the way the game was played in the NFL, building his confidence, and getting his feet under him."

"I remember being surprised that he wasn't playing more that first year," said tight end Ken MacAfee, the former Notre Dame star who was already on the San Francisco roster when Montana and Walsh arrived. "I don't think Bill knew what he had for a while."

He knew. Walsh was determined not to throw Montana into the fray before he was ready. Too often, he had seen promising young quarterbacks ruined by early exposure to NFL defenses, damaged both mentally and physically. Archie Manning, the second overall pick in the 1971 draft out of Ole Miss, played almost immediately for the hapless New Orleans Saints. Fronted by a weak offensive line and feeling the burden to perform for an outmanned team, Manning wound up running for his life week after week. The shots he took turned him into a widely admired profile in courage, and the inevitable dents to his confidence made his example a cautionary tale. Remarking on the experience many years later, Manning said, "I wish I'd had more time to develop. But they needed me to play, and I wanted to play." Similarly, number-one pick Jim Plunkett, the 1970 Heisman Trophy winner for Stanford, was overwhelmed in his early years with the New England Patriots, stunting his development. By the time he arrived in San Francisco in 1976, Plunkett looked like a shadow of his former self.

The cautious and precise way Walsh handled Montana in his first two years would prove critical to his development.

On the practice field, Walsh and Wyche spent a tremendous amount of time working on Montana's fundamentals, including his all-important footwork. Because the new offense was so dependent on precise timing, it could work at full strength only if the quarterback was able to master every nuance of the three- and five-step drops. Each pivot was choreographed, with a specific intent. Forever attuned to the player's posture at specific points, Walsh could be heard yelling "Keep your knees bent, Joe," when it was time for him to release the ball—because the coach had learned that certain passes could not be delivered effectively with straight legs.

To teach Montana his innovative progressive read system, Walsh conducted a drill in which he sent three different receivers on simultaneous routes, while he stood behind the quarterback. At the coach's signal, one of the receivers held up his arms. In the matter of a few precious seconds, the quarterback was expected to precisely negotiate his retreat to the pocket, move through the read, and choose the correct receiver. If he was too slow, the quarterback left himself vulnerable to the rush. If he was too fast, the receiver would not be in position just yet. The timing had to be perfect, and at first, Montana struggled with the high expectations he could feel swirling around him. "Every drop-back I did during drills had to be right," he recalled. "Every pass had to be perfect."

Carefully inserting him into game situations where he could get his feet wet and gain confidence, Walsh brought his pupil along slowly. He never sent him into the game when the 49ers were backed up deep in their own territory, and frequently, when starter Steve DeBerg drove the team across the 50 yard line, he was yanked in favor of his understudy, who could feel good about himself by harnessing the system he was still trying to master in order to move the chains. While helping him grow into the job without the pressure of winning or losing, Montana developed what his coach called the "credibility that gained him the unqualified respect of his teammates." On a windy day at Candlestick, with the Denver Broncos headed for a 38–28 victory, Montana entered the game in the fourth quarter and threw just five passes, including a 16-yarder for a touchdown to Bob Bruer, the first of his career.

The burden of responsibility fell to DeBerg, a third-year veteran out of San Jose State who had entered the league as a tenth-round afterthought. In 1978, DeBerg, who had a strong arm but lacked mobility, was one of the worst quarterbacks in the league, completing just 45.4 percent of his passes for 1,570 yards, eight touchdowns, and 22 interceptions. Pouring over the game films, Walsh struggled to find anything positive to say about the player's performance. However, to the surprise of the entire league, DeBerg quickly learned the new system and experienced one of the truly remarkable turnarounds in NFL history in 1979, finishing as the league's top-rated passer after completing 60 percent (on a record 578 attempts) for 3,652 yards. The stats proved the productivity of Walsh's scheme, in terms of gaining ground, but even as DeBerg drove the 49ers up and down the field, turning all those five-yard gains into first downs, he was prone to making drive-killing mistakes, including 21 interceptions. Time after time, he marched the Niners into the red zone and self-destructed, offering an object lesson about the subtle difference between potency and effectiveness as San Francisco, burdened with the league's twenty-seventh-ranked defense, finished 2–14 for the second straight year.

While positioning himself to compete with DeBerg, Montana was also determined to achieve a measure of domestic tranquility. Toward the end of his senior year at Notre Dame, he had met a beautiful, strong-willed flight attendant named Cass Castillo, and they quickly began a relationship that turned serious. Slightly more than a year later, the quarterback married for the second time, just as he neared another turning point in his football career.

As the new decade dawned, the 49ers' list of needs was long, and in the search for defensive help, Walsh traded for Thomas "Hollywood" Henderson, a Pro Bowl linebacker who had been discarded by the Dallas Cowboys for erratic behavior. Henderson was far and away the best defensive player on the San Francisco roster, but when Walsh invited the new man over to his house for dinner, he noticed that Henderson kept excusing himself to use the restroom. A younger man, wise to the world of 1980, would have recognized the telltale signs. Walsh worried that Hollywood suffered from some sort of urinary problem, not realizing until later that the player was sneaking off to snort cocaine. The experiment lasted a few weeks and Henderson was waived out of football for good.

What the Niners desperately needed more than anything else was a quarterback who could take control of the team and make a clutch play in a critical moment, and anyone who understood football could see DeBerg was not the man for the job. Such a man was on the payroll but he was still warming up in the wings.

"You could tell from day one in training camp [in 1980] that Joe was being groomed to take over," recalled tailback Earl Cooper, who led the Niners in rushing as a rookie. "He had the look of the future about him."

DeBerg opened the 1980 season as the starter, but Walsh began to insert Montana at pivotal moments. In the third game of the year against the New York Jets, DeBerg suffered from laryngitis and was wearing a specially designed speaker inside his helmet, so the other 49ers could hear his signals. After a drive began to stall inside the Jets' 10 yard line, DeBerg pointed to his helmet, indicating something was wrong with his amplifier. But there was no malfunction. Walsh just wanted Montana in the game, and the subsequent time-out allowed Montana to take the field. On the next play, he ran a bootleg for a touchdown.

By midyear, Walsh decided Montana was ready to be thrown into the fire. After a 59–14 rout by the Dallas Cowboys, which exposed the offensive line's weakness and DeBerg's lack of mobility, Walsh turned to Montana, who was impressive but still unable to prevent the weak 49ers from losing. As San Francisco headed for an improved but still disappointing 6–10, he started seven of the final ten games, completing an NFL-best 64.5 percent of his passes for 15 touchdowns and nine interceptions. The competition intensified, and as the quarterbacks shuttled in and out, Montana battled insecurity. "As soon as you made a mistake, you looked at the sideline to see if the other guy was standing next to Bill, or if he was warming up," he said.

The turning point came against New Orleans. By December 7, 1980—the day before former Beatle John Lennon was gunned down outside his New York City apartment, which much of the country first learned while watching *Monday Night Football*—the Saints were headed for one of the most miserable seasons in NFL history. Losing was hardly a new experience in New Orleans. Fourteen years after joining the league, the franchise had never posted a winning season and never qualified for the playoffs. But in 1980, the team tested the depths of its own well-chronicled futility, arriving in San Francisco with a pathetic 0–13 record. Coached by Dick Nolan, who had been dismissed by the 49ers to make way for the short-lived Monte Clark, the Saints were increasingly being referred to, by their own fans, as the Aints, including some who showed up for games wearing brown paper bags over their heads. Since World War II, only the first-year Tampa Bay Buccaneers, who stumbled through 1976 by losing all fourteen games, managed to exceed the Saints' level of ineptitude.

However, in week fourteen at Candlestick, the moribund Saints came alive. Archie Manning dominated the first two quarters, repeatedly scrambling his way out of trouble while passing for 248 yards and three touchdowns. It was 21–0 before San Francisco earned a first down. It was 35–7 at the half. As Montana struggled to move the chains, the 49ers gained just 21 yards before intermission.

After listening to Walsh talk about the fight they would now wage against adversity, Montana led his offensive team back onto the field and quickly hit Dwight Clark for a 48-yard pass. Four plays later, the quarterback scored on a one-yard run, cutting the margin to 35–14. Soon, the defense forced a punt, and once again, Montana connected with Clark, this time for a 71-yard touchdown, slicing New Orleans' lead to 35–21. In the fourth quarter, the San Francisco defense forced two fumbles, leading to two long drives. After Montana's 14-yard pass to Freddie Solomon brought the Niners within a touchdown, he orchestrated a 78-yard march to tie the game, culminating in Lenvil Elliott's seven-yard run, which forced the game into overtime.

"The most amazing turnaround I've ever seen in my life," recalled tight end Eason Ramson.

In the overtime, it took an interception by Dwight Hicks to put the ball back in Montana's hot hand, some tough running by Elliott and Don Woods, and a roughing-the-passer call on Saints defensive lineman Steve Parker to pave the way for Ray Wersching's 36-yard field goal, which gave San Francisco a heart-pounding 38–35 victory. As the Saints tumbled to 0–14, headed for a record-setting 1–15 finish, the Niners celebrated the biggest comeback in NFL history.

Perhaps half of the announced crowd of 37,949 had long since headed for home, many no doubt muttering about the sorry state of their team, but those fans who remained in attendance were suddenly happy and stunned. They had witnessed the dawn of a new age, led by a quarterback who seemed to play better when he was behind.

"We were in a big hole and Joe led us out," recalled Earl Cooper. "I think you could say that's when we all knew, without a doubt, there was something pretty special about Joe Montana."

# CHAPTER FIVE

# The Catch

LIKE ALL GREAT MOMENTS IN sports, it is bathed in both light and shadow.

But before the play that altered the trajectory of Joe Montana's life came a play that Randy Cross will never forget.

From the first snap of the NFC Championship Game at Candlestick Park on January 10, 1982, Ed "Too Tall" Jones filled the air with trash. As his powerful Dallas Cowboys battled the upstart San Francisco 49ers, the six-foot-nine defensive predator inundated the line of scrimmage with one persistent thought: He didn't respect Montana or the Cinderella Niners.

"A lot of guys talked smack. That's part of the game. But Too Tall was especially obnoxious that day," recalled Cross, the Niners' All-Pro guard.

Instead of being rattled by Jones's incessant jabbering, the forever-cool Montana was motivated by it, because, meaningless as it was in the ebb and flow of a hard-hitting football game with enormous stakes, the trash talk reflected a deeper truth. It was more than background noise. It was the sound track of Montana's life. Time after time, he had been doubted, dismissed as too ungifted, too small, too fragile, too inconsistent, too this, not enough that, to become a successful quarterback. He always looked so calm and centered—staring out into the chaos around him with those piercing baby blues and a "What, me worry?" expression—but beneath the surface, he was a tenacious competitor with a burning desire to win who desperately wanted to be respected, pursuing not just championships but some larger validation.

"It took quite a while for Joe to get the kind of respect he deserved, and I think that was something he used as a motivational tool," observed his Notre Dame and San Francisco teammate Ken MacAfee. "He wasn't the type to talk about it too much, but there's no doubt, he felt like he had something to prove."

In the second quarter, Montana rolled out on a naked bootleg, pursued closely by Jones. Suddenly, the quarterback stopped, causing Jones to lose his footing, and lofted a bullet across the middle to his buddy Dwight Clark, who raced into the distance for a 38-yard gain.

Looking up at Jones as the crowd erupted, Montana shouted, "Respect that, motherfucker!"

The towering Jones just glared at Montana as Niners offensive tackle Keith Fahnhorst pulled him away—"Joe! Joe! Joe!"—reminding his quarterback that he still had to block Too Tall, and Montana was not making the job any easier.

"Joe was giving it right back to Too Tall and I told him, 'Just shut the hell up and play,'" Cross said many years later.

Just as Jones's chatter reflected something more profound, so, too, did Montana's forceful reaction. Deep down, the mild-mannered Montana wanted to utter the same throttling sentence to all who had underestimated him on the road to this pivotal day.

But after a moment of ballsy engagement with one of the most intimidating defenders in football, he turned away and returned to the task at hand, heading for a moment that would define him for the ages.

As Montana guided San Francisco to the brink, the world he left behind was crumbling. The long slide started in 1974, the year he graduated from Ringgold High School and moved on to South Bend, as the country slipped into a deep recession, shrinking the demand for steel and causing mass layoffs across the Mon Valley. What many assumed was just another cyclical pause in the great American manufacturing engine was instead the first indication that the smokestack economy, which had blanketed the region in prosperity for the better part of a century, was entering a protracted death spiral, permanently devastated by the accumulated weight of overly generous union contracts, corporate resistance to modernizing obsolete plants, and the increasingly sober realities of an emerging global marketplace, which permanently shifted the competitive advantage to more efficient foreign steelmakers. By the autumn of 1981, as the United States sank into the worst recession since World War II, plants started closing up and down the big river, many for good.

Rampant unemployment ravaged the Mon Valley, causing an economic tidal wave of home foreclosures, shuttered storefronts, bankruptcies, and reductions in municipal services resulting from the decimated tax base. "When the hard times came, it was devastating to this area," said former Ringgold football player Don Devore, who took over his father's hardware store after graduation and guided it through some very difficult years. "The downturn affected everybody, one way or another, because the whole economy was dependent on those jobs."

The once vibrant little town of Monongahela withered in the face of all that destruction, causing the population to shrink by roughly half as many lifelong residents sought opportunities elsewhere, especially those around Montana's age or younger who could see the handwriting on the wall. Many of those who stayed were destined to become permanently unemployed or underemployed, unable to find full-time work for years, even decades.

"Seeing your friends and neighbors lose their homes . . . had an impact on all of us," said Ulice Payne, who stayed in Milwaukee after graduating from law school and eventually became president of the Brewers. "For some people, working at a steel mill was all they had ever known. They had no other skill set and they didn't know how to acquire the skills to do something else. It was really sad. Some people just never got over it."

Steve Russell, one of Montana's teachers at Ringgold, watched various relatives and friends deal with the disruption caused by the disappearance of jobs that once were considered a permanent fixture of the Mon Valley landscape. "It's very traumatic when you've planned your life to do a certain thing and then your income is taken away," Russell said. "There's such a sense of loss. You struggle with how to go on, how to pick up the pieces and start over."

During this difficult period for his hometown, Montana rarely returned to visit, especially after his father and mother moved to California to be near him. He sometimes swept into town to see relatives, including his maternal grandmother, Josephine Bavuso, but he never called his old football teammates to get together for a beer, which rubbed many of the guys the wrong way. "It's very hard to go back, anywhere, it really is," he once explained. "But Mon City is not the kind of place people who leave go back to. Not in spirit, not all the way."

As he was rising on the national stage, such cryptic language, coupled with his persistent standoffishness, angered many of his former teammates who still harbored old grudges. Even as he emerged as a nationally celebrated sports icon, Montana became an ambivalent figure in his hometown. Admired but not quite beloved.

When reporters from around the country began descending on Monongahela to trace the roots of Montana's greatness, Chuck Abramski repeatedly trashed his former pupil, telling one sportswriter, "A lot of people in Monongahela hate Joe Montana." Abramski was overstating the situation, but without a doubt, the community was full of hurt feelings, especially after Monongahela celebrated him with Joe Montana Day on April 17, 1982. The local boy made good was paraded down Main Street before a big crowd, and later gave a speech to a packed dinner crowd. "A very special day for this town," recalled Don Devore. When word leaked out that someone representing Montana subsequently billed the Monongahela Valley Progress Council for his airfare from the West Coast, the adoration cooled. Montana blamed the invoicing on a miscommunication, telling one reporter, "I never knew a thing about it until I read all that stuff in the paper." By then the damage was done.

Abramski needed no additional motivation to spew his venom. He was still steamed about the old days. "Joe broke my heart," the old coach, who was fired from Ringgold several years after Montana graduated, told one sportswriter. "I'd come home at night and cry . . . trying to figure out ways of getting Joe to come [to the off-season conditioning program]. We needed his leadership." Mocking the relationship between father and son that nearly caused him to lose Montana to a rival high school, Abramski told another writer, "If I was in a war, I wouldn't want Joe on my side. His dad would have had to carry his gun for him."

The veiled shot at Montana's courage was particularly galling to the quarterback, who had once written a letter of recommendation for his old coach, helping him land one of his last jobs in football. Rather than responding in the media, Montana reached out in a private phone conversation, in which Abramski kept complaining that Joe had never sent him an autographed picture. They wound up shouting at each other.

"It was a sad situation," said Jeff Petrucci, the former Ringgold quarterbacks coach who went on to become the head coach at California University of Pennsylvania, his alma mater, winning a league championship in 1984. "Chuck just couldn't let go of the bitterness. He was a good football coach, but he had a blind spot about what happened with Joe and the workout program. It was irrational . . . and very hurtful to Joe."

The worst days for the steel mills corresponded with the decline of Terry Bradshaw's Pittsburgh Steelers, so the town's mixed feelings about Montana sometimes included criticism that he played for the 49ers instead of the beloved home team. Beyond the realities associated with the draft system—and the fact that the Steelers had the chance to pick him but chose not to—lurked a deeper truth. By moving so far from home and leading another city's dynastic ambitions—achieving stardom against the relief of their mounting despair—Montana emerged as yet another symbol of loss for an area left reeling by the demise of the industrial revolution.

When the quarterback arrived in San Francisco, the city suffered from an image of decay, crime, and corruption, mirroring much of urban America. At the same time, Bay Area residents took great pride in their reputation on the leading edge of American culture, viewing the world through a sophisticated, intellectual lens, forever challenging the established order, embracing their diversity, often disdainful of Middle America's more conservative impulses. In the nation's consciousness, San Francisco was forever associated with the hippie movement of the 1960s, especially the Summer of Love, when tens of thousands of flower children descended on Golden Gate Park in a drug-fueled frenzy of hedonistic expression. To traditional America, San Francisco was synonymous with decadence in its various forms. A decade after the height of the hippies, counterculture movements and radicals continued to find refuge in a city that took pride in its tolerance for minority viewpoints. One such group was the Peoples Temple, a religious sect founded by the mesmerizing and politically connected Jim Jones, who operated for several years in San Francisco before relocating nearly one thousand members of his flock to the South American nation of Guyana. On November 18, 1978, when Jones directed a mass suicide that rocked the world, the tremor was felt most profoundly in San Francisco, where the horrific scene became a symbol of the danger inherent in the city's various excesses. "Jonestown released a poison cloud over San Francisco," author David Talbot wrote in *Season of the Witch*, his bestselling book about the city's most turbulent age. "There was blood and terror in the air." Nine days later, the civic tumult grew grimmer still when former supervisor Dan White walked into city hall and gunned down Mayor George Moscone and supervisor Harvey Milk, the first openly gay public official ever elected in the state of California. The brazen murders staggered San Francisco.

Five months later, when a third-round draft choice joined the struggling 49ers, the city was still battered with grief, desperately needing something to believe in.

As belching smokestacks all across the industrial Midwest began to cool and the dusty collection of shuttered factories morphed into the Rust Belt, a new revolution stirred in the distance. This movement, centered south of San Francisco in the area around San Jose known as Silicon Valley, was powered not by harnessed fire and sturdy men performing manual labor, but by highly skilled engineers and programmers who exploited the microchip to feed the demands of a still-gathering information age, planting the seeds of an economic renaissance.

The connective tissue between the flower children and many of the early leaders of the computer revolution who gravitated to the South Bay towns around San Jose was easy to see: Both movements challenged conventional thinking, unwilling to be constricted by the older generation's ideas. In their own way, the leaders at Fairchild Semiconductor (which invented the silicon chip) and Intel (which introduced the microprocessor), the pioneers created the technology to make computers smaller and more powerful, were radicals pushing against the establishment, forever fusing the ethos of Golden Gate Park in the flowering of Silicon Valley. It took a couple of college dropouts with long hair and an irreverent view of the world to launch the personal computer age—in the Los Altos garage attached to Steve Jobs's boyhood home. In the years after Jobs and partner Steve Wozniak founded Apple Computer in 1976, stoking demand for chip makers, software designers, hardware manufacturers, and venture capitalists, the world began hurtling at breakneck speed into a future increasingly shaped not just by the San Francisco region but by the San Francisco mindset.

In 1981, three unrelated events converged as the Bay Area moved into a new age. On June 5, the Centers for Disease Control in Atlanta issued the little-noticed report announcing the AIDS virus, which soon would develop into a full-scale epidemic causing millions of deaths worldwide, a scourge destined to ravage San Francisco in the years ahead. On August 12, IBM introduced its first personal computer, bringing standardization, credibility, and demand to a still-nascent industry that would be dominated in the years ahead by Silicon Valley giants including Intel, Hewlett-Packard, and Apple, setting the world on the circuitous road to the Internet. And that fall, the San Francisco 49ers began to win.

Toward the end of the exhibition season in 1981, Tampa Bay head coach John McKay arranged a trade with his colleagues in San Francisco, acquiring James Owens. The speedster who had started his professional career auditioning alongside Montana proved to be a disappointment at receiver, and McKay planned to move him to the backfield. In return, San Francisco received much-needed help in the inside running department from Johnny Davis, a fourth-year veteran out of Alabama.

After the colorful and unpredictable McKay traded him in a fit of rage, following a preseason game against the Falcons, a devastated Davis sat in the Atlanta airport, crying. He lingered for quite a while at a pay phone, breaking the news to his mother. "McKay thought he was punishing me by sending me to San Francisco, and I felt like I was being punished," Davis recalled. "I didn't want to go all the way to San Francisco. That was a long way from home, and besides, they weren't winning out there. Who in their right mind wanted to play for the 49ers?"

Among Walsh's most important attributes was his keen eye for talent. His systematic analysis of a player's skills yielded significant knowledge, much of it overlooked by others, and as he went about the business of acquiring the various parts to power the 49ers engine, his attention to detail often surprised his colleagues. He could be ruthless in discarding players who didn't fit the system—and aggressive in pursuing those who possessed a specific skill. "Bill would look at a player and say, 'This guy can help us for eight plays a game,'" recalled Terry Donahue, the former UCLA head coach who later became the 49ers' director of player personnel. "And I'm thinking, what the hell do we want with a guy who's only good for eight plays? Bill had dissected the individual parts of the team so thoroughly that he understood how those eight plays could make a difference, if we had this one individual. I've never been around anybody else who thought on that level."

Entering his third season, Walsh was still working to assemble the right pieces. The team had grown a bit stronger after the 1980 draft, which produced defensive tackle Jim Stuckey, linebacker Keena Turner, and running back Earl Cooper. But the defense was still woefully inadequate, and 1981 loomed as a pivotal year. In the draft, Walsh selected three players who would be critical in the Niners' rise, including defensive back Ronnie Lott, who became the Joe Montana of the defense, bound for the Hall of Fame; as well as secondary mates Eric Wright and Carlton Williamson. All three players started as rookies. (The emergence of Dwight Hicks, who was on the roster when Walsh arrived, gave the 49ers four solid defensive backs in 1981.)

The transformation of the defense was further bolstered by two key acquisitions.

Linebacker Jack "Hacksaw" Reynolds was like some cartoon version of a football player, right down to his nickname, which he acquired during his college days at Tennessee. Distraught after a loss to Ole Miss, he took out his frustrations on his beat-up old Chevrolet Bel Air, wielding a series of hacksaws to chop off the top. The car was soon discarded but the nickname stuck. It seemed a perfect fit for the intense, tough, scary-looking character who lived and breathed the game. "If you were making a movie and you were looking for the prototypical football player type, Hacksaw would be your guy," Johnny Davis said. After eleven years with the Los Angeles Rams, Reynolds became a free agent and Walsh outbid the Buffalo Bills for his services, not realizing what a profound impact he would have. In addition to his still-good lateral movement, which gave the 49ers new strength near the line of scrimmage, Hacksaw became an inspiration to a defense that needed to be stoked, elevating the players around him with his obsessive film study and his burning desire to win.

Every bit as critical was the midseason arrival of Fred Dean, a two-time Pro Bowler for the San Diego Chargers. When Dean demanded his long-term contract be renegotiated, the Chargers refused and traded him to San Francisco, where he immediately gave the 49ers something they had been sorely lacking: a menacing pass rush.

Both signings required DeBartolo to open his wallet, and in these instances as well as many others to come, DeBartolo's willingness to meet the market price for the players Walsh wanted represented a powerful advantage for the 49ers.

Discussing the moves heading into the season, Walsh said, "We're still not where I'd like us to be, but we're close."

The most consequential deal of all involved the quarterback situation.

Heading to training camp, Montana was firmly established as the starter, based on the way he finished 1980, but DeBerg was a competitor who was determined to keep fighting for the job. "Bill told me I was going to be the number one," Montana later recalled. "But I had my doubts. . . . With Steve around I figured it would be another season of us going back and forth."

The two players got along fine, without any animosity, and competed with each other in a professional manner. "I admired [DeBerg]," Montana said years later. "He had to battle for everything he achieved . . . He knew I was competing for his job but he couldn't have treated me better."

But Walsh, who endeavored to understand the psychological as well as the physiological in all of his players, believed Montana would operate more effectively without DeBerg breathing down his neck. He was beginning to understand what made Montana tick. When the coach announced his intention to trade DeBerg to Denver for a fourth-round draft pick, several key figures in the organization felt he was acting too hastily. What was the hurry? But Walsh knew exactly what he was doing. In one fell swoop, he reassured Montana and put the whole burden on his shoulders, believing the act, loaded with symbolism, would help Montana take the next step in his development. Off to the Broncos DeBerg went, a journeyman destined to play for four more teams, as Montana became the unquestioned offensive leader of the San Francisco 49ers.

Despite the various improvements, the 49ers opened the season surrounded, as usual, by low expectations. Most knowledgeable observers expected the road to the Super Bowl to originate in the NFC East, where defending conference champion Philadelphia and runner-up Dallas looked strong once again. In the NFC West, the Atlanta Falcons, with a powerful running game; a gifted, if frequently battered quarterback in Steve Bartkowski; and a stout defense, were favored to repeat . . . a sentiment vindicated by the third game of the season.

After the Falcons jumped out to a 17–0 lead, it was 24–10 in the third quarter when Montana methodically drove the 49ers from deep in their own territory to the Atlanta 11, relying heavily on a mix of short passes and the legs of tailback Ricky Patton. On third down, Dwight Clark was running a crossing pattern at the goal line, and Montana fired the ball in his direction. But it was a bad pass, way off target. Instead of finding Clark, the ball sailed farther into the end zone, into the waiting arms of free safety Tommy Pridemore, who returned the interception for a 101-yard touchdown.

"I never thought about downing it," Pridemore explained after Atlanta's convincing 34–17 victory. "When I saw the tight end was blocked, I knew I could get out [of traffic]. Once I made the corner, I had clear sailing."

It was an embarrassing moment for Montana, the kind of mistake that so often caused coaches and teammates to lose faith in DeBerg. Beyond the larger implications of the innovative offense, the drive demonstrated a fundamental fact about football: By eating more than five minutes off the clock, coming away empty-handed, and making a mistake that resulted in seven points for the Falcons—the dreaded 14-point swing—San Francisco had made Atlanta's job much easier.

Sylvia Engstrom knew it would be a long flight home.

Sylvia was hired as a stewardess. Only later did the term fall out of favor, replaced by the more gender neutral "flight attendant," which is how she was known when the longtime United Airlines employee was offered the opportunity to work a charter ferrying the 49ers to an away game in 1980. She was hesitant. "Nobody wanted to fly sports charters," she recalled. "They were considered the worst assignment you could get [because] you would hear these awful stories about the way the athletes behaved."

One flight with the 49ers changed her attitude, and she became a fixture on their trips for the next sixteen years, enjoying a first-class vantage point as the franchise experienced one of the most successful runs in professional sports history.

"It turned out to be the best assignment ever," she said. "They treated me very well and I got to take this incredible ride with them."

In September 1981, after the Falcons crushed the 49ers, Walsh walked onto the United Airlines charter riddled with doubts about his team's disappointing 1–2 start, which included a season-opening loss to the Detroit Lions and a victory over the Chicago Bears. The coach always sat in the front row of first class, next to an empty seat. Especially after a painful loss, no one wanted to be anywhere near him. But on this night, like many others, he motioned for Sylvia, a familiar face who always took good care of the boss.

"Get Wayne and bring us two vodkas."

Sylvia was dating Wayne Walker, the sports director of San Francisco's KPIX-TV, the CBS affiliate. Walker, who played fifteen seasons as a linebacker and kicker for the Detroit Lions, hosted Walsh's weekly television show and was an announcer on the 49ers' TV broadcasts.

"You could always tell when they lost," said Sylvia, who married Wayne the following year. "It was always very quiet."

Walker was accustomed to being called to the front of the jet. One of Walsh's confidants, he spent significant time with the coach, much of it talking football. On Monday nights during the season, they usually rented a limo and shared dinner somewhere in the city, unwinding from the grind while chatting about a variety of subjects, including boxing, one of Walsh's passions. (The coach's boxing obsession often extended to his quarterback, who learned to appreciate Walsh's analogy of trying to wear down an opponent with round after round of jabs before delivering a roundhouse right. "The idea is," Montana once said, "set them up, then at the right time, knock 'em on their ass.")

"Bill was a lot of fun to be around," Walker said. "He had a great sense of humor. He was hilarious."

But on this night, at a precarious juncture in his career, Walsh was beginning to wonder about his legacy and whether he would be given enough time to succeed. "I listened to his frustrations and told him he was going to be just fine," Walker recalled. "He needed a pat on the back every once in a while, just like everybody does."

The next Sunday, the 49ers looked stronger in knocking off the New Orleans Saints, 21–14, highlighted by Montana's 60-yard touchdown pass to Freddie Solomon. It was the start of a seven-game winning streak that moved the Niners to the top of the NFC West. While the reinvigorated defense began to shut the door on opponents—exemplified by rookie Ronnie Lott's fourth-quarter interception of Archie Manning, which he returned for a 26-yard touchdown to provide the winning points—Montana led an offensive revival that became the talk of the league.

In Walsh's first two years, the offense was largely dismissed as a gimmick that bespoke desperation, but in 1981, the brilliance of the scheme and the skill of Montana's execution were impossible to deny. Instead of standing in the pocket and zipping the ball way downfield, Montana was propelling the 49ers forward with small chunks of passing yards—five- and six- and seven-yard completions, which set up the strategically applied running game. Some longer routes were thrown into the mix, to spread the defense, but big yardage was gravy for the steak. It was the methodical nature of all those small bites, the passing equivalent of handoffs, that caused defenders such grief, strung together for first downs that kept the offense pointing toward the end zone and burned the clock. It was death by a thousand cuts.

"This whole idea of a ball-control offense based on short passes was just so revolutionary," recalled center Randy Cross. "It could be very frustrating for the defense."

Discussing his intention to stymie the defense, Walsh said, "I want them saying over and over again, 'Dammit, we've got to stop them from making first downs. Dammit, they just completed that five-yard pass again.'"

While sharing playing time with DeBerg in 1980, Montana had sometimes appeared too eager to dump the ball off to his backs. In 1981, his increased confidence produced greater patience in the pocket, which allowed him to increase his yards-per-completion from 10.2 to 12.53.

Time after time, Montana made clutch plays as the offense fed off his confidence. Just as Walsh had intended, he responded to DeBerg's departure by elevating his game. "There has been a metamorphosis with him," Sam Wyche said. "He has truly become the team leader." Freed from DeBerg's shadow, the quarterbacks coach saw him becoming more assertive.

"Once he was the guy and everybody was looking to him, his leadership qualities began to be felt across the team," said tight end Eason Ramson. "He had a way, a very quiet way, of motivating everybody. It's not something that's taught. It's something that was in him, and he used it well."

As Montana began to attract attention while rising to the top of the NFC passing statistics, headed for a season when he would complete 63.7 percent of his passes for 3,565 yards, 19 touchdowns, and 12 interceptions, Walsh told a reporter, "As an instinctive player, Joe Montana maybe is among the best the game has ever seen at quarterback. He's only in his third year, and he can only get better. He will be at his best in four or five years."

The turning point may have occurred in week five, when the 49ers knocked off the Washington Redskins, 30–17. The way Montana methodically worked the offense on three long scoring drives perfectly captured Walsh's philosophy, and coupled with an opportunistic defense, it proved incredibly effective. But the game that caused the country to take notice happened the following Sunday at Candlestick, when Montana passed for two touchdowns, including a 78-yarder to Dwight Clark, to lead a 45–14 rout of the Dallas Cowboys. Nobody embarrassed the Cowboys in such dramatic fashion. Not in those days. "Losing that game . . . was a rude awakening for us," recalled Dallas receiver Drew Pearson.

The winning streak, which included pivotal victories over the Pittsburgh Steelers and the Atlanta Falcons, was halted by a 15–12 loss to the Cleveland Browns in November, secured in the closing minutes by a Montana interception. But it was a rare stumble in an otherwise dominant season.

After clinching the NFC West with a 13–3 record, San Francisco hosted the resurgent New York Giants in the first round of the playoffs. Like the 49ers, the Giants had been down for a long time, suffering through eight consecutive losing seasons. Plagued by years of mismanagement from the estranged heirs of team founder Tim Mara, which produced a kind of institutional paralysis, the franchise pivoted into a new age with the hiring of general manager George Young in 1979. The onetime Miami Dolphins executive seized control with a firm hand, hiring Ray Perkins, the New England Patriots' offensive coordinator, as head coach and moving aggressively to rebuild the roster. Three years later, the 9–7 revival under Perkins produced the team's first playoff bid since 1963.

One of the primary reasons for the turnaround was a rookie linebacker from North Carolina. Lawrence Taylor was a ferocious tackler with tremendous speed and athleticism who would one day be recognized among the greatest players in the history of professional football. Up to this point, the Niners' offensive line had done a creditable job in protecting the quarterback against a long line of defenders trying to disrupt the offense, but the San Francisco coaches were starting to learn how destructive number 56 could be. Fearing his ability to put Montana on his back, they designed something special to stop him. The heaviest burden fell on guard John Ayers, who pulled dramatically during passing situations and repeatedly stymied the NFL's Rookie of the Year. "Taylor is a super football player but . . . I cemented my feet so he couldn't run over me," explained Ayers, who utilized his thirty-pound weight advantage to maximum effect.

With Taylor neutralized, Montana was free to enjoy the greatest passing day of his young career. Throwing both long and short, he completed 20 of 31 for 304 yards and two touchdowns—including a 58-yard bomb to Freddie Solomon—as San Francisco cruised to a 38–24 victory.

It was just the opening act of a bitter rivalry, and Taylor and his teammates would find a way to Joe Montana.

On fall Sundays, Steve Travers spent his afternoons playing in a baseball league at Big Rec, a set of adjoining fields inside Golden Gate Park. Fog descended across the serene enclave in the morning and usually lifted by the time he arrived, casting the fields in a warm glow of sunlight. The twenty-two-year-old Travers, who had grown up in the Marin County community of San Anselmo, was pursuing a career in professional baseball. After spending his first year as a pitcher in the St. Louis Cardinals' organization—at Johnson City, Tennessee, in the Appalachian League— he was back living in the Bay Area and keeping his skills sharp while preparing for spring training. During the games at Big Rec, the various sounds of the city wafted through the park, including police sirens and music flowing from passing ice-cream trucks. By late autumn, Travers could hear another sound rising above the urban cacophony: the authoritative voice of Don Klein, the play-by-play man for the 49ers radio network, crackling through the air as spectators and picnickers followed the action on multiple portable sets.

"Everyone was keeping up with the 49ers and wanted to know how the game was going," Travers recalled. "It hadn't been like that in years."

The renewal produced a new demand for tickets as Candlestick, routinely half- filled throughout the late '70s, began to fill to capacity, attracting not just serious football fans but all manner of locals and celebrities attracted to the glimmer of success. The growing legion included Mayor Dianne Feinstein, who had turned her box seats over to Congressman Willie Brown as a political favor, only to demand them back when the team started winning. Even the widow of murdered Mayor Moscone, who had faded from public view, becoming San Francisco's most talked-about recluse, was sighted at the stadium during the glorious 1981 season, cheering on the red-and-gold and smiling broadly for her team and her city.

The victory over the New York Giants set up a showdown with the Dallas Cowboys at Candlestick for the right to represent the NFC in the Super Bowl. After crushing Tampa Bay, 38–0, the Cowboys headed to San Francisco determined to put the upstart 49ers in their place.

For more than a week, the Bay Area had been inundated with torrential rains, causing massive flooding and at least twenty-eight deaths. The enormity of the natural disaster loomed over every aspect of local life as hundreds of families dealt with the dire consequences of unwanted water gushing through their homes. Two days before the game, the lead story in the *San Francisco Chronicle* carried the ominous headline, "Why Houses Slide."

Located south of the city on the western shore of San Francisco Bay, Candlestick Park was originally built for the baseball Giants, who set up shop in 1960, but eventually was retrofitted to also accommodate the 49ers, who migrated from Kezar Stadium in 1971. The place exuded all the charm of a federal prison. Widely mocked for its swirling winds, bog-like playing surface, and all-around second-rate vibe—including protruding cracks in the parking lot—the stadium had been built on the site of an old landfill, after developer Charles Harney sold the tract to the city under circumstances so suspicious that a corruption investigation ensued.

Through the years, Candlestick hosted various events, including the last American appearance of the Beatles in 1966 and a stop the previous October on the Rolling Stones' 1981 concert tour. As the smell of marijuana wafted through the air, a young woman abruptly climbed up on stage while the band was performing. Mick Jagger looked her over and said lustily, "Well all right! Take your clothes off and let's have a look at ya!" The crowd roared in approval, punctuating another freewheeling moment in the age of sex, drugs, and rock 'n' roll.

The song played most often over the loud speakers at Candlestick that season was "Don't Stop Believing," the recent number-one hit from Journey, the San Francisco–based rock group. The hard-driving ballad, featuring the vocals of Steve Perry, became an anthem for a city that was finally enjoying the success of a sports team and trying to keep the faith that the magic would last all the way to the Super Bowl.

The believing did not come easily for San Francisco fans, especially as the mighty Cowboys came to town.

At the beginning of the Reagan era, Tom Landry towered over professional football, iconic not only for his success but for also for the cold, calculating way he approached the game. In contrast to the fiery coaches personified by the late Green Bay Packers legend Vince Lombardi—who filled every room he entered with a raging intensity—Landry was an emotionally detached figure who commanded his troops like an aloof general, "a cross between the Pope and Gary Cooper," in the words of sportswriter Skip Bayless.

Landry was leading Dallas through the greatest period of sustained success in league history, including five Super Bowl appearances and two trips to the pre–Super Bowl NFL Championship Game. Over a fifteen-year period, the Cowboys had been one of the last two teams standing a staggering seven times. Employing a sophisticated offensive scheme that routinely produced big plays from quarterbacks who worked within a rigid framework—especially the coolly efficient Roger Staubach, who retired after the 1980 season—and the innovative Flex Defense, which pursued through carefully structured gaps by reading certain offensive keys, the Cowboys reflected a precise, mechanized view of football. "The Flex sort of represented Coach Landry's feelings about the way the game should be played," explained linebacker Lee Roy Jordan. "If everybody did his job, the defense worked like a machine."

By embracing the Texas-sized bravado inherent in the "America's Team" moniker, the Cowboys cultivated a large national following and the rhetorical implication that they were the class of the league, which insulted the other twenty-seven franchises scattered about the continent. Even if it happened to be true. The two Super Bowl losses to Pittsburgh, which helped elevate the Steelers to the undisputed team of the seventies, tarnished the luster of the Cowboys somewhat. But despite the proof of their imperfection, the team emblazed with the silver star remained to many envious fans across the league the smug, condescending evil empire.

In the days leading up to the NFC title game—Dallas' ninth in twelve years—the Cowboys made it quite clear they were motivated to seek revenge for the regular-season rout administered by the 49ers. Too Tall Jones went further, telling a Dallas reporter, "They didn't beat the real Cowboys." This time, the "real" Cowboys would show up to restore order to the football universe. Insisting he did not respect the 49ers or even know most of their players' names, Jones ripped into Montana: "All you have to do against that guy is throw off his timing and you blow his game." When word of the flying insults reached Walsh, he privately rejoiced. The Niners' coach believed he had the better team, telling TV show cohost Wayne Walker, after the cameras were turned off, "We've got this thing in the bag. We're quicker than they are and they don't know it." The bulletin-board material helped him stoke the fire, giving the players an additional emotional lift for a showdown in which Dallas was favored by two points.

While the October dismantling of America's Team filled the 49ers with confidence, the fans remained wary. Especially those old enough to be burdened by the memory.

Up to this point, no San Francisco professional sports team had ever won a championship. Across the bay in blue-collar Oakland, Al Davis's Raiders and Charlie Finley's Athletics had brought home several world titles, but the city of San Francisco remained a sports wasteland, psychologically battered by decades of futility. A certain segment of the populace had always embraced the 49ers, despite their pervasive mediocrity, but the cumulative effect of all those heartbreaks was an unmistakable inferiority complex that promoted a defeatist attitude tinged with fear. Because the 49ers consistently let their fans down.

Among the three consecutive playoff losses to the Cowboys during the first term of Richard Nixon, the most gut-wrenching happened on a Saturday in late December 1972, the same afternoon Franco Harris's "Immaculate Reception" allowed the Steelers to beat the Raiders. With San Francisco firmly in control with ninety seconds remaining, the 49ers lost a fumble and an onsides kick and Roger Staubach passed for two touchdowns, leading Dallas to a 30–28 victory that still ranks among the most remarkable comebacks in league history.

"The whole city was just stunned and heartbroken," recalled Art Spander, the longtime *Examiner* sports columnist.

The loss lingered in the San Francisco soul, until a moment of indescribable light buried the darkness for good.

After their memorable meeting at Howard Johnson's, Joe Montana and Dwight Clark developed a strong personal bond. The introverted Pennsylvanian and the outgoing Southerner—who was dating Miss America Shawn Weatherly, his college sweetheart—spent much of their free time playing video games, especially the arcade sensation Space Invaders and the handheld Mattel video basketball game, like millions of adolescent boys scattered across the country.

As the two players ascended from wide-eyed rookies to starters, Montana developed tremendous confidence in Clark's ability to get open and make the catch, whether downfield as a wide receiver or across the middle as a tight end. Time after time, when he needed to make a clutch play, Montana looked to Clark, who recorded a team-leading 85 receptions for 1,105 yards and four touchdowns in 1981. Montana to Clark. The phrase rolled off Don Klein's tongue so often, it took on the cadence of a mantra, burrowing deep into San Francisco's hopeful heart. As the media began to speculate about the impact their friendship was having on the Niners' passing game, the quarterback bristled at the suggestion, which he labeled "a fairy tale." "[Clark's] ability was the key," Montana insisted. "If we had a third down and four yards to go or third-and-eight, Dwight would come up with ten. He would always get you that first down."

By their third year together, after practicing every single pass pattern hundreds of times, learning to time the ball's arrival at the perfect spot on the field at the precise moment the receiver came open, Montana knew exactly where Clark would be in any given situation. The quarterback probably could have worn a blindfold and still found the target—guided not by his eyes but by his memory of where his man would be. One play required the six-foot-four Clark, as a secondary receiver, to run near the back of the end zone and leap high into the air, where Montana delivered the ball at the top of his climb and no defender could possibly snag an interception. It was called sprint right option, and they rehearsed it nearly every day.

As the nation's eyes turned to Candlestick, the rain clouds parted and Sunday dawned sunny and mild, setting the stage for a classic showdown that would test Montana's skills as never before.

Two plays in the first half demonstrated the mobility and accuracy that made Montana such a threat.

On the Niners' first possession, facing a critical third-and-seven from the Dallas 49, he rolled right, chased by Too Tall Jones and Harvey Martin. Nearing the sideline, he turned his shoulder in mid-stride, throwing back to his left and finding tight end Charlie Young across the middle. As the ball took flight, Young, a thirteen-year veteran who had been acquired from the Philadelphia Eagles, was still running a circuitous route through the Dallas defense. Montana knew exactly where he would be when the ball arrived, and the combination of a perfectly thrown pass and a perfectly run route gave San Francisco a first down at the Cowboys' 32, setting up the Niners' first touchdown.

Sometimes Montana's agility was the difference between a sack and a score. A case in point happened midway through the second quarter, when the quarterback made an acrobatic move to avoid a tackle behind the line from one Cowboy and, as another tugged at his legs, stepped forward and fired a bullet to Dwight Clark, who was all alone in the end zone.

Still, Montana played inconsistently, tossing three interceptions. The 49ers also fumbled three times. Yet the Cowboys were only able to convert those six turnovers into 14 points as the lead swung back and forth, with

Dallas ahead 17–14 at the half and San Francisco taking a 21–17 advantage into the fourth quarter.

All the while, Montana secretly feared for his life. On the sideline around kickoff time, a team official informed the quarterback that someone had threatened to kill him. He knew it was probably a hoax, a cruel joke played by an unhinged fan, and he tried to put it out of his mind.

After recovering a fumble early in the fourth quarter, Dallas quarterback Danny White hit Doug Cosbie with a 21-yard strike, giving the Cowboys a 27–21 lead. Three plays later, Montana sent Solomon down the right sideline but overthrew him, passing right into the leaping arms of Cowboys cornerback Everson Walls, who gathered his second interception of the day. It was a deadly error, one of Montana's worst passes all year. Suddenly, Niners fans were beginning to feel the weight of their troubled history.

When the San Francisco defense forced a Dallas punt, the 49ers took over at their own 11 yard line with 4:54 showing on the clock. Eighty-nine yards stood between the 49ers and the Super Bowl. Eighty-nine yards guarded by Too Tall Jones and the "real" Cowboys.

"I can honestly say we had no doubt whatsoever about winning that game," recalled 49ers running back Earl Cooper, a native of Texas who had grown up cheering for the Cowboys. "Yes, we had made a bunch of mistakes. But there was a resiliency to that team, especially the guy leading us. We felt like he would find a way to win."

Most in the stadium did not share Cooper's faith.

By this point in his football career, Montana's predilection for miracles was well established. This time, he was not facing a three-touchdown deficit with eight minutes left. This time, he needed no chicken soup. But he had never confronted a more consequential moment or tried to save the day against a more powerful and feared defense. The Dallas Cowboys had built their well-deserved reputation by pulling out close games, and virtually every neutral observer in the stadium expected the Doomsday Defense to slam the door on the Niners' Cinderella bid. "The Cowboys were just too good," CBS announcer Pat Summerall privately concluded.

But a new day was dawning, led by a cool customer who "handled himself on that long drive just like he did back on Family Day in training camp," recalled tackle Keith Fahnhorst.

"Joe spearheaded a confidence [that] lifted everybody," remembered Freddie Solomon.

In time, Walsh's play-calling acumen would become legendary, and never was this skill more apparent than the final drive against the Cowboys, when the game became a chess match between two of the giant coaches in the history of the sport. With Dallas expecting the pass, Walsh sent Lenvil Elliott into the game. Elliott, an aging veteran who previously played for the Bengals, had missed nearly the entire season with a knee injury, gaining a total of 29 yards on seven carries. Only in recent days had he been activated, to replace the injured Ricky Patton.

Defying logic and the 49ers' own tendencies, Walsh skillfully mixed the run and pass as the Cowboys lined up in a nickel defense. Three times on the drive, Elliott ran the ball on sweeps. Three times, he caught the defense by surprise—gaining a total of 24 yards. With the minutes quickly ticking away, the decision to run the ball so often was inherently risky but it proved to be a masterstroke because it kept the Cowboys on their heels, guessing and vulnerable.

"As that drive progressed, you could see a recognition among the Cowboys that they weren't in control of the situation," Cross recalled. "We just kept moving the ball down the field and they couldn't stop us."

Sandwiched between four running plays—Elliott's three as well as a 14-yard flanker reverse by Freddy Solomon—Montana completed two passes to Clark, one to Earl Cooper, and two to Solomon, including a 12-yarder across the middle that gave the 49ers a first down at the Dallas 13 with 1:15 remaining.

On the next play, Solomon was wide open in the left side of the end zone. Montana overthrew him as Walsh cringed, later telling reporters, "I thought that was the championship right there. We were never going to get that open again."

Two hours after Jones's jabbering touched a nerve that caused him to momentarily lose his cool, Montana exuded a steadying calm. But his motivation to win stemmed at least partially from fear. "The word 'choke' kept passing through my mind," he said several years later. "Despite this perfectly executed drive, I knew if we lost we would be just another bunch of choke artists."

After Elliott ran to the six, giving the 49ers third-and-two with fifty-eight seconds left, Montana called time-out and jogged to the sideline to confer with Walsh. The call was sprint right option, the same pass Solomon had scored on in the first half—the same play the Niners practiced over and over but rarely used. While the quarterback drank water from a paper cup, Walsh told him, "As soon as you see the angle he's breaking, then just drop the ball up there. If you don't get what you want, you'll just simply throw the ball away."

Rolling right, Montana could see Solomon, the primary receiver, covered as he headed into the end zone and cut left. On the opposite sideline, fullback Johnny Davis nervously turned his eyes to the ground. The former Tampa Bay Buc, used primarily as a blocker and a short-yardage runner, had scored the 49ers' second touchdown of the day, on a one-yard dive, before leaving the game to make way for Elliott's outside running. Now he feared the worst. "I couldn't watch," he said. "I believed in Joe but I still couldn't watch."

The play called for halfback Earl Cooper to block Jones and at least slow his pursuit. "I tried to cut him but he was such an athlete, he jumped over me, like I wasn't even there," Cooper recalled.

As Jones chased Montana toward the boundary, with Harvey Martin fast approaching from the other side, the quarterback demonstrated his poise by holding the ball until the right moment. To Walsh, it seemed like an eternity. He could see Too Tall ready to clobber his quarterback, moving in for the kill with his massive arms extended. Montana pumped once. Then again. Finally, he released the ball, awkwardly, slightly off balance, and it rocketed toward the back of the end zone, headed for where the quarterback expected Clark to be. He could not see the end zone or Clark, but he knew where his receiver was supposed to be. With a near-perfect touch, he placed the ball just beyond the reach of Cowboys defender Everson Walls, who was on Clark's heels. "When I saw it," the receiver said many years later, "I remember thinking to myself, 'Holy shit! That's really high!'"

Three years after climaxing the Chicken Soup Game by hitting Kris Haines with a carefully thrown low-trajectory pass—just high enough to be caught, too low to be picked off—Montana once again exploited his superb touch to seize the day. Watching the ball approach, Walls initially thought it was soaring to an uncatchable height but watched with a sense of gathering fear as "instead of floating, I see it dropping." Clark leaped into the air, higher than even he himself thought possible, pushing his fingertips toward the sky and snatching the ball out of the clouds. Touchdown. Tie game. A crestfallen Walls remembered thinking, "History was just made."

Montana didn't see the Catch live. He was flat on his back, knocked to the ground by Jones an instant after the ball took flight. "I knew Dwight had it when I saw his feet come down and then heard the crowd roar," the quarterback recalled. Only later did he learn, while watching the replays, the full measure of Clark's incredible leap forward. Some believed Montana was throwing the ball away, but in reality, the players had repeatedly practiced such a placement, although the quarterback later conceded, "It ended up being a little higher than I expected."

Eason Ramson, who had left the field to make way for Clark as part of a two–tight end set, often played basketball with the hero during the off-season. He was well aware of the former high jumper's impressive vertical leap. "We used to tease him: For a white boy you can really hop!"

After Ray Wersching converted the extra point to give San Francisco a 28–27 lead with forty-seven seconds left, pandemonium gripped the Candlestick crowd. But Danny White quickly pushed the pause button on the celebration, hitting Drew Pearson across the middle. When two nearby defenders collided, Pearson could smell the end zone, but in a play that would go down among the biggest in franchise history, Eric Wright, one of the three rookies in the secondary—known collectively as "Dwight Hicks and the Hot Licks"—grabbed his shoulder pads and yanked him to the ground at the San Francisco 44. (The play probably would have produced a horse-collar flag if it had been subject to twenty-first-century rules.) Otherwise he might have gone all the way, or at least rambled into field goal range. On the next play, Lawrence Pillers sacked White, the ball popped loose, and Jim Stuckey recovered the ball, sealing the biggest win in the history of the San Francisco 49ers.

As fans rushed the field, filling the air with a joy San Francisco had never experienced, Montana made his way to the home locker room and collapsed beside a water fountain while Eddie DeBartolo told the team, "I'm so proud . . . I don't think that anything could top this, anything in my life." Like Montana, DeBartolo had missed the Catch. After rushing to the sideline in the closing moments, he got stuck behind a mounted policeman near the baseball Giants' dugout, causing his view of the end zone to be obstructed by the horse's rear end.

Wandering around the locker room more than an hour after the game ended, an emotionally spent Walsh pulled *Examiner* columnist Art Spander aside. He had a twinkle in his eye. "You can stop writing that the 49ers can't win the big one," he said with a big smile. Indeed. The curse was over and a new age had begun.

After watching the game from the upper deck, baseball pitcher Steve Travers and a friend returned to their car and headed out into the night, bound for the bars of Union Square and Columbus Street. Like many others, they were energized by the victory, overjoyed by the thought of a championship for their city, and didn't want to go home. Not just yet. Upon reaching the Broadway Tunnel, they noticed traffic snarled to a stop as fans honked horns and expressed their 49ers pride toward perfect strangers. "I had never seen San Francisco like that," Travers recalled. "The city looked different. It felt different."

While demonstrating the considerable athletic skill of the quarterback and his favorite receiver, The Catch represented a turning point in professional football history. The age of America's Team was over. The loss to the 49ers signaled the beginning of the end, the start of a slow burn into the history books. Never again would Landry sniff a Super Bowl. Never again would Dallas seem so invincible. The victory launched San Francisco and Joe Montana toward unimagined heights, setting the stage for a new dynasty.

Two weeks later, the possibility loomed that the 49ers might be late for their Super Bowl game against the Cincinnati Bengals in snowy, frigid Detroit. Headquartered at a remote hotel, the second of two team buses was caught in a traffic jam on the way to Pontiac's Silverdome, victimized by the Secret Service, which temporarily shut down the roads to make way for Vice President George Bush's motorcade. Determined to keep the team loose while nervously glancing at his watch, Walsh yelled out, "I've got the radio on and we're leading 7–0. The trainer's calling the plays." Several rows back, Montana was cracking his own jokes, keeping his teammates loose. The bus finally arrived, more than an hour late, just in time for the players to dress and get onto the field for pregame warm-ups.

The roadblock climaxed a crazy week for two teams making their first appearance in the big game, as the media glare intensified and Walsh complained about a practice schedule that accentuated the burden of the three-hour time difference for the West Coast team. "It was so cold and miserable," recalled Randy Cross, "it was real easy for us to focus on football." While the game felt somewhat anticlimactic for the 49ers, coming off the dramatic breakthrough win over the Cowboys, the collision between Paul Brown and Bill Walsh added spice to the matchup. Six years after Walsh departed Cincinnati under a cloud, he relished the opportunity to cap the 49ers' turnaround against his former mentor, who now served as the team's president and remained its guiding force.

For Montana especially, the victory over Dallas was transformative. Simultaneously, he appeared on the cover of *Time, Newsweek,* and *Sports Illustrated,* an unprecedented convergence of journalistic fascination that reflected and hastened his growing celebrity. Almost overnight, the quarterback called by his coach "the most resourceful player in the National Football League" became a star, the man who delivered a pass and a win that rocketed off the sports pages and into the national conversation. The coming months and years would test his ability to remain the down-to-earth figure who was so widely admired by his teammates.

In the locker room before a game, the 49ers reflected their differences.

Some players liked to be left alone with their thoughts, mentally stepping through their assignments. Some filled the air with jokes. Others strapped on their game faces and talked about kicking ass, infusing the atmosphere with electricity. Among the disparate personalities, Hacksaw Reynolds was truly unique: He arrived fully dressed and ready for battle, including cleats and eye black. While the players around him put on their uniforms, he was already headed for a jacked-up state that inspired all who knew him. "You sort of learned how each man liked to prepare and to be respectful of everybody's rituals," recalled Johnny Davis, who slipped on earphones and listened to a specially dubbed tape of classical music. Davis, a talented pianist, annotated the tape with certain motivational phrases and keywords timed to the rhythm of the day, such as, "You are now at the stadium."

Montana struck a subdued chord. The athletes who dressed near him before a game and the sportswriters who peppered him with questions afterward encountered the same businesslike, emotionally detached figure. "Joe was not a rah-rah type of guy," explained Randy Cross. "And that was part of what made him Joe Montana." The example he cast for the team before a game was of the focused, controlled leader, casually going over the game plan and chatting with teammates. His cool set a tone. Never too high. Never too low.

Usually, Walsh prohibited loud music in the locker room before a game, but when the last half of the team finally arrived at the Silverdome, he took a cue from Montana, who had brought a tape of the Kenny Loggins hit "This Is It." The quarterback slipped the cassette into a boom box and it blared across the room:

*This is it!*
*Your back's to the corner!*

Walsh appreciated the message and encouraged Montana to play the song over and over again to fire up the troops.

Although San Francisco had defeated the Bengals, 21–3, at Riverfront Stadium in November, on a day when Montana scored three touchdowns and the defense forced six turnovers, the 49ers entered the Super Bowl as only slight favorites over a team that was widely considered more talented. The AFC champions, who compiled a 12–4 regular season and knocked off Buffalo and San Diego on the road to Detroit, featured an explosive offense led by quarterback Ken Anderson. The pregame hype focused on the likelihood of a high-scoring affair, demonstrating the effect the rules changes were beginning to exert not only on offensive football but on the expectations of media and fans. Determined to confuse and confound his old team, Walsh spent the two weeks between games reaching deep into his playbook, causing his quarterback to absorb a dramatically expanded game plan featuring more than 120 possible plays.

Before an audience of more than 110 million television viewers, Montana guided the 49ers to a commanding 20–0 lead in the first half. After the teams traded a pair of turnovers, the quarterback led an 11-play, 68-yard drive that included one of the trick plays Walsh had installed just for the Bengals. What began as a sweep by the now-healed Ricky Patton actually turned into a flea flicker pass from Montana to Charle Young, which went for 14 yards. The march ended with Montana scoring on a one-yard sneak for a 7–0 lead.

During such situations near the goal line, fullback Johnny Davis had become a powerful weapon for the 49ers, using his strong legs and muscular body to drive through the line for seven touchdowns. The play most commonly used for this purpose was known internally as fullback at zero. "At zero means you run right up the center's ass," Davis explained. More often than not, Montana took the snap, turned, and handed to Davis. However, in the Super Bowl, Walsh instructed Montana to fake to the fullback, which left Davis as a decoy as the quarterback slipped into the end zone. "That really should have been my touchdown," Davis recalled with a laugh. "Joe took my touchdown!"

When Bengals receiver Cris Collinsworth coughed up the ball deep in 49ers' territory, Montana once more took control and presided over the longest scoring drive in Super Bowl history: 92 yards. Twice, he converted on third down, finding Solomon and Clark, respectively, for long completions. The touchdown came on an 11-yard pass to Cooper, which gave the 49ers a 14–0 lead. The addition of two Ray Wersching field goals gave the Niners the biggest halftime lead in Super Bowl history.

In the second half, Cincinnati came roaring back behind Anderson and an opportunistic defense. But the San Francisco defense stiffened, particularly on a memorable goal line stand, holding the Bengals on four downs from inside the four, and Super Bowl MVP Montana drove the Niners for two more field goals to secure the 26–21 victory.

The game plan turned decidedly conservative in the second half, perhaps because Walsh wanted the victory so badly. After a flawless first half, Montana mostly handed off in the second, finishing 14 of 22 through the air for 157 yards, but he made several key plays that sealed the win.

One play in particular demonstrated Montana's resourcefulness. After the Bengals closed the gap to 20–14 in the fourth quarter, the 49ers were backed up to their own 22, where they faced a second and 15. Montana was chased out of the pocket, in danger of a drive-killing sack that might have altered the game's outcome. With his primary and secondary receivers covered, the quarterback found little-used Mike Wilson for a 22-yard completion and a first down. The clutch play kept the 49ers driving toward the field goal that would put the game out of reach.

Struggling for the right words to describe his quarterback's effectiveness, Walsh told reporters, "He's one of the coolest competitors of all time and he has just started . . . He will be the great quarterback of the future."

Wayne Walker would always remember the day after Super Bowl XVI. That's when he knew something special was happening in his adopted hometown.

Soon after landing at San Francisco International Airport, where only a small crowd showed up to greet the new world champions, the team was rushed downtown, where a parade was planned down Market Street. As the players and coaches stepped onto motorized cable cars, many were still trying to recover from a late night of partying back in Detroit. Most wanted to go home.

Like many of his players, Bill Walsh knew enough about the city's diversity and tradition of athletic apathy to shield himself with low expectations. The police expected a crowd of perhaps 25,000, but the coach doubted the 49ers could attract such a large gathering for what amounted to a pep rally on a Monday afternoon. Not in San Francisco. Then the cable cars turned from the Embarcadero onto Market Street, and the remarkable sight of an estimated 500,000 screaming fans—packed onto sidewalks, positioned atop parked cars, dangling from light poles, leaning out of office windows—assaulted the senses of every person in the travel party. It was a scene of complete pandemonium, as if the entire city had shut down to celebrate an achievement that suddenly seemed bigger even than a Super Bowl victory. "The whole experience choked me up," Ronnie Lott recalled. "I had tears in my eyes for most of the afternoon."

When the parade stopped long enough for a short program outside City Hall, Walker, the master of ceremonies, looked out across the sea of delirious humanity and felt a chill run up his spine. "Who says this isn't a sports town!" And the crowd roared.

Taking note of the throng's diversity, which included every conceivable ethnic group, every age, every economic strata, Walsh was deeply moved. "Seeing the outpouring of emotion that day, I realized what an historic moment it was, not just for the team, but for the entire city," he said. "We were salving wounds and lifting spirits that had been very low for a long time."

While battling their way to the top of the football world, the 1981 San Francisco 49ers forged an emotional bond with a city that desperately yearned for a winner. "In this very diverse city, with all these factions, they brought everybody together in a way you hadn't seen before," Walker recalled. Suddenly citizens who had never paid much attention to the 49ers became big football fans, gravitating to a cultural institution that produced a new birth of civic pride. And no player would ever own the city's heart quite like Joe Montana.

# CHAPTER SIX

# The Art of Reinvention

THE EXCHANGE WAS CLEAN, AND Joe Montana took three steps backward. It was a routine practice day, and before the defense could converge on him, the quarterback methodically hit halfback Spencer Tillman with a swing pass. After catching the ball and picking up several yards, Tillman, a studious preacher's kid who had starred at Oklahoma, trudged back to the huddle with a question ringing in his ears.

"I was watching Joe all the way and I noticed that he never looked my way," recalled Tillman, who later became a well-respected college football analyst for CBS Sports.

While the other players were still gathering for the next play, he pulled his quarterback aside. "How did you know I would be open?"

"I looked at the coverage. The safety was cheating over. And I knew they couldn't play the coverage the way it needed to be played to cover you. So I knew you would be open."

Somehow, he just knew. The snap judgment reflected equal parts study, experience, and instinct, providing the recently acquired Tillman with a memorable introduction to one of the attributes that made Montana such an effective quarterback.

"Without even looking at my side of the field, he just flicked the ball out there to me and he knew I would be there and knew I would be open," he said. "This was a result of him looking at half of the field for maybe two seconds! Most quarterbacks would be so discombobulated being put in that situation . . . to make a declarative assessment of what the defense was trying to do to them. But Joe knew everything. There was nothing that got past him."

The offense created by Walsh was a kind of science, and in time, Montana's multilayered understanding of the scheme empowered him to solve every conceivable problem posed by NFL defenses. But it took a player like Montana to prove it as more than a theory. It took Montana to use the science to create a kind of art: Gliding out of trouble and making perfect throws, just one step ahead of disaster . . . buying time for his receivers to get open . . . releasing the ball with a swiftness that left defenders grabbing for air . . . delivering time after time in clutch situations, when the situation appeared especially hopeless.

"What Joe had was a poise, instinct, spontaneity, and intuitiveness that no one else has had," Walsh once explained.

Walsh and Montana were not simply building a powerful offense. They were challenging the very nature of offensive football, which included reinventing what a successful quarterback could look like.

The first unorthodox feature of the offense was the scripting of plays. Like many other facets of the system, this idea originated when Walsh was coaching with the Bengals, and Paul Brown often wanted to know, "What do we have for openers?" It started with four set plays. By the time he arrived in San Francisco, Walsh was scripting the first 15 snaps, which eventually grew to the first 25, a strategic innovation that empowered the 49ers in several important ways. For one thing, it gave Montana and his teammates a clear plan of attack, which promoted mental clarity and confidence. "It helped our players sleep at night," Walsh said. "We could take the field without the butterflies and hypertension, because we had a plan." Recalling the process of receiving and absorbing the list, running back Johnny Davis said, "You could think about [those plays] in your mind the night before and be ready. That was a big thing." In some cases, Walsh deviated from the script, such as when the Niners faced unusually long yardage from deep in their own territory and the preselected play struck the boss as wrong for the situation. But this rarely happened.

Given the green light by Walsh, Montana shared the play list with television announcer Wayne Walker in the locker room before each game. "I don't think there's any doubt, the scripting was a great benefit to Joe," Walker said. "It was one of the things that played so well to his strengths as a quarterback." The inside knowledge, applied selectively, also made the former Detroit Lions linebacker look like a guru to the viewing audience.

By the time Montana arrived in the league, the age of the quarterback who called his own plays was mostly a distant memory. The advent of coaching-directed plays—in what Walsh called "the almost clinical atmosphere of the press box, away from the noise and emotion of the field"—emphasized systems and strategic adjustments at the expense of the once-all-powerful quarterback. The scripting by Walsh elevated offensive strategy to an even higher level of sophistication. When the 49ers jumped out to a big lead in the first half, as they often did, the system was hailed. A triumph of meticulous planning over adrenaline-dripping reaction! Conversely, when San Francisco fell into an early hole, it was easy to blame the script and deride Walsh's rigidity.

The impact on defenses was striking. For decades, coaches across the league had carefully charted opponents' offensive tendencies and trained their defenses to expect certain plays in a given down-and-distance situation or from a particular formation. In the cat and mouse game between staffs, many offenses exploited the prevalence of such knowledge by consciously going against their own tendencies, which, if applied just right, could turn all that preparation into a liability. But Walsh's scripting was not deception. By attacking from predetermined plays without consideration of down, distance, and field position, the system belied the whole concept of offensive tendencies. This made the 49ers less predictable, which represented an unmistakable advantage for the offense.

At the same time, the 49ers coaches closely observed how the opposition reacted to those predetermined plays and used this information to shape calls later in the game. "Once they saw what [the defense] was doing on a certain play on a certain formation, we might come back with the same formation and do something different, which often caught 'em off guard," recalled offensive lineman Guy McIntyre. One small change—such as altering John Taylor's route to draw the safety away from Jerry Rice—could, and frequently did, mean the difference between a short gain and six points.

Like various innovations in football history—the T Formation, the Wishbone, the Shotgun, and later, the Spread—the West Coast Offense succeeded at least partially because it exploited conventional defensive wisdom and tactics to create vulnerabilities and mismatches, which, in time, produced a new array of compensating defensive adjustments. But perhaps more than any scheme ever devised, Walsh's creation represented an assault on the sport's guiding offensive philosophy, which cemented the team's bond with a place that was all about challenging the status quo.

For many residents of the Bay Area who saw their metropolis on the vanguard of American society, forever pushing the country to think outside the box, the rise of the 49ers reflected the triumph of intelligence and innovation. By breaking free of the traditional primacy of establishing the run, and further shattering the mold by completely rethinking how the forward pass could be used, Walsh and Montana were remaking the sport with a San Francisco slant. Intellectually and spiritually, the West Coast Offense was of San Francisco, flowing with the DNA of all those disaffected souls and innovators who questioned fundamental assumptions about the world. While emerging as a different sort of quarterback leading a different sort of offense, Montana was changing the very nature of an American institution, which made him an exemplar of the most sacred of all San Francisco values: the power of the unconventional thought.

The latest shift in offensive football came at a time when various segments of American industry and culture were coming to grips with revolutionary change.

No innovation loomed larger than the advent of the personal computer. In the space of less than a decade, the computer had been transformed from a massive machine occupying an entire room and requiring special expertise to an affordable consumer appliance small enough to rest on a desktop. At the very time Walsh and Montana were proving the viability of the West Coast Offense, Steve Jobs was leading a small team of programmers, engineers, and designers to develop the Macintosh computer, which debuted in 1984, featuring the groundbreaking graphic user interface, better known as the mouse. Each in their own way, the two Bay Area operations represented the power of bold thinking against an entrenched establishment.

Cable was rapidly transforming the television business. As the wired universe expanded at a torrid pace, destined to surpass 50 percent of American households by the end of the 1980s, the consumer who had been largely limited to three broadcast channels for decades was suddenly liberated by a new age of abundance. CNN introduced the twenty-four-hour news cycle; MTV altered the way young people related to popular music; and ESPN became a validating destination for sports fans.

The availability of extensive game clips and breaking news on ESPN's *SportsCenter*—which soon found an able competitor in CNN's *Sports Tonight*—conditioned fans to a new level of informational entitlement. The heroics of Montana and various others who came of age during this period could be dissected, understood, and viscerally experienced in much greater depth. In 1987, ESPN acquired its own package of NFL games, expanding the broadcast schedule for the first time since the 1970 birth of *Monday Night Football*. The NFL economic model would never be the same. Under the direction of former *Inside Sports* and *Rolling Stone* editor John Walsh, who arrived in 1988, the network moved aggressively into news-gathering, setting ESPN on the road to becoming the most authoritative and influential brand in sports media.

In the network's early days, late-night host Chris Berman frequently received letters from viewers who thanked him for providing something to watch in the wee hours of the morning while they fed their infant children or arrived home from the late shift. "When they invented this place, the outcry from some was, 'Who's going to watch sports twenty-four hours a day?'" Berman said. "Well, the realization that we saw [in those letters] was that your twenty-four hours and that guy's twenty-four hours may be different. Not everybody was working nine to five. There was an understanding in general that our lives were changing, and we were trying to service that changing world."

At the same time, the Gannett Company was placing a gigantic bet on a new approach to an old medium. Not only was *USA Today,* which launched in 1982, attempting to become the first truly national newspaper, it was reinventing the newspaper concept. The paper featured much shorter stories than conventional competitors, eschewing journalistic depth for the kind of brevity the company's executives believed the TV generation desired, plus the sort of bold graphics and color photographs that would soon become the industry standard.

No innovation affected the vast American public quite like the advent of the Automated Teller Machine, which reached critical mass in the early 1980s. No longer did you have to show up at your bank during business hours and wait in a long line to access your own money. The ATM transformed the banking industry and promoted a new age of consumer freedom.

Like many of the changes roiling American society in the Reagan era, Walsh's offense represented a profound challenge to a conservative institution resistant to change.

Unlike the long line of coaching greats who saw football ultimately as a test of wills—hard-charging icons including Knute Rockne, Paul "Bear" Bryant, Vince Lombardi, and Woody Hayes—Walsh believed above all else in the power of precision. His game was football through a more cerebral lens. Without a doubt, the West Coast Offense reflected finesse much more than any of its contemporary rivals: Raw power was not as important, in most cases, as precise passing routes and a ball thrown just so at the proper time. Unlike many other coaches, he did not believe in molding his players through physically grueling practices; his teams spent much of their practice time walking through their assignments and learning every nuance of every play. He was determined to get inside each defender's head, to win a game of psychological warfare by causing confusion and frustration. "Walsh modeled everything on mentally breaking down the other team," said offensive lineman Bruce Collie. This included frequent use of motion and other tactics designed to confound the defense.

The subtleties of this often escaped the general public, but if Montana yelled, "Strong Right Change" during his signals, Roger Craig switched positions with Tom Rathman. Because one linebacker was schooled to look for the position of the tight end, which had not changed, this typically left Craig facing the slower linebacker, which was a mismatch the gifted former Nebraska star would win most every time.

Despite all this trickery, the suggestion that the 49ers were not a hardnosed team was frequently overstated. Walsh resented the "finesse" label that so often was attached to his offense.

"Bill wanted to give you the impression that they were all about finesse," Terry Donahue said. "In reality, while you were distracted by the finesse, they were all about physicality and tearing your kneecaps off. He had some of the most brutal and devastating blocking designs any defense ever had to play against."

Steve Wallace understood the helplessness many defenders felt while playing San Francisco. Before he was drafted by the 49ers, destined to become a key figure in protecting Montana, the Atlanta native repeatedly watched with a sense of frustration in the early 1980s as Montana victimized his Falcons. "I remember sitting there in front of the TV as they ran those seven-and-outs and the guy's wide open," said Wallace, who spent his college career blocking for Bo Jackson at Auburn. "So much of the time, the [receiver] is getting a 10-yard cushion. They keep doing it and they keep moving the chains. And you start to understand, hell, this is an easy completion and a sure thing. Why not take advantage of it?"

The inherent sophistication of the scheme required intense study and comprehension by all who competed for playing time. "If you wanted to stay on the football team, you had to know not only your job but what the backs were doing, what routes the receivers were running, and the concept of why the blocking assignments were the way they were," recalled offensive lineman Bruce Collie. "Because everything meshed. There was a reason for everything."

Because of this mind-set, the daily walk-through in sweats took on a much greater significance. After learning the plays on paper and on video, the Niners reinforced their understanding of each aspect of the 120 possible plays with repetition that was every bit as much mental as physical. "Out of that you got a very three-dimensional feel to your playbook," Collie recalled. During this process, Walsh and Montana could be heard talking about the various details of the plays and making adjustments to fit that week's opponent.

During a practice early in his rookie year, Collie learned a valuable lesson that illustrated the depth of Walsh's scheming. When Montana threw a short pass to Roger Craig, Collie pulled in front of the receiver and began moving to take out the cornerback, which he thought was his job. In a conventional offense, his instinct would have been right on the money. But in this case, Walsh wanted to override his instinct for a more complex purpose.

Stopping the action, he asked Montana to start again and guided Collie through every step of the play. With his hands placed on the lineman's hips, he slowly moved him through the play, explaining, "I want you to run a route. And what this route does, because of Roger's position, it makes the cornerback make a decision, because his job is to contain. So you keep stretching him out. Well, at some point in time, he's got to make a decision. Is he gonna run off the sidelines or is he gonna come up and Roger will bring him to you?" By this, Walsh meant that Craig's downfield running would eventually make containment fruitless, forcing the defender to commit himself. Time after time, this sort of technique sprang the 49ers for big gains that contributed to victorious Sundays.

"If I have any talent," Walsh once explained, "it's in the artistic end of football. The variation of movements of 11 players and the orchestration of that facet of football is beautiful to me."

Beyond Walsh's meticulous planning and the precision of all those gifted athletes working in unison, the offense hummed because it was perfectly suited to Montana's various skills, especially his mobility, his improvisational skills, and his uncanny ability to hit a receiver with a perfect pass just as he became open—or an instant before. "There's no magic in a system," Buffalo Bills head coach Marv Levy observed. "Joe Montana was the guy that made the magic."

The first three or four seconds after the snap loom large for any quarterback. No matter how far he can throw the ball or how fast he can run, the offensive leader must be able to quickly read the defense—especially whether he's facing zone or man-to-man coverage, or if the blitz is coming—and exploit this knowledge while getting rid of the ball. Many gifted athletes have struggled in making the transition to the NFL because of the mental requirements of those few seconds. For some the pressure can be overwhelming. The mind of every quarterback works differently, but the most successful usually have the ability to zone out all the external mental noise and concentrate on the information needed to make the all-important decision of where to go with the ball.

"When you're in that situation, you don't have time to think," explained Ken Stabler, the longtime Oakland Raiders quarterback. "The trick is knowing your team so well . . . and the other team so well . . . and having so much confidence in your own abilities . . . that you react without thinking."

Montana thrived in this pressure-packed atmosphere. Empowered by his own instincts and Walsh's rigorous training, he possessed the ability to see the unfolding play in his mind like a movie. Looking out into the defense, he saw only colors, which simplified the decisions he needed to make in split seconds. "If the 49ers are wearing red jerseys and our opponents white, my vision picks up the color changes," he once explained. "If the wall of colors quickly changes from red to white in the first two steps of my drop-back, things register automatically."

Flooding the field with receivers, which usually guaranteed that at least one man would eventually find an open seam if the quarterback was accurate enough and quick enough to reach him, the West Coast Offense worked on a series of progressive reads. First the quarterback looked to the primary receiver, then on to the various others in the chain, progressing from one to the next in a systematic fashion. Boom. Boom. Boom. Because he was so quick, because he understood the offense in such intricate detail, and because he possessed such good football instincts, Montana could make the crucial decision of where to go with the ball in the blink of an eye.

"Joe could read his coverage on the second step, and by the third, the ball was flying," said halfback Earl Cooper.

A good example of the progressive read system could be seen when the

49ers ran a so-called double go pattern, which sent both wide receivers sprinting deep down opposite sidelines. First Montana would look toward the two wide outs and size up the position of the defending cornerbacks: If the coverage was too tight on both, he would move on to the tight end running a hook across the middle. If the tight end, too, was covered, the quarterback moved quickly to a running back.

The plays typically developed faster because Montana operated from three- or five-step drops and roll-outs and because of all those short routes. The quarterback was able to pull the trigger so quickly because he knew exactly where each receiver was supposed to be, a key component in the system's precise timing between passer and receiver. The unit spent hour upon hour in practice rehearsing where and when a receiver was to stop, allowing the quarterback to throw to a particular spot on the field believing Jerry Rice or John Taylor or Freddie Solomon would be there in time to snag the ball.

"Joe's pass was halfway to you before you made your break," tight end Eason Ramson said. "You knew when you turned around the ball was gonna be there."

The system made especially good use of the tight end, influencing an entire generation of offenses, and especially when the defense blitzed, the tight end needed to be prepared for a hot read. "You better be ready," Earl Cooper said. "If not, [the ball] might catch you before you catch it . . . right in the bread basket."

Through the years, Montana proved his arm was stronger than some gave him credit for, but the reality that he did not possess a cannon comparable to bombers like Dan Fouts, Dan Marino, or Joe Namath was largely rendered a moot point by the requirements of the system. "He didn't have the strongest arm," Fouts said, "but he didn't need the strongest arm. And his accuracy was excellent."

Montana's superb touch allowed him to put the ball where he wanted to put it at precisely the right time—able to choose, for instance, whether to hit a receiver on the four or the nine from 10 or 15 yards away. Few quarterbacks have ever mastered such routine precision. His quick feet, which Walsh noticed right away during their first encounter, proved crucial to the 49ers' success. It wasn't just that he was nimble enough to avoid trouble and force defenders to fear his legs. He could also move through his drop quickly enough to keep pace with the developing play. Because the offense relied so heavily on the perfectly choreographed timing between quarterback and receiver, the difference between a completed pass and a missed opportunity could be measured in two or three seconds.

"Joe's mechanics were perfect, almost overnight, because he's such a beautifully coordinated athlete and he just has a natural flow to what he does," Walsh said. "The mechanics have to be there to time the passes. It all has to fit together, and Joe could do that better than anyone I've ever seen."

Some combination of instinct and training allowed him to understand when a receiver was about to be open, which reflected a quality that was central to the success of the offense. "Montana's eyes are so fast," Everson Walls said. "He just sees things faster than other quarterbacks." Flooded with information and options, and forced to react instantaneously, he consistently made good decisions about where to go with the ball. In some cases, the right decision was to throw it away, which often made the difference between a stalled drive and a touchdown.

"In the current day Joe would never win the passing efficiency contest because, on second-and-seven, he would throw the ball away rather than take a sack—because he played the quarterback position like you're supposed to," offensive lineman Steve Wallace said in 2013. "Guys today, they want to go to the Pro Bowl and be MVP and all that stuff, so they're too caught up in passing efficiency. Joe's rating could've been a lot higher, but he always found a way to win 'cause he took the selfish part out of the equation."

In various ways, a succession of quarterback coaches—Sam Wyche, Mike Shanahan, Mike Holmgren, and Paul Hackett—influenced Montana's development, but his rise to greatness was profoundly shaped by Walsh, down to the smallest detail. During one practice session during the mid-1980s, offensive linemen Guy McIntyre observed Walsh instructing his quarterback on the mechanics and timing of one particular pass. "You need to throw the ball right here," he said, demonstrating with the ball while mimicking his drop. "You've got to be here at [the receiver's] third step. And you can't let him take more than five steps because if you do, then the safety will come over and be able to break up the play. But right at this point, at two steps, the defensive back can't cover him, the corner can't cover him, and the safety hasn't quite reacted to the play yet. So that's when the ball has to be delivered. That little window."

Somewhere along the way, the practice habits that had troubled Dan Devine faded into a mature professionalism. Montana became a dedicated student of the game who worked hard to master every nuance of Walsh's system. "After the first few years, Joe was a walking encyclopedia," said Randy Cross. "He always said, 'Bill taught us all we knew but he didn't teach us all he knew.'" When he joined the staff, San Francisco offensive line coach Mike Solari was immediately impressed by Montana's understanding of the scheme. "He knew that offense backward and forward—what Walsh used to call the 'dynamic of the play,'" Solari said. "Because of that, he had this incredible confidence that he could always find a way to move the chains."

As he learned the system like a language and began to experience and recognize every conceivable defense, Montana slowly grew into an audible master. By the mid-1980s, he was checking off 15 to 20 percent of the time, to avoid a play the defense seemed especially ready for or to exploit an exposed vulnerability. His signals always included a color. Each week, the live color changed, which meant, for instance, that "red" was a signal that he was changing the play at the line. Any other shade uttered was meaningless and yelled out to confuse the defense.

At times, Montana also transcended the offense, empowering the 49ers with his remarkable ability to improvise. As Sam Wyche once noted, "Sometimes Joe makes things happen that really don't have much to do with the system." Watching from the sidelines as his quarterback routinely glided out of trouble and somehow found a way to move the ball, teammate Ronnie Lott learned to appreciate his gift to "find something when something's not there." Time after time, when an opposing defense appeared to have him trapped, he quickly seized on one vulnerability and exploited it. Atlanta head coach Jerry Glanville, who was repeatedly burned by Joe Cool, lamented, "Montana is the guy who, when you do everything right defensively, still gets away and makes the big play." Of this particular skill, the man who watched his offense raised to an art form with number 16 at the controls, once said, "Joe Montana stretches our limits. He redefines what is sensible."

Beyond the various skills Montana brought to the offense loomed the intangible of leadership. "Joe was just a natural leader," said fullback Johnny Davis. "He had a presence. You could feel it."

It mattered greatly that he could apply his knowledge of the system in the blink of an eye and that he could put just the right touch on a pass across the middle. But it also mattered that he could infuse his teammates with confidence, urgency, and calm, all at the same time. This was the quality that empowered all the others.

"There was something about the way he looked at you in the huddle when you knew he was depending on you," tight end Eason Ramson said.

The link between his ability to focus on the task at hand and his apparent immunity from the tension of the situation was demonstrated on a regular basis, causing Walsh to observe, "Joe could be in the most difficult circumstances and keep his poise. He wouldn't lose any of his control." As defensive back Dave Waymer explained, when the pressure arrived, "We knew he was the guy who wouldn't overheat." Even he struggled to get a handle on this ability, once telling a reporter, "I don't go seeking pressure situations out there but the pressure doesn't bother me. I'm always too busy concentrating on my assignment to get caught up in the moment." More to the point, he once explained, "It wasn't that I played better under what other people called pressure. It was that I played the same, Super Bowl or season opener."

As the 49ers rose to the top of professional football and the West Coast Offense emerged as a widely studied strategic breakthrough, Bill Walsh became known as "The Genius," reflecting his unusual place in the pantheon of coaches. Even as he took great pride in the nickname, it represented an enormous burden for a football coach who was not spending his days trying to split the atom or find a cure for cancer. Some uttered in sincere respect for his achievements, rooted in his intellectual approach to the game. Hank Stram, the former Kansas City Chiefs coach, once said with great admiration that taking in a game coached by Walsh was "like watching a seminar." Others wielded it like a slur.

While the label sometimes landed like a backward compliment to Walsh, it represented a veiled insult to Montana, whose skills proved instrumental in making the offense successful. By 1982, he started to chafe at the implication that it took The Genius to make him a winning quarterback.

Three months after Super Bowl XVI turned him into a sports star rivaling Magic Johnson and Pete Rose, Montana sat backstage in a Los Angeles television studio, taping an episode of the CBS game show *Tattletales* while wearing bright yellow headphones. Now, in this moment, it was official: The quarterback was no longer just a quarterback. Success on the field had turned him into a full-fledged celebrity, competing for applause and laughs alongside former *Bonanza* patriarch Lorne Greene. The music ringing in the quarterback's ears prevented him from hearing the on-screen conversation between host Bert Convy and his wife, who needed to predict how he would answer a question in order to score points against Pa Cartwright and his bride.

Responding to one question by the host, Cass Montana said, "My husband hasn't had many failures so I will say he has learned more from his successes. But he may be modest and say failures."

When the time arrived to see how well Cass knew her husband, the forever glib Convy—a fixture of daytime television throughout the 1970s and '80s—turned serious and asked the quarterback, "Joe Montana, have you learned more from your successes or your failures?"

Thinking quick on his feet, as if facing a fast-approaching blitz, Montana said, "Successes."

As the audience members who shared in the resulting cash and prizes exploded into applause, the quarterback interjected, "But you know, you can also learn from your failures. They teach you who your friends really are."

The response offered a snapshot of Montana at a turning point in his life: equal parts candor and modesty about his good fortune, mixed with a healthy dose of circumspection. Like the West Coast Offense, he was a work in progress, a twenty-six-year-old man coming to grips with overnight celebrity while trying to figure out who he was and what he wanted out of life. Three years after he walked out of the 49ers locker room without being recognized, he could no longer dart into a grocery store for a loaf of bread without causing a scene. Suddenly flooded with offers for commercial endorsements and public appearances, which soon had him crisscrossing the country, the 49ers front office tried to shield him, because he had a difficult time saying no.

The financial security resulting from his professional success allowed the Montanas to live comfortably, overlooking San Francisco from a large house, surrounded by an acre of land, in the coastal hills of Woodside. The quarterback bought two Arabian horses and a red Ferrari and indulged various other interests, but he seemed determined to avoid the pitfalls of sudden fame and fortune—to prevent success from changing him.

Constantly aware of the spotlight, Cass appeared wary of it, telling a reporter, "I've done everything in my power to play this thing down. There is nothing that appalls people more than somebody walking around glowing in newfound fame . . . thinking, 'Oh, boy, the Montanas think their shit doesn't stink,' because ours sure does—a lot."

As the quarterback soon learned, once you've yukked it on national television with Pa Cartwright, you can never truly retreat to the shadows.

As Montana and the 49ers ascended, the NFL entered a turbulent age. Like the game on the field, the institution of professional football began to challenge once-sacrosanct assumptions about itself, grappling, like all businesses of a certain age, with the various implications of its own success. In 1982, the NFL endured a year like no other.

The first devastating blow was delivered in a Southern California courtroom. Two years after signing a long-term deal with Los Angeles Memorial Coliseum and announcing his intention to abandon Oakland for more-lucrative L.A., Raiders principal owner Al Davis won a jury verdict that prevented the league from blocking his ambitions. It was the decisive

battle in a long-simmering war. Davis's disdain for the NFL power structure could be traced to his short tenure as the commissioner of the upstart American Football League in the mid-1960s, a feud that intensified
when cooler, more pragmatic heads engineered the merger of the two cir-
cuits without him, transforming the wily, combative disciple of Sid Gillman into a Jolly Roger caricature, minus the eye patch, who taunted Pete
Rozelle and the league establishment at every opportunity. By fighting for
and winning the right to transplant his team in order to fatten his bottom line, starting in 1982, Davis fundamentally altered the NFL paradigm
by forever shattering the gentleman's agreement of territorial order. (The
timing of the move enabled the 49ers' rapid rise as a cultural force for the
entire Bay Area, as both success and geography tilted in favor of Walsh's
new dynasty, freed from competing directly against the Raiders.) Two
years later, Robert Irsay, empowered by Davis's precedent, moved the Colts
to Indianapolis in the middle of the night, causing the entire city of Baltimore to feel violated, in a way that many—including the great Johnny
U—struggled to adequately express. Soon, discarded fans in other cities
would come to understand the sting of loss, the feeling of betrayal and
abandonment that first assaulted Raiders supporters in Oakland and across
the East Bay in 1982. This was one of the first signs of a new age of cyni-
cism and disaffection bubbling up out of the stands, just as Montana and
the 49ers climbed to the top of the football world.

Four days after Davis's landmark victory, a group of businessmen gathered in New York to announce the formation of the United States Football League. The latest attempt to capitalize on professional football's
popularity landed, at first, with a less-menacing thud, because the new
circuit planned to avoid direct competition with the NFL by playing games
during the spring. But the seasonal issue quickly turned out to be a rather
minor detail in a bitter rivalry—and a smokescreen for a full-on, frontal
assault on the NFL. This too was war.

"What you have to understand about our league," explained Bruce
Allen, general manager of the new Chicago Blitz, "is that we're a whole
league of Al Davises. Most of our guys had been promised NFL expansion franchises but had never received them. Most of our people are just

as rich as the NFL owners, if not richer, but our guys are hungry. Hungry and imaginative."

It was only a matter of time before the upstart league—featuring twelve franchises scattered across the continent in markets both served and unserved by the NFL, including Baltimore, Birmingham, Los Angeles, and Memphis—began competing for the nation's outstanding college players and driving up the price for talent. The New Jersey Generals shattered a longstanding taboo by signing Heisman Trophy–winner Herschel Walker to a three-year, $4.2 million contract before his college eligibility expired, establishing a precedent destined to fundamentally transform the college and professional games. The USFL was headed for the crowded graveyard of NFL wannabes, but in the stormy year of 1982, it loomed as yet another threat to the NFL's aura of dominance and stability.

"After all those years of tremendous growth, the NFL was entering an era of very public turmoil on several fronts, and we certainly contributed to the perception that the NFL brand was being battered," recalled Chet Simmons, the longtime television executive who became the USFL's first commissioner.

With the Davis decision and the USFL launch still fresh in the minds of football fans across the country, *Sports Illustrated* published a shocking exposé that pulled back the curtain on illicit drug use in the NFL. The riveting first-person account by former Miami Dolphins defensive back Don Reese represented a turning point for the league. Admitting he had become addicted to cocaine soon after joining the NFL, and alleging widespread substance abuse across the league, Reese forced Pete Rozelle and the owners to acknowledge the problem, the sort of problem that mirrored the white-powdered haze then blanketing various segments of American society.

Reading the *SI* article in the weeks before training camp, 49ers receiver Eason Ramson sweated bullets, silently wondering if anyone knew about him. But his paranoia soon subsided, and like other 49ers of the time, Ramson continued to snort cocaine, negotiating the lonely road from experimentation—which began during his rookie year with the St. Louis Cardinals—to full-blown addiction during his four years with the Niners.

Only later would the world learn that he had sniffed a line in the locker room at the Silverdome before the kickoff of Super Bowl XVI against the Bengals.

"When I got to the NFL . . . cocaine was introduced to me as a status symbol, a symbol of success," Ramson explained many years later. "It was the rich man's high . . . 'You're on top now. This is what we do.' . . . It was peer pressure that brought that into my life, because I wanted to be accepted."

In 1982, when Ramson still had everybody fooled, his addiction remained a symbol of a powerful undercurrent threatening the NFL and undermining the 49ers' attempt to repeat as Super Bowl champions. He was on his way to becoming a cautionary tale, but Walsh later estimated that as many as eleven San Francisco players of the time struggled with habits that impacted their football careers. In the year of Don Reese, the truth of the rich man's high was no longer a secret but it remained a fact of life in a world of talented young men who often felt bulletproof and entitled, exalted figures coming to grips with sudden wealth, peer pressure, and the seductive tease of mind-numbing euphoria.

Amid the gathering storm clouds, the league owners and the National Football League Players Association approached the season on a collision course. After years of impotence, the players' union had entered a new era of assertiveness under the direction of veteran labor lawyer and political activist Ed Garvey, who convinced the players to demand a bigger cut of the pie. As the collective bargaining agreement expired, the two sides reached an impasse centering on the most contentious issue: the NFLPA's desire for 55 percent of the league's gross revenues, which translated to an estimated $1.6 billion over the next four years. The owners refused to discuss such a revolutionary concept, insisting the NFL business model could not sustain such high labor costs.

Despite seeing the average NFL salary more than triple in the space of a decade—from $23,000 in 1970 to $79,000 in 1980, or about five times median American household income—many players were convinced that they were not sharing equitably in professional football's rapid growth into America's favorite spectator sport. "There were some bitter feelings on both sides," explained New York Giants defensive end Gary Jeter. "We hadn't seen the owners' books and when we finally were able to see them, we were upset at the percentage (of revenue) we were receiving . . . We were called professional ballplayers, but we weren't being paid like professional ballplayers."

One year after a devastating strike by Major League Baseball players, Garvey was determined to play hardball with the NFL owners, and he proved to be a convincing salesman with his membership. But the strike he engineered was a disaster for all concerned. The walkout, which began three weeks into the season, lasted fifty-seven days; caused the cancellation of eight weeks of games, which cost the two sides more than $250 million in revenue and salaries; stoked a new level of animosity among the various factions; and gave rise to a caustic wave of cynicism among fans who, deprived of their Sunday-Monday fix, struggled to comprehend the justifications proffered by all those highly paid athletes and well-healed owners. More than any other moment, the '82 strike introduced the concept of unbridled greed to the steadfast multitudes who enriched the sport with their money and their (equally valuable) eyeballs; many would never look at their heroes in quite the same way.

In San Francisco, the strike produced significant locker room dissension. Like many others, Montana, who declined to join the union, believed Garvey was pursuing an impossible goal in demanding the 55 percent. His position mirrored many others across the league who were growing distrustful of Garvey and former Raiders offensive lineman Gene Upshaw, one of the other union leaders: Why not push the owners on free agency?

"There was anger among some players . . . a lot of bad-mouthing," Montana later conceded. "When I tried to make my point my own teammates put me down."

The strike-shortened 1982 season turned into a 3–6 disaster for San Francisco—including 0–5 at home—as the chemistry and focus of the previous year faded into a morass of bickering and finger-pointing. Statistically, Montana played about as well as he had in the championship year of 1981 (completing 61.6 percent of his passes for 17 touchdowns), but the defense proved to be much more porous, which caused Walsh to replace defensive coordinator Chuck Studley with George Seifert, who was to become the architect of the much stingier units of the coming years.

Amid the grim descent from the lofty Super Bowl perch, Montana's ability to move the ball was forever evident. During one stretch that started before the strike, he became the first quarterback in league history to amass five straight 300-yard games, completing a cumulative 68 percent of his throws for 1,739 yards and 12 touchdowns. The record owed a huge debt to San Francisco's offensive desperation: The twenty-eighth-ranked running game provided little help, and the Niners frequently fell behind, forcing Montana (who led the league in attempts, with 346) to put the ball in the air more often than he or Walsh wanted to.

"When it's third-and-six, and guys across the line are digging in with their cleats," Montana remarked, "it's tough on an offensive lineman."

The final game of the streak was a microcosm of San Francisco's season. Candlestick rocked on a chilly December day as Montana and San Diego Chargers gunslinger Dan Fouts engaged in a high-powered air war, combining for 806 yards and a league-record 65 completions. Late in the fourth quarter, Fouts drove the Chargers 72 yards, culminating with his fifth touchdown pass of the day, for a 41–37 lead. Then came Montana's chance to win yet another game in the clutch . . . but he threw an interception. Game over.

The most far-reaching impact of 1982 was how the season transformed the relationship between Montana and Walsh.

As the losses mounted, Walsh publicly criticized Montana for pursuing outside endorsement opportunities during the season, which he saw as a distraction. "It's taking away from his concentration," Walsh told Glenn Dickey, who covered the 49ers for the *San Francisco Chronicle*. "He doesn't always have time to learn all the system, so he's going into a game not fully prepared. I'm really concerned that a potentially great career is going to dwindle away."

Montana bristled at the suggestion, since he limited the outside work to his off days and since there was no demonstrable decline in his productivity.

But the quarterback took the hint. The next season, he stopped appearing on a local television show and moved nearly all endorsement activities to the off-season, which sent a signal to Walsh and his teammates.

When Ray Wersching missed a chip-shot field goal that would have beaten the Los Angeles Rams in the season finale, Walsh walked across the field with a friend, wearing the look of a beaten man.

"Can't even kick a goddamn field goal!"

One year after the magical day in the Silverdome, Walsh was deeply depressed and considering the unthinkable.

When he failed to show up for a postseason team meeting, many of the players took it like a punch in the gut. What none knew quite yet was that their head coach was so distraught by the '82 collapse—and his inability to get a handle on the drug situation—that he seriously considered walking away from the sidelines. To make matters worse, his relationship with DeBartolo was growing more contentious; the honeymoon was over, and DeBartolo was growing more confident in his football knowledge. Walsh's vacillation continued for several weeks, which caused a shake-up in the coaching staff and cast a cloud of uncertainty across the entire organization.

"Bill had been through a very trying year and he was worn out," recalled his friend Terry Donahue, one of the coaches he approached about taking over the 49ers if he stepped away from the field and remained general manager. "He was so competitive, so driven . . . and yet he had insecurities and doubts."

Imagine the tumbling dominos. If Walsh had stepped away from the sidelines after the '82 season, the next age of professional football might have evolved very differently, and Joe Montana might never have become the Joe Montana venerated by history.

No player was more offended by Walsh's year-end no-show and the insult it suggested than his quarterback, and after the Genius finally put an end to his Hamlet act, their professional relationship entered a new, more complicated phase.

Two years after Walsh demonstrated his faith in Montana by jettisoning Steve DeBerg—fully aware of the psychological implications of the trade—the coach now felt free to ratchet up the pressure on his quarterback. He knew how good Montana could be, was determined to push him toward his true potential, and appreciated the dutiful way he accepted coaching. "Joe is a coach's ideal quarterback because he will take directions," Walsh said. "He's been able to avoid becoming self-satisfied and selfish, qualities all too inherent in stardom."

However, Montana felt increasingly resentful of Walsh's pointed criticism of the smallest details of his performance, of the psychological warfare he sometimes practiced in withholding praise, and the way the quarterback was often forced to call plays he disagreed with. "Hey, guys, I just work here," he would sometimes say in the huddle, and his teammates knew exactly what he meant.

Forever damaged by his difficult relationships with Chuck Abramski and Dan Devine, Montana was able to cultivate a much more professional interaction with Walsh, whose people skills vastly surpassed the quarterback's previous coaches. But the echoes of Abramski and Devine never fell totally silent in his mind, and whether Walsh realized it or not, he had stepped into a role fundamentally influenced by men who had not known how to handle an athlete so gifted and yet so in need of just the right balance of structure and freedom—a man with the self-discipline to be an individual without being individualistic. When the quarterback sniped about Walsh to his teammates, as he frequently did, it reflected a certain resistance to authority, a certain independent streak that was deeply engrained in his psyche. Yet this tension was closely tied to Montana's success. He needed a little edge, and Walsh was the man who supplied it. Ultimately, one of the reasons the partnership—which evolved into something approaching a father-son relationship—worked so well was because they were, in two fundamental ways, very much alike. "They're both very competitive and they're both perfectionists," said quarterbacks coach Mike Holmgren.

"Maybe Joe didn't realize it at times, but part of Bill's job was to make Joe feel uncomfortable," observed offensive lineman Steve Wallace. "Joe wasn't completely fond of how aggressively Bill coached . . . what he had to do to make Joe play better. But it worked."

What truly rankled the quarterback was the suggestion by media and others who fawned over the Genius that he was merely a highly paid cog in Walsh's intricately designed machine. Such talk assaulted the quarterback's pride, and also belied the reality that Montana was a superb athlete who routinely made plays that very few men in the history of the game have been able to make—wielding Walsh's system like a magic wand, churning all that science into art. The resulting tension caused Montana no small amount of mental anguish through the years, but it also motivated him to prove all those people wrong.

As the 1983 season approached, Joe Montana desperately needed help. For Walsh's offense to work on the highest level, it required a consistent running threat that could take some of the pressure off the quarterback. Faced with the collapse of the 49ers' ground game in 1982, Walsh engineered two draft-day acquisitions to shore up this deficiency: In the second round, the Niners placed a bet on Nebraska's rather underrated Roger Craig, who had been overshadowed by the Cornhuskers' Heisman Trophy–winning tailback Mike Rozier. Exploiting the Rams' desire to start a new era with Southern Methodist star Eric Dickerson, who would become one of the leading ground gainers of the decade, Walsh and his right-hand man, director of football operations John McVay, traded for Wendell Tyler, an explosive back who had also demonstrated his ability to catch the ball.

In the season opener at Candlestick against Philadelphia, Tyler immediately validated Walsh's maneuvering, amassing 91 total yards, including a 32-yard touchdown run and an 11-yard reception. But the quarterback struggled to stay vertical. Twice, Montana was knocked out of the game by the hard-hitting Eagles defense. With 4:15 remaining, backup Guy Benjamin hit Earl Cooper for a 73-yard touchdown strike, cutting Philadelphia's lead to 22–17. Three minutes later, with the starting quarterback still on the sideline, San Francisco self-destructed: Guard Randy Cross was flagged for holding, nullifying a game-winning touchdown pass to Dwight Clark. On the next play, Tyler sealed Philadelphia's victory by fumbling inside the 10, giving voice to the skeptics who insisted his fleet feet were not enough to offset his propensity to put the ball on the ground.

"Offensively, we sputtered the entire day," Walsh said. "It wasn't a great performance, but I think we will end up a very good football team."

The following Thursday, with number 16 back under center, San Francisco exploded for 41 first-half points in a 48–17 destruction of the Minnesota Vikings. Montana was virtually flawless, tossing four touchdown passes, including a six-yarder to Tyler, who also rushed for 107 yards. Ten days later, San Francisco crushed St. Louis, 42–27, as Montana threw for three more touchdowns—including a 69-yarder to Freddie Solomon—and Tyler rushed for 108 yards.

One year after the Falcons steamrolled into Candlestick and pushed the franchise a bit deeper into the darkness that was 1982, two of the best quarterbacks in the league finished a late-September Sunday relatively even statistically. Steve Bartkowski, who would lead the NFL in passing, completed 19 of 23 for 243 yards. Montana hit 27 of 32 for 261, including two touchdowns to Dwight Clark and another to Earl Cooper. But while the reinvigorated 49ers' pass rush sacked Bartkowski eight times, Montana repeatedly glided out of trouble, staying free long enough to dump it off short or tucking the ball tight and scooting out of bounds as San Francisco scored a 24–20 victory to go 3–1 in the NFC West.

"Sometimes you watched what Joe could do, the little moves he could make, and you just shook your head," recalled Bartkowski. "He made it look easy."

Sometimes it was what he did not have to do. Tyler (who rushed for 856 yards and four touchdowns in '83) and Craig (725 and eight) added a new dimension to the 49ers' offense, which Walsh was now calling "the best I've ever been associated with." The league's eighth-ranked running game, which improved its productivity by more than 60 percent in one year, lifted the West Coast Offense to another level, as did the pair's combined 712 receiving yards. After George Seifert's defense held New Orleans' powerful rushing attack to 90 yards in a 32–13 road victory over the Saints, Walsh could see his team taking a powerful shape. "I'm just in awe of this football team," he said in one of his less guarded moments.

Seven days later, with the division lead up for grabs, Montana and Rams quarterback Vince Ferragamo lit up the Anaheim sky with one of the year's most memorable passing duels. With slightly more than eight minutes to play, the Rams led, 35–24, on the strength of five touchdown passes by Ferragamo, the onetime Canadian Football League star who was best known for leading the 9–7 Rams out of the wild card bracket to Super Bowl XIV. Working from near midfield, Montana—headed for a 358-yard day, second best of his career thus far—sent former Olympic hurdler Renaldo Nehemiah on what amounted to a decoy pattern. Nehemiah had already caught one touchdown pass, although he would never live up to the tremendous expectations that attached to his blazing speed; soon, he would leave the NFL and return to track-and-field. In this case, the threat he represented became a weapon in Montana's arsenal, clearing the way for the quarterback's 46-yard scoring pass to Dwight Clark, which cut the margin to four. Less than ninety seconds later, Ferragamo, facing a critical third down from deep in his own territory, retreated into his own end zone and was summarily crushed by defensive end Dwaine Board, who stripped the ball for a 49ers touchdown. "It was just a reflex play," Board explained. Now San Francisco had the lead. On the next series, Ferragamo threw into the open arms of the 49ers' Willie Harper, who returned the ball to the Rams' seven. Two plays later, Bill Ring's four-yard run sealed the Niners' dramatic 45–35 victory. "To come back on a team like the Rams in the fourth quarter was fantastic," said Walsh, who praised his team's "will to win."

At midseason, however, San Francisco tumbled from division leader to a team in danger of missing the playoffs altogether, losing four of five to fall to a very troubling 7–6. Among these was a humbling 13–3 defeat to the Bears on a frigid, windy day at Soldier Field. Facing Buddy Ryan's innovative 46 defense for the first time stymied Montana, who completed 26 of 43 for 255 yards but tossed two interceptions, was sacked five times and, for the first time in his three-plus years as the starter, was unable to penetrate the end zone. "[The defense] confused me," he said, "because I didn't know which defender would be blitzing and which defender was going to drop back to cover our receivers."

Entering the final weekend of the regular season, San Francisco needed to shove Tom Landry's Dallas Cowboys a bit further into the history books to secure the division title. Two years after the Catch reordered the football universe, millions of fans across the country tuned in to ABC's *Monday Night Football* expecting a battle of heavyweights. The Cowboys had lost just three games and thereby locked up a wild card berth. But Dallas was fading fast. With the quarterback in red throwing four touchdown passes—including two to Roger Craig—and the defense forcing four turnovers, the Niners cruised to a 42–17 victory, completing a roller-coaster 10–6 regular season and clinching home-field advantage in the playoffs.

In the first round, San Francisco faced a team making only its second playoff appearance since 1970, led by the man who had been the most direct victim of the Joe Thomas debacle. For three quarters, Monte Clark's underdog Detroit Lions were battered by the 49ers but somehow avoided a knockout punch. Five Gary Danielson interceptions—including two by rookie linebacker Riki Ellison—gave Montana numerous opportunities but San Francisco's lead was just 17–9 heading into the final quarter. "The defense kept us in the game," Walsh conceded. Then Detroit stormed to life, cutting the margin to 17–16, and with less than six minutes to play, the quarterback made a deadly error. Looking across the middle, he fired a ball into the waiting arms of cornerback Bobby Watkins. The interception set up Billy Simms's three-yard touchdown run, which gave Detroit a 23–17 lead with 4:54 left. Just then, the Comeback Kid punched in for the day.

Taking over at his own 30 yard line, Montana started moving the 49ers downfield, taking the short gains Detroit was willing to give, earning one first down after another. At the Detroit 27, the quarterback rolled right, facing an intense rush. His field of vision was consumed with shades of white shirts. Just before being leveled, he lofted a pass to tight end Russ Francis, the aging veteran who had been retained despite a rather strained relationship with Walsh. Francis caught the ball on his knees at the 20, sprang to his feet, and ran for another six yards. For this clutch play alone, Francis was worth all the aggravation he caused the head coach. On the next play, the ninth of the drive, Montana hit a streaking Solomon across the middle for a 14-yard touchdown as the Candlestick crowd of 58,286 erupted, celebrating the ninth fourth-quarter comeback of Joe Cool's NFL career. Ray Wersching's extra point gave San Francisco a 24–23 lead with 1:23 remaining.

Detroit was not quite beaten. Not just yet. After the quarterback watched nervously as Eddie Murray's game-winning field goal sailed just wide right with five seconds left, which allowed San Francisco to advance to the NFC title game by the margin of perhaps two feet, aided by the unsteadying effect of Candlestick's spongy grass, sportswriters on hand for the memorable finish began comparing Joe Cool's latest rally—in which he completed 6 of 6 passes for 52 yards—to the legendary drive against Dallas. The conditions were eerily similar, but Montana explained, "They have different meanings. This one just keeps us going. The other one put us in the Super Bowl."

The script was as derivative as *Rocky III*, but the impact of the performance was no less profound on those who witnessed the quarterback's latest heroic turn, which, in this case, prevented his ill-timed interception from losing the game. "Montana," Monte Clark said afterward, searching for the right word, "is incredible."

Returning to the Super Bowl would require knocking off the defending world champion Washington Redskins at RFK Stadium. No one outside San Francisco wanted to touch such a bet. As 1984 dawned, Joe Gibbs's Redskins, winners of thirty-one of their last thirty-four games, cast a menacing shadow across the National Football League, featuring John Riggins, the most bruising fullback in the game; league MVP Joe Theismann at quarterback; All-Pro receiver Art Monk; a powerful offensive line known as the Hogs; and a stingy defense led by sack specialist Dexter Manley. *Miami Herald* writer Larry Dorman captured a sentiment shared by many of his colleagues, declaring, "No one, in good conscience, could give the 49ers the edge at any position in this game."

Heavily favored Washington dominated the first three quarters. Leading 7–0 in the third, Theismann, the former Notre Dame star, sent Monk downfield on a sideline pattern. The pass fell incomplete, but Ronnie Lott was flagged for a questionable interference call, giving the Redskins a first-and-goal at the six. The penalty set up a one-yard touchdown run by Riggins, which made it 14–0.

Lott was not a man who made many mistakes, and his teammates were inclined to take his side about the contact that took place near the boundary. Three years after arriving from Southern Cal, the precise son of a career Air Force officer was widely acknowledged as the leader of the San Francisco defense. Once describing the rage that propelled him on the field as "like riding on a twisting, twirling, skyrocketing roller coaster," Lott delivered thunderous hits. He chased with a speed and fury few defensive backs of his time could match. He infused his teammates with just the right mixture of emotion, intensity, and purpose. Like Montana, Lott was a player of extraordinary ability who was able to lift those around him. The two men shared a mutual admiration and developed a close friendship. And they were both having a bad day.

By late in the third quarter, the Redskins held a commanding 21–0 lead as a chill wind blew in off the Potomac.

With about a minute to play in the third, Montana gathered his team at his own 21. Up to this point, the quarterback had struggled to find his rhythm, tossing two interceptions and enduring a second quarter when the 49ers managed just eight total yards. But as the fourth quarter dawned and the teams traded ends, he started completing passes, especially on outside routes. Nine plays into the drive, he hit Mike Wilson, subbing for the injured Dwight Clark, for a five-yard touchdown, cutting Washington's lead to 14 points.

After Washington missed a field goal, Montana took over at his own 24. Fading into the pocket on first down, he looked first to Nehemiah, who was running down the left sideline. "I thought we could set Renaldo free," he recalled. But when safety Mark Murphy moved toward Nehemiah, the quarterback quickly recognized the opportunity his commitment represented. Freddie Solomon, still stinging from his third-quarter fumble, which set up the Skins' second touchdown, reacted to the safety's movement by improvising his route. "I went outside to get loose," he remembered. Suddenly Solomon was wide open, and Montana hit him in stride for a 76-yard touchdown, the longest in playoff history. Now it was 21–14 and the mighty Redskins were starting to sweat.

When the San Francisco defense held once again, forcing a punt, Montana drove the Niners 53 yards in four plays, hitting Wilson with a 12-yard pass to make it 21–21 with 7:18 left to play.

The way Montana brought the 49ers back from the dead was something to see. He finished with a playoff-record 27 completions on a playoff-record 43 attempts for 347 yards, including 18 completions during the rally. But it was too little, too late.

In the closing moments, Theismann led his own furious drive, aided by a controversial pass interference call on Eric Wright. Minutes after Mark Moseley's 25-yard, game-winning field goal, the losing quarterback slumped over a locker room bench. Washington 24, San Francisco 21. Staring blankly into the distance, speaking in hushed tones, he struggled to make sense of a game that slipped away despite his brilliance.

"It's my fault," he said. "If I had played better earlier, we would have won."

Failure can be a marvelous teacher, especially when it comes wrapped in such an ambivalent package, and Montana would always remember the pain of losing one step short of the Super Bowl.

As a mob of sportswriters descended on the San Francisco locker room after Montana's failed rally, the loud, angry voice bursting through the door belonged to Eddie DeBartolo.

"They're trying to get to me! The officiating was terrible!

"They're trying to get to me because my father owns the Pittsburgh Maulers of the United States Football League and they think it's a conflict of interest. But they can't get me through this team . . ."

The 49ers' owner always stood up for his team, and like everyone associated with the organization, he took the loss to the Redskins hard. He took all the losses like he had played sixty minutes and personally drawn up every play, exuding a genuine passion for the game that helped endear him to his players.

After one especially bitter defeat, DeBartolo arrived in the locker room before the players and coaches and spent several minutes taking his frustrations out on an innocent soft drink machine. By the time the team started filing through the door, the massive box had been reduced to a useless pile of glass and metal. Everyone saw it, and everyone knew it must have been demolished by the fiery little man standing nearby in the immaculately tailored suit, but no one said a word until Ronnie Lott walked past, carefully inspected the rubble, and turned to his owner.

"What happened? You didn't have correct change?"

DeBartolo just glared at him.

Six years after purchasing the 49ers, DeBartolo had established that he was a very different sort of owner. He rarely attended the owners' meetings—preferring to send a surrogate, usually Carmen Policy, his one-time personal lawyer who eventually became vice president of the team and played a large role in shaping the 49ers' dynasty—and seemed genuinely uninterested in working with his counterparts. When the owners created the scouting combine in 1982, allowing for a systematic evaluation of players before the draft, the 49ers declined to participate. "When you go to those things, you're all pulling on the end of the same rope," explained John McVay. "We feel confident enough in our scouts and coaches to do it all on our own." Such independence was made possible by DeBartolo's willingness to employ a larger front office staff and devote a greater budget to scouting than his rivals.

Determined to build a winning franchise, and secure in the belief that the answer to most challenges was a big, fat check, he spent lavishly in various areas to turn the once-moribund outfit into a first-class organization, from its sparkling new practice facility and utilization of charter planes with extra seats to the incentives he provided for the players.

"The players genuinely loved and respected Eddie," Steve Wallace said. "How many owners can you say that about? He wanted the absolute best for his players and wanted his players to feel like they were part of a first-class organization."

Everything had to be bigger and better, including the glistening diamond-encrusted Super Bowl rings worn by every man in the organization. "That's the kind of gesture that makes players say, 'I worked my butt off to win this championship for a good man, and in return, he's shown us his gratitude,'" Montana said. "That's respect, and that creates a winning attitude."

The approach often produced jealousy and resentment from the league's old guard. "Some people think they can buy anything," sniped Cincinnati's Paul Brown, who presided over the NFL's thriftiest operation. "That might be the way for some people, but not for the Bengals."

Beyond his irrational postmortem rant in Washington, which reflected the volatility that often made him look like an Italian-American cliché, it was true that league officials and his fellow owners felt threatened by the DeBartolo family's investment in the rival USFL, which served only to exacerbate their disdain for the brash young man who seemed so disrespectful of their old boys' club. But they proved powerless to stop it.

A frustrated athlete who had been too small and too untalented to play the game, DeBartolo achieved a certain vicarious thrill by cultivating close personal friendships with various San Francisco players through the years, especially Montana. This sometimes led him down a dangerous path. DeBartolo often infuriated Walsh by negotiating directly with players, undermining the authority of the head coach/general manager, who was left to deal with the consequences of a newly elevated pay scale resulting from yet another generous contract. "Now what am I going to do when Ronnie Lott comes knocking on my door?" he vented to one friend after another preemptive bump.

Competition from the USFL forced the Niners to act decisively to retain several key players heading toward the 1984 season. Montana exploited the climate to renegotiate his contract, doubling his salary to more than $1 million per year. Now one of the highest paid players in football—making slightly less than Houston Oilers quarterback Warren Moon and New York Giants linebacker Lawrence Taylor—Joe Cool was about to show the world he was worth every penny.

Eight weeks into the 1984 season, Bill Walsh discovered another weakness. The Genius spent much of his time looking for flaws, in his own team and in his opponents, and this time, while watching film, he located a glaring hole in the Los Angeles Rams, rivals for supremacy in the NFC West. The way the Rams' safety attacked in one particular situation, leaving a narrow seam, created an opportunity for a quarterback who could make a perfect throw at just the right time. He just happened to have such a man on the payroll.

Several days later, Montana danced around the Anaheim Stadium field and repeatedly exploited the intelligence with several perfectly timed slants. If he was just a second or two late, the safety could converge and make the play. But he was never late. He was never off target. It was the Walsh/Montana partnership in microcosm: pinpoint execution as a valuable currency. (As Dolphins defender Doug Betters once observed, "Football is a game of inches and Montana knows what to do with those inches.") On these routes and on the various other mostly short patterns in San Francisco's repertoire, the quarterback methodically put the ball in the right place at the right time, stringing together one first down after another in a 33–0 demolition of the Rams.

"They take the four- and five-yard pass and think of it as a run," lamented Rams defensive end Jack Youngblood, who spent much of his day lunging for the ballcarrier moments after another short completion.

Montana connected on 13 consecutive passes and wound up hitting 21 of 31 for 365 yards and three touchdowns.

"The way our offense is designed, Bill feels we can throw against anyone," Montana explained. "It can be small things [that make the difference]. It could be something like throwing the ball just a little lower, or Freddie [Solomon] getting low enough in the end zone."

Devastated by the loss to the Redskins the previous January, the 49ers approached the 1984 season as a very hungry football team. "Losing in the championship game will leave a bitter taste in your mouth," Earl Cooper recalled. "We felt like we had something to prove." Still trying to get the loss "out of my system," Montana was still stinging from the controversial interference penalty on Eric Wright. "Man for man we knew we were cheated [out of the NFC title]," he said. The quarterback spotted "a certain intensity" in training camp that reflected a team fully invested in the goal of getting back to the Super Bowl. "We were going to do everything in our power not to be denied."

After opening the season with a 30–27 victory over Detroit, San Francisco hosted Washington, which had lost some of his luster after suffering a decisive 38–9 defeat to the Raiders in the Super Bowl. Throwing for 381 yards, Montana answered Theismann drive for drive and made several clutch plays down the stretch, converting a crucial third-and-eleven that allowed the 49ers to run out the clock on a hard-fought 37–31 victory.

As the season moved into October, the 49ers boarded their United Airlines charter for the long cross-country trip to New York for a widely anticipated *Monday Night Football* game against the Giants, who were under new management and starting to show signs of life.

One year after leading the Giants into the playoffs for the first time in two decades, Ray Perkins abruptly resigned to succeed his mentor Paul "Bear" Bryant at Alabama. "The only job I would have left New York for," said the stern onetime receiver. When Perkins stepped into Bryant's enormous shadow in December 1982, general manager George Young moved quickly to promote defensive coordinator Bill Parcells, who immediately imposed his gigantic sense of purpose on every aspect of the franchise. A hard-charging New Jersey tough guy who was the stylistic opposite of the cerebral Bill Walsh, Parcells had worked his way up through the college and pro ranks before landing on Perkins's staff, where he was directly responsible for the emergence of Lawrence Taylor. He was abrasive, demanding, and driven. "Even when we were doing well," he told biographer Nunyo Demasio, "I was on their asses." After he was hired as head coach, the Giants regressed. Beset by injuries and his own mistakes, New York tumbled to 3–12–1 in 1983, a season so horrible that Young began maneuvering behind his back to hire Howard Schnellenberger, the NFL veteran who had just captured the national championship with the University of Miami Hurricanes. The deal never materialized, and Parcells returned for the 1984 season.

Every week, the 49ers faced a team eager to prove that Walsh's unconventional system could be neutralized with the right combination of pressure and deception. As San Francisco arrived at the New Jersey Meadowlands, the Giants loomed as more than a 3–1 team that seemed to be headed in the right direction. They were slowly maturing into the most serious challenger to the 49ers—and Walsh's attempt to impose his precision-oriented stamp on the game. Unlike the Genius, Parcells believed in the enduring power of the old-school physical approach: Play hard-nosed defense. Run the ball. Dominate the line of scrimmage. It would be an oversimplification to say that Walsh believed in outsmarting his opponent while Parcells believed in kicking his opponent's ass, but there was in this verbal shorthand the ring of truth. In time, the stark contrast between the two teams would provide the sport with significant competitive tension, investing every game with the feeling of a referendum, stoking a fierce rivalry that helped define the sport from the mid-1980s to the early '90s. It was East versus West. Old versus new. Muscle versus finesse. Run to set up the pass versus pass to set up the run. They weren't simply competing for championships; they were battling to control what football was.

On the first Monday in October of 1984, Montana quickly demonstrated the power of the new. Six plays after the opening kickoff, on third-and-seven from his 41, Montana took three steps backward and saw Renaldo Nehemiah, the world record–holder in the 110-meter high hurdles, blow past Mark Haynes in single coverage. The quarterback rifled a bullet that hit Nehemiah perfectly in stride, and he raced 59 yards for a touchdown. It quickly turned ugly. Less than four minutes later, San Francisco owned a 14–0 lead after Montana culminated a 75-yard drive with a one-yard pass to rookie tight end John Frank. Four plays later, Dana McLemore gathered a Giants punt and raced 79 yards for another San Francisco touchdown, giving the 49ers a commanding 21–0 lead halfway through the first quarter. The 31–10 rout moved the 49ers to 6–0, alone atop the NFC West and one of only two remaining undefeated teams in the NFL.

Across the country, another powerful team was rising in the AFC East. Two years after Miami lost to the Redskins in Super Bowl XVII—the bullish image of John Riggins trampling Dolphins cornerback Don McNeal to score the winning touchdown remained a vivid nightmare in Miami, especially in the McNeal household—Don Shula had added one key ingredient to his veteran team. Dan Marino was the kind of player who could make a good team great.

A native of Pittsburgh, with deep roots in blue-collar western Pennsylvania, Marino became the latest model to emerge from the cradle of quarterbacks, four years behind Montana. Arriving in Miami as a first-round draft pick after an outstanding career at the University of Pittsburgh, he burst onto the scene at midseason in 1983, supplanting the veteran David Woodley en route to the Pro Bowl. In the autumn of 1984, as NBC's *Miami Vice* exploded into a Friday-night phenomenon, exploring fictional South Florida sleaze through a hip lens, Marino's record-setting aerial show brought a new energy to Sunday afternoons. By the time the Dolphins won their first eleven games to command the AFC East by four games, the full-color poster of the smiling quarterback, dressed in a classic black tuxedo with the Miami skyline unfolding behind him, was selling even faster than the Don Johnson–inspired white sports jacket.

Week after week, Marino plundered defenses at a torrid pace. In a 36–28 victory over the Cardinals, he threw for a staggering 429 yards. In a 31–17 demolition of the Jets, he piled up 422 yards. The strength of his arm and the quickness of his release often drew comparisons to Namath. Always looking to break one long, he attacked with a rare combination of power and savvy, whipping bullets downfield to favorite receivers Mark Duper and Mark Clayton, leaving defenses defenseless and demoralized. In October, he shattered Bob Griese's franchise record for touchdown passes in a season (22). In November, he surpassed Y. A. Tittle's twenty-two-year-old NFL standard (36) and kept going.

Marino's aerial assault left football people across the league scrambling to place him in perspective. "The quickest arm I've ever seen," said his own coach, who won two league titles with Johnny Unitas. "Phenomenal," said Buffalo nose tackle Fred Smerlas. "Scary," concluded New England executive Dick Steinberg, who added, "He's ripping up the NFL like nobody's ever done . . . I don't know what you can do to stop the guy."

As fans across the league began to talk about the possibility of a San Francisco–Miami showdown in the Super Bowl, this unanswered question hung in the ether like a riddle.

Seven weeks into the season, the Pittsburgh Steelers handed the undefeated 49ers a 20–17 loss at Candlestick. The game turned on a controversial play: Near the goal line in the fourth quarter, Eric Wright batted the ball away from Hall of Fame receiver John Stallworth, but was flagged for an interference call, producing a cascade of boos from the home crowd and giving the Steelers new life. Two plays later, Mark Malone hit Stallworth in the end zone for the winning touchdown.

While Marino's big numbers attracted most of the attention, the twenty-eight-year-old Montana—who completed 64.6 percent of his passes for 3,630 yards, 28 touchdowns, and 10 interceptions—quietly hit his stride while leading a team that approached perfection. It was also the year when Wendell Tyler, who rushed for a franchise-record 1,262 yards, proved he was still one of the most elusive backs in the league. Roger Craig forcefully demonstrated the dual threat ability that made him such a valuable commodity, accumulating a combined 1,324 yards rushing and receiving. George Seifert's defense, featuring Pro Bowl linebacker Keena Turner and the best secondary in football—all four regulars were invited to the Pro Bowl—allowed the offense room to breathe by yielding just 14.2 points per game. The team's giveaway/takeaway of plus 16 led the league. Unlike the 1981 Super Bowl champions, who overachieved despite key weaknesses, the 1984 San Francisco 49ers were a dominant football team with precious few flaws. As all the pieces fell into place, the six-game winning streak was quickly followed by a nine-game winning streak. San Francisco thundered to a 15–1 finish, the most regular-season wins in league history and the best mark since Miami's 17–0 in 1972.

Sometimes it looked easy: In a 51–7 rout of the Minnesota Vikings, Montana tossed three first-half touchdowns, including a 44-yarder to Dwight Clark, and then watched backup Matt Cavanaugh play most of the second half. Sometimes not: After throwing four interceptions against the Cincinnati Bengals, the quarterback rallied the 49ers for a 23–17 win, secured by his four-yard pass to Freddie Solomon with 1:39 remaining. "I don't remember throwing four interceptions before," he said. "I just hope it never happens again. We were lucky to get out with a win, turning the ball over that many times."

It was the offense that allowed the quarterback to overcome so many costly mistakes, and it was the quarterback who knew how to use the system to find his way home in the dark.

More often than not, Montana empowered the 49ers by making good choices and finding the end zone, as demonstrated by a crucial moment in a December rematch with the Rams. Facing third-and-goal from one, he engineered a textbook play-action, faking to Wendell Tyler up the middle and then coolly hitting Earl Cooper all alone in the end zone for the winning touchdown in a 19–16 victory.

"Joe was the master in those situations," Cooper said. "You can say, well, Bill Walsh was calling the plays, and that's true. But it took a guy who could execute perfectly, make the read, make the throw, and that's what Joe did, time after time."

The road to the Super Bowl began with a playoff game at Candlestick against the New York Giants, who upset the Rams, 16–13, in the NFC wild card game and arrived in San Francisco eager for revenge. "They took us to school that night [back in October]," admitted running back Rob Carpenter. "But I'm glad we've got a chance to show them how much we've improved. And believe it, we have improved."

The play of quickly maturing, if still somewhat impatient, quarterback Phil Simms was central to New York's 9–7 season. "He has surprised a lot of people in the league," said Walsh, who clearly was not the least bit surprised by the man who might have been his Joe Montana. But the turnaround, which strengthened Parcells's once-precarious hold on his job, owed a larger debt to a punishing defense led by linebackers Lawrence Taylor and Harry Carson, who appreciated how complicated the task of defending Montana could be. "There is a lot of talk about Montana and Dan Marino," observed Giants defensive end George Martin. "But Montana is better because he is more versatile. That's what makes the 49ers so tough to prepare for."

With Walsh eager to jump out to an early lead, Montana quickly lunged for the jugular, throwing two touchdown passes in the first seven minutes—21 yards to Dwight Clark and nine to Russ Francis—to stake San Francisco to a 14–0 advantage. But he later tossed three costly interceptions, allowing New York to pull within four, before a third Montana touchdown pass—29 yards to Freddie Solomon—made it 21–10 at the half. "Sometimes our offense kind of goes downhill for some reason," Montana said. "This time it was because of me." The second interception came immediately after a 53-yard scramble by Montana, the longest of his career, which brought the home crowd to its feet. The second half became a scoreless battle of defenses, as the 49ers' pass rush clamped down on Simms, sacking him six times and forcing two interceptions, to preserve the 21–10 victory, which sent San Francisco to the NFC Championship Game for the second straight year.

In the aftermath, Walsh exuded a rather contented vibe, while conceding that his team's offensive performance in the second half had not been "as artistic as we'd like." Meanwhile, in the visitor's locker room, Bill Parcells was spewing obscenities and growing impatient. Not only had he been beaten by the 49ers again, he had been beaten by a man who talked about football like he was reviewing a Mozart concerto at the New York Philharmonic.

Like the Giants, the Chicago Bears represented the antithesis of the emerging San Francisco approach to the game. Mike Ditka's teams won in the traditional style, featuring the powerful running of Walter Payton, the league's all-time yardage leader, and an intimidating brand of defense. Ditka and defensive coordinator Buddy Ryan were often at each other's throats, but Ryan was a wily tactician and an inspirational leader who knew how to get the most out of his personnel. Led by the ferocious middle linebacker Mike Singletary, the Bears stampeded to a 13–3 season, ranking first against the run and second against the pass while holding eight teams to a touchdown or less. Confronted with those eight men in the box, and all that stunting and blitzing, Joe Gibbs adjusted by putting Joe Theismann in the shotgun, so he could have a little more time to maneuver. It didn't work. The Bears still forced Theismann to run for his life, and the Monsters of the Midway eliminated Washington, 23–19, to earn a date with San Francisco. Chicago advanced to its first NFC title game since the merger with the swagger of a favorite, filling the newspapers with trash talk, convinced that they were too tough, too mean for the high-flying, highfalutin 49ers.

Well aware of the significant challenge the Bears' defense posed, Walsh devised a gimmick and planned to save it for just the right moment.

The road to this milepost began the previous April, when Walsh, no longer overwhelmed by immediate needs, drafted offensive lineman Guy McIntyre in the second round. Given the strength and stability of the men who provided the human fortress protecting Montana—Randy Cross, John Ayers, Fred Quillan, Keith Fahnhorst, and Bubba Paris—McIntyre, who spent his first three years at Georgia blocking for Herschel Walker, arrived as a demonstration of the Niners' newfound luxury of planning for the future. He would not be needed right away, but his time was coming. His ability to absorb the intricacies of the West Coast Offense would make him one of the central figures in protecting Montana as he aged, a daunting task that was far from his thoughts when he first encountered the quarterback during the 49ers' minicamp in the spring of 1984.

"My first impression of Joe was seeing him standing next to Dwight [Clark] by their lockers," McIntyre recalled. "I remember thinking to myself: That's Joe Montana?"

Him?

The guy with the spindly legs?

"He wasn't this impressive-looking person, and I was really sort of shocked, sort of amazed," McIntyre said. "He was this little skinny guy. *The* Joe Montana!"

As he made the roster and began playing on special teams and occasionally as a backup lineman, McIntyre experienced up close the various nuances at work in making Montana such an effective quarterback. "You watch him work and you realize, [if we] give him time, he'll do what he needs to do to win the game. He'll find a way."

On the Monday before the Bears game, a large contingent of 49ers, accompanied by wives and girlfriends, headed out to dinner at Stuart Anderson's Black Angus Steakhouse. The boys had a good time blowing off steam, and when somebody slipped a quarter into the jukebox and the Isley Brothers' hit "Shout" began blaring across the restaurant, McIntyre, the onetime Georgia frat boy, leaped to his feet and led his teammates onto the dance floor, where they started singing at the top of their lungs and mimicking the "gator" dance made popular by John Belushi and friends in *Animal House.*

At practice the next day, Walsh unveiled his latest offensive wrinkle: lining up McIntyre in the backfield as a blocking back to help offset the mismatch caused by the way the Bears stacked the middle of the line.

Watching the scene, San Francisco linebacker Mike Walter, who had witnessed the floor show, yelled out, "Angus in the backfield."

Thus the Angus Formation was born.

"I don't know when Coach Walsh decided to do it, but we only practiced it the week before we played Chicago," McIntyre recalled.

Walsh saved the gadget play for a crucial moment. In the third quarter, with the 49ers leading 6–0, the six-foot-five, 285-pound McIntyre exited the huddle and lined up behind Montana, in place of Roger Craig. It was an odd sight, and in the seconds before the snap, the insertion succeeded in confusing the Bears. Wendell Tyler took the handoff and followed the big fullback through the line, rambling nine yards to score the first touchdown of the game for a 13–0 Niners lead.

"The Bears had a great defense, but they were certainly caught off guard," said McIntyre, whose maneuver inspired Ditka to use William "The Refrigerator" Perry as a short-yardage runner the next season.

If the Angus Formation demonstrated Walsh's predilection to tinker and devise new ways to outsmart defenses, the task of beating the Bears and reinforcing the viability of his brand of football rested disproportionately on the shoulders of the instrument he had been fine-tuning for six years. To beat the 49ers, Chicago needed to disrupt Montana before he could distribute the ball. It was that simple. Walsh's game plan called for Montana to get rid of the ball even faster than normal. "We speeded up the process, with Montana throwing the ball to a wide receiver or running back before the pressure could develop," Walsh said. "Everything depended on our receivers beating their cornerbacks quickly with Joe taking three steps and getting rid of the ball."

On a day when the San Francisco defense was outstanding—limiting the Bears to just 186 total yards—Montana proved too nimble in his three-step drops, too quick in his release, too accurate in his throws, too masterful in his reads, too instinctive in his audibles, too mobile in his escape. Even though he tossed two interceptions and completed only slightly more than half of his passes (18 of 34 for 233 yards), Montana led an attack that amassed 387 yards and 25 first downs, piloting a decisive 23–0 win that could have been much worse.

The game's final touchdown was vintage Joe Cool. When the ball was snapped and the Bears' rush converged while Freddie Solomon took the initiative of adjusting his route to find a seam, Montana calmly rolled right, buying time until his receiver could get open. He danced and waited, waited and danced, until he could see, a split second before it happened, that Solomon was about to be free in the end zone, releasing a perfectly thrown pass that arrived in the slightest window in time and space. Touchdown. Object lesson. Art melding with science.

"That's why Joe Montana is the greatest quarterback in football today," observed John Madden, the former Oakland Raiders coach who was quickly emerging as the preeminent football analyst on television. "The amazing thing is that Montana seems to do it all the time, so often that you almost expect it of him . . . People expect him to do over and over what other quarterbacks can't do once."

Of course, he was no Dan Marino.

By the time San Francisco punched its ticket for Super Bowl XIX at Stanford Stadium in Palo Alto, Miami had completed a 14–2 regular season and earned its way to football's championship game by eliminating Seattle (31–10) and Pittsburgh (45–28). The media's insistence on framing the game by comparing and contrasting the two Pennsylvania-born quarterbacks quickly became tedious, especially to the largely overlooked 49ers defense. No showdown of field generals had ever attracted the hype of Montana versus Marino on the last Sunday in January of 1985, when Joe Cool stepped onto the biggest stage as a decided underdog.

At every turn, Montana, already the most efficient passer in the history of the NFL, was confronted with a near-consensus opinion: The bigger, stronger Marino could be the greatest quarterback who ever pulled on a jockstrap. Don't you agree, Joe? What's it like to face such a gifted passer, Joe? Don't you just wish you could air it out like Marino, Joe? Assaulted day after day by the implication that he was taking the field in the other guy's shadow—that he lacked the tools to direct the sort of high-powered offense employed by the Dolphins—Montana refused to challenge the premise of such questions, preferring to respond in a haze of humility.

"I'm just an ordinary Joe," he insisted nonchalantly. "I can't even throw that hard. I'm just fortunate to be in a great system surrounded by some great players. I just hope I'm worthy of this game."

If such answers struck some reporters as false modesty, the truth was actually more complicated. Montana was not the sort of athlete who liked to blow his own horn. Broadway Joe, he wasn't. He didn't need to beat his chest and tell you how great he was. He wasn't a good quote. He was gracious in the spotlight but he didn't crave it. Deep down, in a place very few people saw, he was enormously confident. He knew how it felt to own a moment, to be able to make a football dance in the breeze. He understood that he possessed some special quality of leadership and a competitiveness that kicked in whenever somebody started keeping score. But because of the various struggles he had faced on the road to this critical juncture, because of the swirling doubts that had played such a significant role in his athletic development, he never stopped feeling the genuine need to prove himself. With some athletes, this can promote debilitating insecurity. With Montana, it was a raging fire churned into motivational propellant. "Even after he had been in San Francisco for years," noted former 49ers offensive line coach Mike Solari, "Joe approached every day like he was trying to make the team." Because he had been conditioned by his father and various others to keep his ego in check, he was always mindful to let his play speak for itself. As Randy Cross once said, "Joe's very confident in his abilities. He's just smart enough not to blow his own horn. He knows other people will do that for him." There was a power in

Montana's ability to restrain himself, to be the placid athlete with the self-deprecating wit who could poke fun at his arm strength and his skinny legs even as he pushed himself—and those around him—to win. "Joe had this rare combination of strength and humility," said offensive lineman Steve Wallace. "He didn't need to be the prima donna, and I think that was a big part of his success."

Beyond the Marino lovefest lurked a deeper truth. The 49ers and the Dolphins represented two very different approaches to the passing game, each enabled by the 1978 rules changes and now battling for primacy in a sport slowly beginning to resist decades of offensive inertia.

Seven years into the so-called live-ball era, the scoring average had jumped from 17.2 to 21.2, driven by the gradual tilt in favor of the air game, from 25 passing attempts per game to 32. The cumulative completion percentage increased from 51.3 to 56.4—headed ever skyward, as the San Francisco ethos began to exert its influence—and the typical league offense evolved from a ratio of 60 percent running/40 percent passing to 51 percent running/49 percent passing.

"By the early '80s, you had coaches who had been reluctant to throw the ball all that much in the past who began to realize, hey, you can win this way," said Dan Fouts, the powerful arm throttling San Diego's Air Coryell. "Is there a better example than Don Shula?"

The contrast between 1972 and 1984 was particularly striking. During the perfect season in the year of the Watergate break-in, Shula's Dolphins threw just 28 percent of the time—18.5 passes per game. After the climate started to change and he drafted a player who could drill it as well as anybody who ever lived, Shula altered his philosophy to fit the times. In 1984, while setting NFL records for yards (5,084), touchdown passes (48), and completions (362), and earning unanimous acclaim as the league's Most Valuable Player, Marino put the ball in the air 35.3 times per game—54.1 percent of all snaps. Like Fouts, he became one of the leading figures of the offensive revolution, a prototypical pocket passer unleashed in the still-gathering live-ball age. (Marino's superior supporting cast would allow him to eclipse Fouts, who could not overcome his team's various weaknesses and never played in the Super Bowl.)

The accumulated evidence suggested a convincing narrative. Marino was a special talent who could do things with a football Montana could not. This was undeniably true. It was also largely irrelevant as the nation's eyes turned to Palo Alto, located less than an hour's drive from Candlestick.

In the first quarter, the lead changed hands three times as the country watched the two offenses try to impose their will. Marino, who completed his first 10 passes, quickly drove Miami close enough for Uwe von Schamann's 37-yard field goal. Then Montana engineered a 78-yard, eight-play drive, culminated by his 33-yard toss to Carl Monroe. As the quarter drew to a close, Marino, shifting to a no-huddle offense, methodically picked the 49ers apart, marching 62 yards and taking a 10–3 lead on his two-yard pass to Dan Johnson.

In the second quarter, two things happened to alter the game's complexion. Montana kept moving the ball at will. And Marino was stifled by a critical change in the San Francisco defense.

Realizing Miami was unable to muster much of a running game—indeed, the Dolphins set a Super Bowl record with just nine rushes, yielding a paltry 25 yards—George Seifert switched to a nickel defense, which placed enormous pressure on Marino for the rest of the game. Now the riddle was solved. How do you stop a problem like Marino? Throw all your resources at him and make him beat you all by himself. Even the great Marino could not operate effectively when he was being chased and pummeled by half of the San Francisco defense on every play, especially Fred Dean and Dwaine Board, who seemed to be clawing at his face mask every time he drew a breath, their pursuit given weight by the masterful performance of Ronnie Lott and the rest of the secondary, who smothered the Dolphin receivers and forced the quarterback to hesitate and hold. Marino wound up with 318 yards but all the harassment forced two interceptions, 21 incompletions, four sacks, and countless hurries. He led the Dolphins close enough for two more field goals but was completely outclassed by his less-celebrated rival.

Montana played one of the greatest games of his life. "About as perfect a game as a quarterback can play," said an admiring, if dejected, Dolphins linebacker Jay Brophy.

Early in the second quarter, with Miami leading 10–7, he spotted an opening in the Killer B's defense and took off, scrambling 19 yards to secure a first down at the Dolphins' 28. Three plays later, he faded into the pocket and fired a pass across the middle to Roger Craig. The play, known internally as 20 Bingo Cross, had been added to the playbook because the head coach believed the Miami linebackers—who were typically left to cover the backs while the wide receivers attracted double coverage—could not effectively handle Craig. It called for Craig and Tyler to move between the tackle and guard and then cross, just past the line of scrimmage, and it worked beautifully. The eight-yard touchdown gave San Francisco a 14–10 lead.

With Marino faltering, Montana quickly took control of the game. Two more long scoring drives—culminated by the quarterback's six-yard run and Craig's six-yard run, respectively—made it 28–16 at the half. By the time Montana led the 49ers close enough for Ray Wersching's 27-yard field goal and threw a 16-yard touchdown to Craig in the third quarter, the game was essentially over.

"They drilled us," Dolphins defensive end Doug Betters said. "It was embarrassing . . . There's no other way to put it."

Calling his team's performance "almost perfect," Walsh later recalled, "We felt like we were one of the great teams of all time."

By any measure, San Francisco's 18–1 record in 1984 ranked among the most dominant seasons in professional football history, comparable to another team that captured the league championship with a single loss: Vince Lombardi's 1962 Green Bay Packers. Almost as impressive as the 1972 Dolphins' 17–0. Almost perfect.

Humbled by his team's second Super Bowl loss in three years, cornerback Don McNeal said, "The 49ers looked better on the field than they do on paper. We didn't."

The way Montana operated Walsh's system while leading San Francisco to a 38–16 rout of the Dolphins made a powerful statement. He didn't complete a long pass all night. No matter. He just kept stringing together all those short and intermediate throws: hitting Solomon near the sideline, Craig across the middle, Clark underneath.

Moving effortlessly through his reads, manipulating the system like a machine, he completed 24 of 35 for a Super Bowl–record 331 yards and three touchdowns. Time after time, he used his mobility as a weapon, running for a Super Bowl–record 59 yards—averaging 11.8 yards per scramble—and repeatedly evading the rather subdued Dolphins rush just long enough to move the chains.

"[Montana] was outstanding in every way," Shula said. "He knew just what to do with the football the entire day."

Weighing in on the question that had just been settled rather definitively, at least for one day, Walsh said, "Marino is a great young quarterback but in my mind Joe Montana is the greatest quarterback in football today." Then he paused. "Maybe of all time."

Only after making his case to an estimated 100 million television witnesses would the San Francisco hero, who was named the Super Bowl MVP for the second time, confess to a certain irritation adding fuel to his fire. "All week, all we heard was, 'Miami, Miami, Miami,' " he said. "What about us? That motivated the entire offense. It wasn't so much me against Dan. Our whole offense was overlooked the last two weeks."

Like Too Tall Jones and many others, the Dolphins had been forced to contend with a quarterback who had something to prove—about the offense he was leading and about himself. He never said a word to his teammates. He didn't have to. "I'm sure it motivated him," Clark said.

Six years after a long line of NFL experts looked Montana over and saw what he wasn't, he had completely validated Walsh's faith by harnessing the power of an offense that perfectly suited his particular gifts while minimizing his weaknesses. By walking off the field as a two-time Super Bowl champion, he added his name to a short list of high-achieving quarterbacks who towered over the sport. Terry Bradshaw. Bart Starr. Bob Griese. Roger Staubach. Joe Montana. Two rings put him in elite company. But the man from Monongahela was headed for a still-distant horizon, and he would be forced to contend with an array of challenges on the bumpy road to football immortality.

# CHAPTER SEVEN

# No Pain, No Fame

In the 1985 motion picture *Jagged Edge*, the line between fact and fiction momentarily blurred. Looking up at a large seaside mansion, a young boy yelled out to his mother, "Who lives here? Joe Montana?" While meaningless to the plot about a murdered newspaper heiress, the line gave the character the ring of authenticity, because at that time, no name suggested San Francisco quite like Joe Montana. It was the narrative equivalent of flashing a sun-drenched shot of the Golden Gate Bridge. The scene demonstrated the quarterback's rapid ascension to American cultural icon, but the impact of his celebrity would not always be so benign.

As the country moved into the conservative Reagan era, amid the climactic years of the cold war with the Soviet Union and an economic boom that sent the stock market surging to new heights, the way the public viewed sports stars was undergoing a metamorphosis. Long gone were the days when fans viewed athletes through a mythic lens. With the media more aggressively reporting bad news—including a steady stream of law enforcement matters—and many fans struggling to relate to figures who earned enormous salaries and yet still participated in work stoppages and holdouts, often demanding to renegotiate contracts before they expired, the sports stars of the 1980s encountered a much more skeptical public. Every athlete who was arrested or acted boorishly in public contributed to a new-age narrative: These people may have special skills but they are prone to the same weaknesses as the rest of us, thus tilting the fans' perspective from an upward gaze to something more closely resembling eye to eye.

Out of this cynical cauldron, Montana became one of the most popular athletes in America, not just because of his success but also because of the way he handled his success. In addition to his ranking as one of the greatest football players of the age and his reputation as a clutch performer who so often found a way to win, he projected an unmistakable likeability, a disarming, boyish charm. Amid the rampant bad behavior in professional sports, he exuded a refreshing maturity, resonating with a nation growing weary of arrogance and self-importance. There was a certain everyman quality about him. Unlike Chicago Bulls superstar Michael Jordan, who constantly did things with a basketball that caused jaws to drop all across America, Montana didn't seem superhuman. He was relatable.

The public no longer demanded, or believed in, squeaky-clean heroes, and Montana was no choirboy. By 1983, he was a two-time loser in the marriage game. When his relationship with Cass ended, the details of their acrimonious divorce appeared in Bay Area newspapers, introducing him to the downside of fame as he felt the sting of a very personal failure. It was a time when the divorce rate was soaring, and Joe Cool was just another young man still looking for the one. Fans still yearned for athletes who mirrored their values, but what the public sought more than anything else was the sort of star who could perform on the field and rake in the big bucks without acquiring a sense of entitlement, and Montana defined this archetype better than any other athlete of the period.

The daily onslaught of living in the Bay Area and being its greatest sports icon was frequently overwhelming. Even pumping gas could be an ordeal—Joe Montana pumps his own gas?—and when he went out to dinner with friends, the fans invariably converged, thrusting ink pens and scraps of paper. He was always polite. In most cases, he happily signed his name, posed for a picture, shared a smile, demonstrating not only his graciousness but also the realization that one stranger who interrupted his dinner and walked away in a huff could tarnish his reputation. "I've seen him sign autographs for people when his food's sitting there getting cold," said Bruce Collie, recalling one meal when a lady reached toward his face to get something signed and collided with the quarterback's fork, which was headed for his mouth. After games, win or lose, fans young and old mobbed the entrance to the San Francisco locker room, just hoping to see those baby blues up close. At the 49ers complex, the mail piled up like the judge's desk in *Miracle on 34th Street*, from zip codes across the land and beyond. He dedicated time once a week to autographing pictures, footballs, and odd scraps of paper, but he could never keep up with the surging demand. On Halloween, kids across the Bay Area donned number 16 jerseys and Montana masks in the frantic pursuit of candy and heroic connection. His name produced such sizzle across the country that one Kentucky beauty was even duped into marrying a man who claimed to be the famed quarterback, only to have the imposter skip town before their planned Hawaiian honeymoon.

A reluctant celebrity who did not crave the limelight, Montana nevertheless enjoyed many of the perks that accompanied his sudden fame and fortune as he became firmly entrenched in the 1980s Zeitgeist. He was not political but he had a fan in the White House. Prior to Super Bowl XIX, President Reagan appeared via satellite from the Oval Office, becoming the first sitting president to flip the coin. Immediately after the 49ers' decisive victory over the Dolphins, ABC employed a split screen of Walsh, surrounded by his players in the victorious locker room, talking with Reagan. "There ought to be a bigger word than congratulations for all we saw tonight," the president said. "But I just want to say congratulations to you and, of course, congratulations to Joe Montana . . ." The tradition of hosting the champions of the major professional and college sports at the White House was just starting to develop, and although the Walsh-era 49ers never convened at 1600 Pennsylvania Avenue, the former sports announcer invited Montana to a private dinner in the residence, peppering him with questions about his team and the NFL. When he told a reporter about his case of nerves upon entering the White House, Joe Cool was asked if he had consumed an adult beverage or two to relax.

"Are you kidding? I was drinking orange juice. I was afraid to have any drinks."

Around this time, Montana and buddy Dwight Clark were hanging out backstage at the Bay Area Music Awards, where they had been invited to present one of the Bammies. Soon they were chatting with Huey Lewis and the News, the San Francisco–based rock group who had just scored their first Billboard hit with "Do You Believe in Love."

"They professed themselves to be fans, and of course, we were fans of theirs," Lewis recalled.

The small talk eventually led to discussion of a career-bending bargain. "Why don't you let us sing on one of your records?" Montana suggested, pointing out that Clark was a talented singer. "We'll let you take a few snaps!"

"It was kind of a joke," Lewis said.

Out of this chance encounter, Lewis and Montana became friends who played golf, drank beer, made silly wagers, and shared each other's stories about the bumpy ride to fame and fortune. The rock star often prowled the sidelines at Candlestick, sometimes performed the national anthem, and frequently traveled on the team plane to away games. (He never got his snaps.)

After releasing two hit albums and scoring a number-one song with "The Power of Love," featured in the blockbuster 1985 Michael J. Fox film *Back to the Future*, Lewis started writing a tune that reflected a compelling societal trend.

> I used to be a renegade
> I used to fool around
> But I couldn't take the punishment
> And had to settle down

"It was meant to articulate a phenomenon . . . a current . . . going from the '70s to the '80s," Lewis said.

As the eldest baby boomers approached middle age, the vast wave of adults obsessed with pursuing their own version of the American Dream—among them, the materialistic, self-absorbed bunch widely derided as yuppies—included a large number of onetime hippies and antiestablishment types who had spent their youth experimenting with drugs, protesting the power structure, and mocking traditional America. The crowd that once wore tie-dyed shirts, grew waist-length hair, and spurned their parents' example at every turn now dutifully drove off to work neatly groomed, wearing Brooks Brothers suits with bright yellow rep ties, consumed with paying the mortgage and saving for the kids' college. Their reluctant conformity struck a nerve with Lewis and many others who could relate to the experience.

"Because the bohemian thing got to be too frightening . . . with the drug overdoses and [lack of] family . . . they dropped back in and became bourgeoisie," Lewis explained. "But their artistic tastes are still rooted in bohemia. So they look square but they're not. That phenomenon was what I was trying to articulate."

When the time arrived to record "Hip to be Square," Lewis wanted to give one line the punch of a gang shouting. Flashing back to the backstage encounter at the Bammies, he enlisted the help of Montana and Clark, along with fellow 49ers Ronnie Lott and Riki Ellison, who sang backup vocals, including the line "Here, there and everywhere." The song rocketed up the charts in the autumn of 1986, reaching number three, forever connecting the quarterback of his generation to an incisive cultural statement embedded in the sound track of the 1980s.

By the time he made news with Huey, the combination of Montana's on-field success and All-American image was already making him one of the leading advertising pitchmen of his time. Initially represented by Larry Muno, then by Bob Woolf, before embarking on a longtime relationship with International Management Group, the quarterback made up in authenticity and charm what he lacked in acting skill and polish.

His first television commercial, for the fuel additive Propel, proved to be a grueling experience. Moments after someone handed him a script, the director cued him and he began his career as a spokesman in a haze of confusion and nerves. After about thirty takes, he came away with a new respect for the professionals who made it look so easy. "The hardest part is seeing yourself and hearing yourself," he said. "You think it's all right, and then you see it and realize it isn't."

Determined to strike while he was a hot commodity—well aware that "my football career could end tomorrow"—he cut lucrative deals with a long line of consumer products companies, including Pepsi, Schick, Sega, Hanes, Concord watches, and LA Gear, which inked him to a three-year pact to promote its sneakers worth up to $5 million. Even as his salary with the 49ers eventually peaked at $4 million per year—15 percent of the 49ers' payroll, the league's highest—he was earning about as much through endorsements. Often his ads for different products appeared back-to-back on network television, raising fears of overexposure. But supply never exceeded demand.

As many television commercials evolved toward a more sophisticated narrative approach, using their endorsers as characters in quick-developing plots, the effect promoted a measure of marketing symbiosis. The series of thirty-second spots Pepsi invested millions to produce and air, which featured the quarterback in little skits with music icon Ray Charles and several others, succeeded in drenching the cola in cool, driving sales ever higher in the perpetual war against Coca-Cola—while also contributing immeasurably to *his* popularity. Because Montana was more than a football player. He was also a brand with an identity that needed to be carefully managed.

One commercial changed his life. To film a 1984 spot for Schick razors on a Los Angeles soundstage, Montana was paired with Jennifer Wallace, a vivacious, leggy blonde who was cast to play the Schick Sherriff. The twenty-seven-year-old model, who stood six feet, looked him over and was immediately impressed. "They finally got somebody they don't have to prop up on orange crates," she thought to herself. He was nervous. At one point, the director called the veteran actress over and asked her to do something to loosen up her costar. She pinched him on the butt and said, "Relax. The sheriff always gets her man." He turned beet red.

By this time, Montana had become one of San Francisco's most eligible bachelors, tooling around the Bay Area in his red Ferrari with one lovely lady after another. During this period, having lost his hillside house in the divorce, the quarterback spent several months living with Dwight Clark and new wife, Ashley, who became a combination confidant and cook. "I felt like a mother to him," she once said. "He'd talk to me about the girls he was taking out . . . When he went out at night, I'd wake up when I heard him drive in."

One woman who went on two dinner dates with Montana during this period remembered him as "charming" but "incredibly insecure."

"He struck me as a guy who was seeking reassurance, not in an arrogant way, but as someone who genuinely wanted to know if people thought he measured up," she said. "It was really surprising and quite sweet, for someone who was already admired by so many."

After completing the Schick commercial, the man with two Super Bowl rings kept the beautiful model waiting for quite a while before working up the courage to ask her to dinner. Still nervous, he nearly missed his moment, but once more, Joe Cool came through in the clutch. The connection was immediate.

For decades, Herb Caen's notes column in the *San Francisco Chronicle* reflected the pulse of Bay Area culture and gossip, from the rise of the beatniks to the latest celebrity sighting. On an August morning in 1984, Caen's column included yet another item that started tongues wagging from the East Bay to Silicon Valley.

> *The best show at the Golden Gate Theater Thursday night was not 'La Cage aux Folles' onstage but 49er star Joe Montana and his blonde date in the orchestra section, necking so furiously that smoke was coming out of their ears. Every now and then, the amorous lady would come up for air, give herself a shot of mouth spray and spritz Joe. The patrons in the immediate vicinity gave the sprightly couple a standing ovation.*

The blonde was Jennifer Wallace. Soon she became the third Mrs. Montana. While his first two marriages filled him with pain and regret, which he sometimes shared with his teammates over beers, Montana found long-term happiness with Jennifer, who became a positive force in his life and career, providing him with a level of stability, nurturing, and love he had lacked. She was the last piece of the puzzle, slipped into the picture to make it complete. She understood that part of Joe Montana hated being Joe Montana. "This image of the athlete as public figure, star, hero—he's not into that," she once said. But she also realized he could not turn off the fame, helping him make peace with this sometimes debilitating truth resulting from his enormous success.

One morning in the summer of 1985, hundreds of people lined up at Macy's in New York, many of them waiting for hours just to say a fast hello and have a photograph signed by the hero. He was pleasant to one and all. He smiled and joked and acted the perfect gentleman. But he kept looking at his watch, because as much as he appreciated the attention, being surrounded by adoring fans actually made him feel uncomfortable. In such situations, the shy young boy inside him felt compelled, as he once explained, "to dodge the light." He kept looking at his watch because he couldn't wait to step into the waiting limo, be close enough to hold Jennifer's hand, and escape.

The mother of his four children quickly emerged as a popular figure among his San Francisco teammates, who appreciated her various kindnesses through the years.

On the way out of town for road games, the quarterback always walked onto the charter with an ample supply of Jennifer's homemade fried chicken, which was quickly devoured. "That chicken was awesome," recalled Bruce Collie. "Joe would show up and we didn't care about him; we wanted at that chicken. She always made enough for the offensive line."

Nothing was too good for the big strong men protecting her husband. But the same force that led Montana to the love of his life left him increasingly vulnerable.

The quarterback hunched over center Fred Quillan, cradled the ball in his hands, and trained his eyes on the defense. That's when he saw something he didn't like.

"Red Ninety-Oh!"

His teammates immediately recognized the live color for that particular Sunday in September 1985, meaning Montana was changing the play at the line of scrimmage.

"Red Ninety-Oh!"

Across the neutral zone during an afternoon game at Los Angeles Memorial Coliseum, Raiders linebacker Matt Millen quickly took three steps toward the line, into the hole where Wendell Tyler soon would be running. He looked directly at the quarterback.

"Oh, no, Joe! Not *Red Ninety-Oh!*"

Startled, Montana started laughing, and snickering spread up and down the offensive line, forcing the quarterback to call a time-out.

"Matt ran like an old washer woman but he was such a stinking mental guy," recalled Bruce Collie. "He was playing a hunch. It was one of the funniest moments . . ."

After Montana regained his composure, he threw for two touchdowns to lead a 34–10 romp that lifted the defending Super Bowl champions to 2–1 on the year.

Unlike 1982, when the strike divided the team and the new season exposed various flaws that had been papered over on the way to Pontiac, undermining San Francisco's attempt to repeat, the 49ers approached 1985 with great expectations, armed with one of the most talented rosters in the league. No franchise had won back-to-back Super Bowls since Pittsburgh in 1978–79, and Walsh believed his team could make a serious run at another Lombardi Trophy.

Largely unseen by the public was Walsh's constant evaluation of personnel, driven by the cold calculus that even the most productive player reaches an expiration date. On the practice field and in games, he was forever attuned to the nuance of each position: Whether an offensive lineman was exploding off the ball with the same fire. Whether a receiver was running a route with the same precision. If a once-dependable running back was suddenly becoming fumble-prone.

"Bill made everybody uncomfortable with their position," recalled offensive lineman Steve Wallace. "You'd better be good or they'll tap you on the shoulder . . . because there's a guy standing right behind you who's waiting to take your job." Age and physical issues can prove to be the most stubborn foes, and like all coaches across the league, the 49ers' boss periodically faced difficult choices. His ability to act decisively in such situations proved central to his success. Several of the athletes who played significant roles in one or both Super Bowls were nearing the end of their careers—including linemen Keith Fahnhorst, John Ayers, and Montana's best friend and favorite target, Dwight Clark—but perhaps the most difficult transition involved receiver Freddie Solomon, a popular and high-profile player who had been instrumental in San Francisco's rise to the top of professional football. Nagging injuries and the unyielding calendar had convinced Walsh that Solomon's best days were behind him, so as he approached the 1985 draft, finding another talented receiver for Montana loomed large in his plans.

The solution to this particular problem first presented itself in 1984, on a road trip to play the Houston Oilers. Relaxing in his hotel room on the night before the game, Walsh happened upon a local television sportscast featuring highlights from a small college game way off the football map. Narrating one long pass play after another, the anchor made no attempt to conceal his amazement. Jerry Rice was that good.

Somehow ignored by the nation's major colleges, the brickmason's son with the reserved bearing and the sort of perfectionist streak that so often drives greatness, wound up at tiny Mississippi Valley State, a small, historically black school with an enrollment of less than three thousand. Because the competition he faced in the Division 1-AA Southwestern Athletic Conference was far below big-time college football, NFL scouts and coaches looked upon his statistics with skepticism. But after catching an NCAA-record 112 passes for 1,845 yards and 27 touchdowns as a senior in 1984—teaming with quarterback Willie Totten, who led a potent attack that averaged a stunning 59 points per game—Rice could not be easily ignored. Most teams projected him to last until at least the third round, but Walsh was not prepared to take such a chance. Despite significant opposition from his scouting operation, he paid a high price—much higher than some thought prudent—to acquire Rice: trading three draft picks to procure the seventeenth overall selection in the first round, which he used to take the player who would become one of the cornerstones of the franchise. Then he started pushing Solomon toward the door.

By this time, defenses were employing various tactics to try to counter Walsh's ball-control passing game. One of the most effective was the advent of man-to-man coverage on the short and intermediate routes, which made it imperative that the 49ers feature a wide receiver who could stretch the defense vertically. Not only would this give Montana significant options downfield, the requirements of protecting against such a threat would leave the defense even more vulnerable to the 49ers' pass-catching backs, especially Roger Craig. Watching him in action, Walsh believed Rice could prove to be such a transcendent force for his offense.

The transition proved bumpy. As San Francisco opened the 1985 season with a loss to Minnesota and a victory over division rival Atlanta, Rice stunned teammates and coaches with his deceptive speed and a knack for getting open, but his hands suddenly betrayed him. Time after time, he dropped perfectly thrown passes. "[Montana] didn't say it, but you could tell that he was starting to have doubts," Rice remembered. Trying to be patient, Montana could see "he was trying too hard. You try so hard and when you screw up, you think everybody's looking at you, thinking how you don't belong—even if they're not." Montana and other teammates tried to soften the blow, but many San Francisco fans were not so understanding, filling Candlestick with cascading boos when the man who once had been nicknamed "World"—because there was no pass in the world he couldn't catch—let another ball slip inexplicably through his fingertips.

Breaking in a rookie receiver was not the only problem confronting Montana. He was forced to deal with nasty rumors that threatened to disrupt his football career.

The whispers began early in the season, after Montana played poorly in several games, including a 20–17 home loss to the struggling New Orleans Saints, when he completed just 12 of 26 for 120 yards and tossed two interceptions. By the second week in November, with the 49ers 5–5 and in danger of missing the playoffs, the talk reached the media. The quarterback called a news conference to deny he was using cocaine.

"I've taken one [drug test] for the 49ers, and I told Bill anytime he or the players or Eddie—the only people I feel I owe anything to—think that is what it is, I'd be happy to take another one," Montana said.

The various stories, which ignited a media frenzy, included one sordid tale in which the quarterback was arrested with drugs in his sports car, only to have the matter covered up by Walsh or some high-ranking politician, prompting *Los Angeles Times* columnist Scott Ostler to joke: "Joe Montana sightings have replaced UFO sightings. All that's left is for someone to produce fuzzy photographs of Joe being busted. Or for the *National Enquirer* to publish an eye-witness account: 'Joe Montana Took Me Captive in his Red Ferrari and Forced Me to Snort Cocaine and Listen to Barry Manilow Cassettes.'" (His resemblance to the pop crooner was deeply embedded in the football shorthand of the day.)

For Montana, the situation was no laughing matter. The quarterback who so effortlessly glided out of trouble on the field was staggered by the allegations, telling reporters, "I wish there was somewhere I could point the finger and take some kind of action . . . It's like the old thing when the girl screams 'rape' and they prove the guy innocent. No matter what, the doubt is still there, and that's the sad part of it."

During a period when several high-profile athletes—including long-time nemesis Lawrence Taylor—struggled with drug problems that affected their careers, Montana understood the stakes. The allegations threatened his livelihood, not only as an athlete but as a commercial spokesman.

After investigating the various rumors, the head coach concluded, "I can categorically say none of these instances have occurred." No evidence to substantiate the charges ever materialized, Montana passed his urinalysis, and the matter slowly faded away, affecting neither his playing career nor his endorsements. Four years later, on the eve of Super Bowl XXIV, a similar allegation hit the media but was widely dismissed. Walsh applauded the way his quarterback handled the situation, later writing, "I think by confronting the issue head-on, he defused most of the rumors."

The controversy swirled just before and after Jennifer gave birth to their first child, daughter Alexandra. Looking back several years later, Montana could see how profoundly having a family of his own shifted his priorities and altered his outlook. The difficult year at the office "wasn't the end of the world," he said. "I had a wife and a daughter to go home to."

Even before the talk surfaced, the man who vowed not to let fame change him was feeling increasingly burdened by his celebrity. "Everyone wants a piece of him and he's never known who to trust," Jennifer once said. He avoided certain public places where the clawing crowds might get out of hand, becoming more cautious in various aspects of his life. He was increasingly guarded with the media, feeling abused by certain local reporters, especially with regard to the drug situation. One columnist even suggested it was wrong for the Montanas to have scheduled the birth of their second child during football season. The jovial figure from the locker room became intentionally bland and aloof when the notebooks and cameras showed up, erecting a defense mechanism that often exacerbated the tension. "I am two different people from the locker room to the press, and I hate being that way," he said. Watching the transformation, offensive lineman Guy McIntyre said, "I think Joe became a prisoner of his own fame." (Despite this, a measure of his decency could be seen in 1988, when the quarterback and his wife used their celebrity to make a televised appeal for the safe return of a kidnapped nine-year-old girl.)

Not long after he signed with Pepsi, feeling the enormous accomplishment of being courted by a corporate giant that featured only the biggest stars, the trade-off represented by such deals began to make him feel completely devoid of personal space. "It reached the point where it was, 'Oh, God, how can I hide?'"

The irony that the fame brought Joe and Jennifer together was never lost on the couple, but they always took great pains to create a life in which Joe could exploit his immense popularity to fatten his bank account without surrendering every last ounce of his privacy. Shortly after marrying, they bought a big house, concealed by iron gates, in the fashionable community of Palos Verdes Estates, near Los Angeles. At least in the off-season they could escape some of the attention of being Joe Montana in the city where Joe Montana was a mythical figure who carried the metropolis on his back.

The drug rumors exacerbated the situation, causing Montana to be even more leery of going out on the town. What if someone saw him walking to the bathroom and assumed he was heading for a toot? When he came down with a cold, he worried what some people might think, hearing him sniffling. Beyond such annoyances, the situation demonstrated something more fundamental: the power of his own celebrity to cause him very personal pain.

At midseason, as the rumors swirled, Montana started backing out of his driveway in a big hurry. Newborn Alexandra was sick, and the worried father was headed for the hospital, cradling his child in his arms. Just then, a bus pulled up to the curb and temporarily blocked his car. The bus driver recognized the quarterback and began making disapproving faces at him and thrusting a downward thumb in his direction. The most famous athlete in San Francisco had never felt so trapped. "I just sat there thinking: Please go away," he recalled.

When the quarterback was introduced at Candlestick the week after his name was tarnished in the papers, the crowd embraced him with a thunderous ovation. It was a moment he would never forget. Then he threw for 235 yards and two touchdowns in a 31–3 demolition of the Kansas City Chiefs, the first of five victories over a six-week span that allowed San Francisco to finish 10–6, second to the Rams in the division but good enough for a wild card berth to the playoffs.

In the lone loss during the stretch, 27–20 to the Rams, one aspect of the Niners' future began to emerge: Jerry Rice found his hands.

After weeks of struggling to live up to the potential Walsh and the other coaches saw in him, Rice caught 10 of Montana's passes for 241 yards, including a 66-yarder. The breakout game marked the unofficial start of one of the greatest batteries in football history.

In the wild card game, San Francisco faced the increasingly powerful and frustrated New York Giants, who viewed the 49ers with a disdain approaching contempt. Five straight losses can get under your skin, especially when two happen in the playoffs, with the Super Bowl looming in the distance like the emerald city.

By the time the 49ers traveled to the New Jersey Meadowlands, Bill

Parcells was no longer worried about his job. The 10–6 season was the Giants' best since the days of Y. A. Tittle and Frank Gifford in the early '60s, and the Big Tuna was on his way to becoming the Big Apple's most beloved wiseass. Howard Schnellenberger had indeed left the Miami Hurricanes, but instead of replacing the embattled Parcells, he had been hired to coach a USFL team that would never play a game. Soon the USFL would be nothing but a memory, and Parcells was still standing, filling every room he entered with the pulse of great expectations, consumed with leading the Giants to the Super Bowl, well aware that the path led through San Francisco.

With the injury-prone Phil Simms healthy and making one clutch play after another—including the winning touchdown in a late-season showdown with the Washington Redskins—and Bill Belichick's increasingly menacing defense leading the league in points allowed, New York hosted San Francisco with a full head of steam. The Giants were right on the cusp.

While dealing with a drug addiction that would eventually consume him and cause him to be suspended for four games in 1986, Lawrence Taylor produced the most shocking moment of the season: Slamming Redskins quarterback Joe Theismann so hard during a *Monday Night Football* game that the collision mangled his leg, prematurely ending his career. No one who saw the hit would ever forget it.

Six weeks later, as the Giants hosted their first playoff game since John Kennedy occupied the White House, the 49ers arrived at the New Jersey Meadowlands a very battered team. Several regulars were hobbled by injuries, including Montana, who required repeated injections of painkillers to dull the ache from a pulled abdominal muscle.

The Giants' defense proved relentless, sacking Montana four times, intercepting him once, and hounding him all day. He completed 26 of 47 for 296 yards but, for one of the few times in his career, could not find the end zone. When Taylor charged through the line, swung his big right arm and missed the quarterback, he tumbled to the ground anyway, losing his balance, betrayed by his usually nimble feet. Another time, he was speared. His receivers dropped passes—one in the end zone—and struggled to make first downs, chased down by defenders including Harry Carson and Jim Burt.

One memorable moment in the third quarter demonstrated Montana's long day. Moments after the quarterback whipped a pass into the distance, Giants defensive end Casey Merrill filled up his world, knocking him violently to the turf. This time, Merrill stopped and looked into his face.

For years, football fans across the country had grown accustomed to the familiar sight of Montana holding his arms high while his blue eyes gleamed through his facemask, reflecting another triumphant moment in the San Francisco dynasty. It was an image deeply engrained in the culture of the 1980s, as familiar as Michael Jackson wearing his single white glove. But against the Giants, Joe Cool spent much of the day on his back, and had no reason to celebrate.

"When he was getting up off the ground, his eyes weren't exactly sparkling," Merrill said. "They weren't sparkling like they usually do when he throws a touchdown pass. I'm sure it was the accumulation of hits."

Awash in vindication after New York's 17–3 victory, taking a step toward his future as one of the leading coaches in league history, Parcells stood in the home locker room wearing a sly grin. "What do you think of that West Coast Offense now?" he crowed. The question hung in the air, needing no reply. Not only had Parcells devised a very effective defense to stop Walsh's scheme, he had strapped a label on it, a name dripping with sarcasm, a moniker reflecting his disdain for any sort of football but his own.

The pop caught Montana's attention. He was accustomed to various disturbing sounds rising out of his body, especially during violent collisions with clawing defenders driven by no greater thought than knocking him out of a game with a mighty thud. The fears associated with his rather fragile-looking frame contributed to the swirling doubts about him coming out of Notre Dame, causing many to wonder how such a skinny specimen could possibly survive the punishment required to play the position. Part of the answer could be found in his mobility, which so often allowed him to dip and dodge. But he also proved remarkably durable in the inevitable crunch. Teammates and defenders alike grew to admire the gutty way he sustained thunderous licks without retreating. "You could knock the living snot out of him," recalled Bears defender Mike Singletary, "and he'd get up, spit out the blood, wink at you, and say, 'Hey, that was a great hit.'"

In the 1986 season opener against the Buccaneers, no one touched him. The pop he heard after twisting his body to throw back to his right, in order to hit Dwight Clark, resulted from the punishment he was inflicting on himself. He finished the game without giving the sound much thought, until the pain in his back grew much more intense and his leg started turning numb. The quarterback had experienced this feeling in the past, but never so severe. "I knew this time it was bad," he said.

Doctors determined he had ruptured the fifth vertebrae in his spine, causing the pulpy filling of the disc to leak, a situation exacerbated by a previously undiagnosed case of congenital spinal stenosis. The specialists recommended surgery, not just to repair the damage but to keep the rupture from affecting the sciatic nerve, which could permanently affect the feeling in his left leg. "I was real scared," Montana later conceded. "You hear a lot of war stories about something going wrong in surgery . . . about how tricky it is around there." Eight days after the pop, Joe Cool put up a good front for Jennifer and his mother and father, making jokes as the nurses wheeled his gurney into an operating room at San Francisco's St. Mary's Hospital. As a team led by Dr. Arthur White placed him under the knife for two hours—leaving a four-inch incision—a headline on the front page of the *USA Today* sports section shocked sports fans across the country: "Montana's Career at End?"

"We'll have to wait and see about whether he'll ever play again," advised Dr. Robert Gamburd, one of the 49ers' team physicians.

A pall fell across the team. "We just weren't prepared to hear that," said offensive lineman Steve Wallace. "We're getting ready to play a game and there's talk that Joe Montana might never play again! How scary is that?"

Turning to backup Jeff Kemp, the onetime Rams starter he had acquired during the off-season, Walsh prepared to scale back his offense, telling reporters, "We expect to face this entire season without Joe."

The mood around the 49ers complex may have been best described by the *San Francisco Examiner*'s Art Spander: "It was hard to tell which thought was more sobering: that Joe Montana might never have the opportunity to display his skills again or that the 49ers might never have the chance to exploit those skills again."

The specter of serious injuries and mandatory medical procedures hung like a perpetual cloud over the 49ers and all other professional football teams, forever framed by the various traumas associated with all those colliding bodies. "You knew [the possibility] was always there . . . [that] you could get hurt . . . but nobody liked to talk about it," recalled running back Johnny Davis, who by 1986 had moved on to the Cleveland Browns. Unlike earlier eras, when modestly paid players often concealed many injuries for fear of losing their jobs, the franchises of the 1980s and beyond benefited from top-flight medical and training staffs who closely monitored every athlete's body. At any given time, several 49ers nursed one or more significant injuries that affected the team and forced the coaching staff to adjust and sometimes make painful decisions. The league's collective bargaining agreement prevented teams from cutting players who were injured beyond their capacity to practice and play, but beyond the purgatory of the injured reserve list—which allowed coaches to temporarily free up a needed spot on the fifty-man roster while giving an athlete time to heal—the combination of age and physical stress eventually exacted a heavy toll on all. "We all sort of knew we were living on borrowed time," recalled running back Earl Cooper, one of the heroes of Super Bowl XVI, who had been traded to the Raiders and soon would be out of football, teaching high school math back in his native Texas.

Even as San Francisco fans descended into melancholy, wondering if they had seen the last of their beloved Joe Cool, Walsh reluctantly prepared to release popular running back Wendell Tyler. Once the answer to a glaring need, the former Ram had teamed with Roger Craig to give the 49ers a powerful running game, which proved crucial in making the West Coast Offense hum. But as the younger, stronger Craig surged to the forefront—becoming, in 1985, the first man in NFL history to amass more than 1,000 yards rushing and receiving in the same season—the thirty-one-year-old Tyler was fast becoming a shadow of his former self. Hobbled by various injuries, he had grown increasingly fumble-prone, including an especially costly turnover near the goal line in a road loss to the New Orleans Saints, in what would turn out to be his last professional football game. Walsh called the decision to cut him "the most difficult task in my eight-year tenure as head coach."

The possibility of losing Montana loomed much larger, with much more devastating consequences for the organization. His combination of skill and institutional knowledge of Walsh's offense could not be easily duplicated. The possibility of relying on Kemp, a former Dartmouth star who had been jettisoned by the Rams to make way for Canadian Football League import Dieter Brock, was comforting to no one. He was signed to be Montana's backup, not his heir. As the Niners began processing the news, offensive lineman Keith Fahnhorst gave voice to a widespread feeling. "You don't replace a Joe Montana," he said. "He's probably the best quarterback in the league." When Fahnhorst, who would retire in 1987, added, "But stuff like this is going to happen," the statement resonated with all who understood even the greatest players could and would eventually be replaced.

At the time, the widely admired Fahnhorst, one of the best offensive tackles in the game, offered a powerful example of resilience. Early in his career with the 49ers, before Walsh and Montana arrived, the former Minnesota Golden Gopher had sustained a devastating blow to one of his kidneys during practice. The pain that sent him to the doctor resulted from a rupture to the organ, and even as this situation slowly healed, he was diagnosed with genetic kidney disease. Despite doctors' warnings, Fahnhorst continued to play football for a decade, wearing a specially designed pad, and never suffered any consequences—until many years later, long after he retired. A case of the flu caused an infection, forcing him to undergo a kidney transplant.

Three days after his operation, a frail-looking Montana took the first tentative steps toward his recovery, dragging himself up and down the hospital corridors with the aid of a walker, connected to an IV pole. "My legs were wobbly and my back was still a little unstable . . . but it made me feel good that I was at least up and moving around," he recalled. Seeing him in this condition shocked Clark, who later said, "He looked and acted like a little eighty-year-old man." Watching him stumble around, even the usually sanguine Ronnie Lott thought the worst: A man he greatly admired had played his last game. It was over. No chance he comes back. Heavily medicated, Montana battled feelings of depression, experienced some interesting hallucinations, even thought about retiring. Then the drugs started wearing off and he could think of nothing but getting back on the field.

The surgery was successful, but as the 49ers progressed through the season without him—led with mixed results by Kemp, son of the former San Diego Chargers quarterback and Congressman Jack Kemp—Montana moved into a grueling rehabilitation phase. He was working up to five hours per day with conditioning coach Jerry Attaway when the man who repaired his spine delivered an ominous warning. "You're physically able to play football," Dr. White told him, "but you're crazy if you do it."

*Crazy.*

Given his violent line of work, the doctors could not guarantee he would not suffer another rupture or more serious consequences.

With Jennifer at his side, Montana patiently listened to his doctor's advice—and then disregarded it. His decision to try to play football again turned out to be a defining moment in his life. At the age of thirty, he was already one of the most accomplished quarterbacks of his time. Rich. Beloved. The owner of two Super Bowl rings and two Super Bowl MVP trophies. The highest-rated passer in NFL history. With nothing to prove, he could have walked off into the sunset, enjoyed his family, focused on a less-obsessive career far beyond the spotlight. But quitting would have been inconsistent with his character. The quarterback's latest comeback powerfully demonstrated not only his love of the game but also his remarkable hunger to compete.

"Joe still wanted to play," said teammate Guy McIntyre, who watched the comeback with a sense of gathering admiration. "I don't think it was any more complicated than this guy who was so incredibly competitive still wanting to play."

Adding an interesting dimension to the situation was the publication, just prior to the season, of *Audibles: My Life in Football,* an autobiography

Montana authored with journalist Bob Raissman. In the book, the quarterback went public with the tension animating his relationship with Walsh, addressing the question then being debated across the league: Was it the system? Or was it Montana? "The underlying basis of any friction between Bill and me is his desire for people to believe I am one of the better quarterbacks in the game because of his offensive system," Montana wrote, adding: "I don't care what Bill or anyone else says, there are things I know I can do on a football field that no one else is capable of doing." In this rare instance of proclaiming his greatness—which few other journalists appeared capable of pulling out of him—Montana no doubt found catharsis. (When reporters tried to engage him on the subject, Walsh wisely demurred, saying, "All we're doing in this conversation is trying to provoke me or Joe, and I don't want to have any part of it.") The quarterback also skewered some of his least favorite sportswriters, especially regarding the drug rumors that made his life so difficult in 1985.

Proof of the system's portability could be found as Montana negotiated his arduous road back, as the journeyman Kemp, who would suit up for four teams in seven years, completed 59.5 percent of his passes and tossed 11 touchdowns. When Kemp went down with an injury, third-teamer Mike Moroski even started two games. Neither man could make the plays Montana routinely made, which weakened Walsh's hand in play-calling, and their leadership lacked that special spark. The 49ers rolled into November 5–3–1, facing a difficult road to the playoffs.

Even as Montana started to recover much faster than anyone thought possible—throwing a football, without contact, three weeks after the surgery—Walsh tried to tamp down the mounting speculation that his marquee attraction would return to action before the end of the 1986 season. "I know there's a campaign going on [to get him back in the lineup], but it's a medical situation," he told reporters. The coach worried about Montana's strength, his range of motion, his persistent circulation problems (he would still be dealing with numbness in his leg for months). He worried if the new Joe Montana could play like the old, especially if he was rushed back into uniform before he was truly ready.

As soon as the doctors cleared him, Montana demanded to play. Beyond his private warning to his patient—which eventually became public, adding drama to the situation—Dr. White told reporters the quarterback's recovery was the fastest he had ever seen.

Fifty-five days after the surgery, on November 9, Montana jogged onto the turf at Candlestick to lead the 49ers against the St. Louis Cardinals. One banner tacked to a wall said it all: JOE'S BACK!

When his name was called in the pregame introductions, the sellout crowd bathed him in a standing ovation and "an electric chill went through the whole team," said safety Tom Holmoe. He later confessed to being too nervous to notice the cheering, but by the time he took the field, wearing a flak jacket with a specially designed tale drooping over his back, the butterflies quickly subsided.

Ten plays into San Francisco's first drive, facing a second-and-seven from the Cardinals' 45 yard line, the quarterback gathered the snap and quickly picked up the blitz. Now he was in his element. No more watching the game on television, ablaze in frustration, wondering, deep down, if the sport had passed him by. In this moment like so many others, he was propelled forward by an unseen force, by an innate competitiveness lubricated by the voices of all those who had doubted him—even his doctor. "We're all crazy, in one manner of speech," he said when asked about Dr. White's advice, poking a little fun at the man who had given him his spine back. "I'm crazy about the game."

Now more than ever, he was prepared for the pressure of a blitz, because Jerry Rice had added a whole new dimension to his passing game, giving the 49ers a deep threat who could stretch the defense. Rice was on his way to a brilliant season, catching 86 passes for 1,570 yards and 15 touchdowns. One year after his career began in such frustration, World was on fire. By the time the rush arrived, the quarterback who could not throw the long ball had rifled a bomb deep into the clear blue California sky. It hit Rice in stride and he swept into the end zone. Touchdown. The euphoria was not complete until Montana, victimized by a late hit, climbed off the ground and started clapping. In that moment, the fans knew Old Joe was back.

"I'm telling you, it was surreal," recalled Steve Wallace. "Candlestick was on fire. You really felt like you were in a dream. Is this guy really *that* good, where he can have surgery [and] come right back and throw like that? Be right on target? Have incredible timing? . . . It didn't make any sense."

After Montana lofted a second touchdown pass toward Rice, who raced downfield, Cardinals defensive end Bubba Baker smashed him to the ground, turned to see the officials' hands reach toward the sky in the distance, and turned back to the prostrate quarterback. Leaning in, headgear to headgear, Baker said, "You're a helluva man."

In this transcendent moment, Montana inspired his teammates with a remarkable performance that opened a new chapter in his career. "He's like Lazarus," cornerback Tim McKyer said. "You roll back the stone, Joe limps out—and throws for 300 yards." In the retelling, it mattered not that Montana completed 13 of 19 passes for 270 yards and three touchdowns, and that he benefited from a 105-yard game by recently acquired running back Joe Cribbs, to spark a 43–17 rout. These were just details. What mattered was that he came through the surgery, battled his way back faster than anyone thought possible, and was still Joe Montana. In fact, he was now on his way to becoming even more Joe Montana than he had previously been. He was now on his way to becoming the man he was supposed to be.

That he could play so well after such a long layoff shocked all who saw it, including veteran tight end Russ Francis, who said, "He's a tough son of a bitch. There's a lot of competitor in his heart. That was not necessarily just ability there; a lot of it was heart."

*Fifty-five days.*

The interval between surgery and triumphant return quickly became interwoven in Montana's identity, a stat every bit as relevant as his passer rating and his accumulated Super Bowl rings.

"The greatest comeback I've seen in fifty years in football," said Sid Gillman.

Seven days later, Montana threw for a franchise-record 441 yards but lost to the Redskins, 14–6. Most memorable was the play when he rolled left, stopped to throw, and was manhandled by Dexter Manley, crunched to the turf as San Francisco fans everywhere cringed. Then he got up, relieved that he could still sustain such a vicious hit. With Montana leading the way, San Francisco won five of its last seven, clinching the NFC West with a 10–5–1 mark to earn a playoff rematch against the NFC East champion New York Giants, who came in as the clear favorites after a dominant 14–2 regular season.

About two minutes into the game, Montana hit Rice on a slant near midfield. Before he arrived in the league, many scouts discounted the receiver's worth because of his rather unimpressive time in the forty-yard dash. But once he found his hands, the man from Mississippi showed many of his doubters the difference between stopwatch time and play time. On the field, when he gathered a ball to his chest and mashed the accelerator, very few defenders could run him down. If he had a seam, he was gone. In this instance, the quarterback hit him when he was wide open, and as he pumped those big legs, he was headed for an apparent touchdown. But, uncharacteristically, Rice stumbled at the Giants' 27, which caused him to lose his grip. The ball tumbled to the ground, rolling all the way into the end zone, where it was recovered by the Giants. Thus began one of the most gut-wrenching games in San Francisco history.

Near the end of the first half, with the Giants leading 21–3, Montana stepped into a throw just as linebacker Jim Burt barreled down on him. An instant before league MVP Lawrence Taylor picked off the ball and started returning it for a touchdown, Burt leveled Montana with a full head of steam. "He hit through the target . . . [with] every ounce of energy he had," recalled Steve Wallace. "Hit him so hard that you saw Joe's body eject backward, like he was in a Hollywood movie and they had a wire strapped behind him." After looking for someone to block as Taylor headed for the end zone, Burt turned to notice Montana sprawled motionless on the ground. He approached the quarterback with an eerie feeling before being waved away by an official. Sobered by the sight, Burt later told reporters, "I didn't want to hurt him."

Knocked out cold, Montana woke up in a fog, complaining of double vision and a bad headache. By then, the Giants had completed a 49–3 romp that sent them to the road to the Super Bowl, where they would earn their first league title of the modern era with a decisive victory over the Washington Redskins. As doctors at New York's Cornell Medical Center attended to the quarterback, diagnosing him with a severe concussion and keeping him overnight for observation, the San Francisco team, tagged with one of the most crushing defeats ever administered in the NFL playoffs, flew into the gathering darkness facing the prospect of a miserable off-season. No one felt the sting more acutely than center Fred Quillan, who had missed the block that left Montana vulnerable. "I wanted to jump off the plane," he remembered.

The next day, the quarterback headed west no worse for the experience. After suffering consecutive first-round playoff losses to the Giants, the 49ers were beginning to look like a team in decline. The magical season of 1984, when the Niners very nearly finished undefeated, was growing more distant every day. Montana's increasingly fragile body was starting to look like a liability for a franchise conditioned by its own recent success to consider anything less than a Super Bowl championship a failure. But now more than ever, as he headed toward his ninth season, number 16 was consumed by a hunger to lead San Francisco back to the top. The year that very nearly broke Joe Montana had instead made him stronger than anyone realized—even Bill Walsh.

# CHAPTER EIGHT

# The Other Man

THE FIRST TIME STEVE WALLACE heard the term, or at least the first time it registered in his mind, was in a sentence uttered by Jennifer Montana. At a team party in the late 1980s, as the drinks and hors d'oeuvres flowed, the quarterback's wife approached him with a big smile. "We really appreciate you protecting Joe's blind side," she said. Wallace, still early in his professional football career, literally shrugged his massive shoulders. "I appreciated her thanking me . . . for doing my job," he recalled. "I mean that's special. But I didn't know what the blind side was."

The road to and from this moment helped shape the most contentious period of Montana's professional life.

Bill Walsh entered 1987 feeling increasingly frustrated. It was hard to see the 49–3 thumping by the Giants as anything less than a gigantic step backward. It was tempting to view the beatdown as a changing of the guard, with New York ascending and San Francisco descending. The concussion Montana suffered exposed a glaring vulnerability: The 49ers were relying heavily on an aging quarterback who could not sustain such devastating blows indefinitely.

No one felt the responsibility associated with this inconvenient truth more acutely than offensive line coach Bobb McKittrick, a former Marine who drove an old Volkswagen Beetle and filled his troops with one overriding thought: "We've got the greatest quarterback in the world behind us. Our job is to give him the time to do his job."

Through the years, Montana cultivated a strong bond with his linemen, sharing his good fortune by twice buying the entire unit Rolex watches. They also appreciated the vagaries of his understated leadership. Whenever some defensive player charged through the line and slammed him to the ground, Montana was not the sort of quarterback who returned to the huddle breathing fire, demanding accountability. Usually, in such situations, he would say, "My fault. I held the ball too long." Even when it wasn't, and he hadn't. In these moments, his teammates found the sort of strength that built confidence and the kind of humility that promoted loyalty. "Joe was always there to take the blame," said lineman Guy McIntyre.

This desire to shoulder the responsibility of leadership and shield his teammates could be seen during one practice session when Walsh became incensed after a botched snap count. Center Fred Quillan quickly accepted the blame for his mistake, only to have his quarterback contradict him in front of the entire team, insisting that, no, the fault was his.

After practice, Montana pulled Quillan aside. "Fred, don't you ever do that again. You keep your mouth shut and I'll take the blame. Always."

"Why?"

"Because, Fred, I'm a quarterback and you're a center. You will always get yelled at more than me. If I take the blame, they won't yell so much."

For years, the memory of one sack filled Steve Wallace with guilt. Lining up at right tackle, Wallace ran the wrong way because he was so accustomed to playing on the left side of the line. His man immediately blew past, untouched, and landed a devastating shot on the quarterback, who staggered to the ground. "Joe's eyes were red when he came back [to the huddle], and you could tell he was thinking, 'How did that guy get in there so clean?'" Wallace recalled. "He just looked at me and I know he wanted to yell. But he didn't. He knew I felt really bad. He didn't have to yell."

Like every component of Walsh's offense, the line took shape through a systematic framework, broken down by McKittrick into thirty-eight different techniques. While the fans focused on Montana and his receivers and backs, the linemen moved through their various assignments with a keen understanding of where and how the play was developing and what each man needed to do to create openings in time and space. It was not enough for one player to accomplish his assignment at the precise time; in order for the play to work, the unit needed to act in unison. All those large bodies crashing into the defense were connected to a very detailed strategy, and mental mistakes were not tolerated. "If you wound up in the wrong place at the wrong time . . . you weren't going to play," McIntyre said. In the mental game Walsh expected his players to master, one body out of step could grind the entire machine to a halt.

The desire to promote players imbued with a certain intellectual approach to the game who could execute consistently was a big part of the equation, but all those technicians were also expected to project the sort of fiery aggression that could not be reduced to a formula. "There's a real juxtaposition," said lineman Bruce Collie. "[The 49er way] was all about learning and professionalism. But we're real men and we're out there to dominate the guy across from us. To be mean and nasty."

The tension between these two impulses could be seen each day during practice, when Collie fired off against defender Michael Carter, driven by a raging animosity. "Off the field, we had a good relationship. But at practice, I wanted to kill him," Collie remembered. Snap after snap, they attacked each other like mortal enemies. One day, Collie punched his fist through Carter's face mask and ripped a gash in his lip, which required stitches. Another day, Carter kicked Collie in the nuts, which also required stitches. "The thing is, you knew you'd better get [the damage] done in the first two or three seconds, because Bill would not tolerate fighting." In San Francisco, players and coaches were programmed to break up fights soon after the fists started flying.

By contrast, several years later, after Collie was dealt to Philadelphia, he wound up trading blows with teammate Jerome Brown for five minutes, until neither man could stand up. "When I can't even swing anymore, I looked over and [head coach] Buddy Ryan's got his wallet out, passing money back and forth with the defensive line coach," said Collie, recalling a moment that taught him one of the secrets to San Francisco's success: They were professionals, and even the raw animal aggression at the heart of the sport needed to be controlled in the larger pursuit of perfect execution.

As key players including Keith Fahnhorst, Fred Quillan, and John Ayers retired, a second generation of blockers—including Steve Wallace, Bruce Collie, Jesse Sapolu, and Guy McIntyre—supplanted those who had cleared the path to the first two Super Bowls. By 1987, only Randy Cross, who moved from guard to center, remained from the 1981 starting unit. "This really is sort of a transition team we have," Walsh said. Their tactics evolved to fit the dawning of a new age.

As defenses reacted to the advent of the modern passing game, the most important pushback came from a new style of rushing linebackers in the mold of New York Giants star Lawrence Taylor, hybrid athletes with size, speed, and elusiveness capable of blasting through the line to hammer right-handed quarterbacks outside their field of vision—from their left, or blind, side. Traditionally, run-oriented NFL teams had stationed their most dominant offensive lineman at right tackle. "That's where you wanted your big stud, because that's where you ran the ball the most," Dan Fouts noted. But as every franchise went searching for its own Taylor to help counter the passing game, the offensive line's center of gravity inevitably shifted leftward. In time, the left tackle became the leading figure in protecting the passer from the destructive force he could not see.

The task of guarding Montana's blind side eventually fell to Bubba Paris, a six-foot-six former University of Michigan star who struggled to keep his weight under control, often ballooning well over three hundred pounds.

Especially after Montana's body began to fail him in 1986, the offensive line felt the burden of protecting an aging athlete who seemed increasingly fragile. Opposing defenses began to talk about him as less mobile, more conscious of the rush, and not quite as capable of darting out of trouble, feeding the perception of mounting vulnerability and diminishing skills that prompted *San Francisco Chronicle* sports columnist Glenn Dickey to conclude, "He's clearly on the downside of a brilliant career."

"There was a lot of pressure on all of us," McIntyre said. "You felt enormous pressure to protect Joe. Nobody wanted to miss the block that caused Joe to get hurt."

All it took was one blow, one Joe Theismann-esque, body-crunching moment, to end Montana's career and devastate the franchise. This thought animated many San Francisco nightmares, especially after Jim Burt slammed into him with the force of a freight train, knocking him into a deep sleep as millions of television viewers held their collective breath.

But the possibility of a marauding linebacker charging in from the blind side and landing a clean shot at Montana was not the only existential threat facing the quarterback as he approached his ninth season in the NFL.

Not even Bubba Paris could shield him from the man who wanted to take his job.

In the shadow of 1986, Walsh was convinced. The end was near. Making such judgments represented a significant part of his job, because every man on the roster ultimately faced the moment when, ravaged by some combination of time, trauma, and competition from a younger or more gifted athlete, he could no longer defend his position. Montana was no different. His time was coming. Soon. Of this, Walsh was convinced, and so he began preparing the franchise to turn the page, looking not just for a backup but for a worthy heir.

The search quickly focused on Steve Young. After an outstanding college career directing LaVell Edwards's sophisticated passing offense at Brigham Young—where he followed in the footsteps of future Chicago Bears quarterback Jim McMahon, shattering 13 NCAA records, including his 71.3 completion percentage as a senior—the left-handed Young quickly became one of the most recognizable names in American sports. Exploiting the bidding war for talent between the NFL and the USFL, he spurned the Cincinnati Bengals to sign a record-setting $40-million contract with the fledgling league's struggling Los Angeles Express. The shocking number quickly transformed Young into a symbol of USFL excess and hype.

By the time he escaped the USFL in 1985, just as it was beginning to die, and signed with the NFL's Tampa Bay Buccaneers, Young was a damaged figure caught in a downward spiral, a once-promising talent battered by the pressures of trying to carry two bad football teams. While struggling to adjust to NFL defenses, he could be impatient in the pocket, and his impressive scrambling ability, empowered by very good speed for a quarterback, became a crutch. He forced way too many throws, leading to way too many interceptions, finishing his one year as the starter as the twenty-fourth-ranked passer in the league, unable to affect the Bucs' 2–14 disaster.

Soon after leaving the University of Alabama to become Tampa Bay's head coach and general manager in January 1987, Ray Perkins conducted an intensive study of his personnel, carefully evaluating Young and his backup, onetime 49ers quarterback, and Montana rival Steve DeBerg. Perkins, the former New York Giants coach who had drafted the virtually unknown Phil Simms, doubted Young's ability to ever become a winning quarterback in the NFL. "Steve Young was a guy with great potential who was still trying to prove himself," Perkins said many years later. "I wasn't sure he had what it took to lead us to that next level."

Armed with the first pick in the draft, Tampa Bay prepared to place a $8.2-million bet on Heisman Trophy–winner Vinny Testaverde, a strong-armed pocket passer who had led the Miami Hurricanes to an undefeated season before losing the Fiesta Bowl's national championship game to Penn State. (Testaverde wound up as one of the era's biggest quarterback busts, contributing to Perkins's eventual demise.) This decision placed Young on the trading block, where, despite his recent struggles, he generated significant interest from several franchises, including the Dallas Cowboys and the Green Bay Packers.

Like his peers, Bill Walsh tried to look beyond the Tampa Bay debacle on his résumé and imagine what Young could be in his system. After surreptitiously traveling to the BYU campus in Provo, Utah, and putting the player through an unofficial workout—watching him in much the same way he had once eyeballed an underrated Montana—the coach came away impressed with the way he delivered the ball. "Most coaches and general managers . . . thought he was too inconsistent to be a starting quarterback, not realizing that with hard work on the mechanics and techniques, you can measurably develop a man's consistency," Walsh said. He saw Young as a lump of clay waiting to be molded into something special.

The deal Walsh and DeBartolo eventually struck with Tampa Bay required San Francisco to give up one second-round and one fourth-round draft pick and a sizeable amount of cash, and because Young was granted virtual veto power over his future home by Bucs' owner Hugh Culverhouse, the trade swung at least partially on the quarterback's willingness to buy into the narrative it appeared to be hastening: Joe Montana was on the way out.

In announcing the acquisition, Walsh assured reporters, "This move is not a reflection on Joe Montana. We fully expect Joe to continue as the leader and mainstay of our team."

Expressing his excitement over the opportunity to be tutored by "a genius in coaching quarterbacks" and to learn from "a legend like Joe Montana," Young also made clear, "I'm not here to sit on the bench."

Anyone who understood a thing about football knew that Young was not brought to San Francisco as an insurance policy or even, as Walsh envisioned in the immediate future, as part of an alternating one-two, left-right punch to bedevil defenses. He was hired to take Montana's job. The only question was, when?

Approaching his ninth year of professional football, and his thirty-first birthday, Montana had thrown for 21,498 yards and 141 touchdowns. His career completion rate 63.2 percent was the highest in NFL history. But, especially after the back surgery and the concussion, he understood he was engaged in a contentious struggle with the creeping calendar. Determined to strengthen his body, and to replace the roughly ten to fifteen pounds he lost while recovering from the operation, he moved aggressively into an off-season weight-training program. "Joe is doing things that he never did before in his life," said DeBartolo, who added, "We truly now believe his future is in front of him." Walsh was willing to concede he had lost a step, but insisted, because of the weights, "Joe is at least as strong as he was earlier in his career."

Still troubling, however, was one lingering effect of his surgery. He remained without feeling in parts of his legs and feet—including a six-to-eight-inch area just above the knee—due to the damage to the nerve endings. Sometimes, this caused him to trip. In time, the numbness would subside.

Always his toughest critic, he told a reporter he believed he still had room to improve his decision making. "The biggest part of playing quarterback is mental," he said. "Last year there were times when I missed blitzes, called the wrong audible, or called an audible when I didn't have to. I want to be more assertive in that area."

Several weeks after the blockbuster trade, during a break from the team's minicamp, Montana sat in a small office at the 49ers headquarters, signing his name over and over across a large stack of photographs and bubble gum cards sent in by his fans. While holding an impromptu news conference with several reporters, he revealed that he had been flooded with letters from fans wondering if he was planning to retire prior to the 1987 season. Addressing such speculation, he said, "If I had wanted to retire, I would not have come back after the surgery. Why would I have gone through all the agony of fighting back?"

When someone asked him about the prospect of Young taking his job, he flashed a confident smile. "I have to lose it," he said. "Hopefully, I leave when I want to. I won't get forced out."

Insisting he planned to treat Young no differently from the other San Francisco quarterbacks he had competed with through the years, Montana conceded, "Sure, you wonder what they [the organization] are thinking. Did they bring in the guy intentionally to take my place? . . . When I sit back and think about it, it makes me mad, but I have to look at it from their point of view . . ."

Five months after leaving the Meadowlands in an ambulance, Montana said he planned to play five or six more years. "I want to make it as difficult as I can to replace me."

Forced to defend his job, Joe Cool could not imagine the counterintuitive truth lingering just over the horizon. Steve Young's arrival was the best thing that ever happened to Joe Montana.

The clock showed two seconds as Montana hunched over center, quickly picking up the man-to-man coverage on Jerry Rice.

The most bizarre finish of the quarterback's career began five plays earlier, with Cincinnati leading San Francisco 26–20 in the second game of the 1987 season at Riverfront Stadium. Facing a fourth and long from deep in 49ers territory with slightly more than one minute remaining, Walsh elected to punt the ball away, counting on his defense to somehow get the ball back. No one expected what happened next. Unable to run out the clock, the Bengals soon faced a fourth down of their own, and instead of risking a blocked punt—or a successful kick that gave the 49ers the chance for one more play—Cincinnati head coach Sam Wyche, the former San Francisco quarterbacks coach, called for a handoff to James Brooks. Wyche's decision to go for it with six seconds left was surprising and fraught with peril. The call worked only if Brooks managed to make the first down or dance around long enough to run out the clock. Instead, reading the play perfectly, Niners tackle Kevin Fagan slipped into the backfield and smothered the ballcarrier, giving San Francisco a first down at the Cincinnati 25 yard line.

Two seconds.

With time for one play, Montana and his teammates raced onto the field and quickly lined up to execute Walsh's call. With three receivers split to the left and Rice lined up to the right, facing a rookie cornerback, the quarterback would not be requiring any progressive reads. Not on this play. Not on Hail Jerry. "Anytime you have one-on-one coverage on Jerry, I'll take my chances," he explained. "I just lined up over center and tried not to stare over there."

The pass soared toward the corner of the end zone as the clock ticked to zero. In this instance like so many others, Montana placed the ball exactly where it needed to go, and the man covering Rice never had a chance. Gliding past the defender and timing his leap perfectly, the acrobatic Rice snatched the ball out of the sky and gathered it forcefully to his chest. Hail Jerry. Hail Joe. The extra point gave San Francisco a remarkable 27–26 victory, sealing the most efficient miracle of Montana's career.

After turning a certain defeat into a stunning victory, the San Francisco players filled the visitors' locker room with a joyful noise, shouting and banging lockers and slapping skin. Walsh could not wipe the toothy grin off his face. As he undressed, Steve Wallace tried to process what he had seen. "It just makes no sense how we possibly could have won that game," he recalled many years later. "The game was over. We had no chance." Beyond Wyche's controversial decision to run the ball, he would always remember the victory as a profound demonstration of Montana's uncanny gift to somehow find a way to win. "Games like that convinced us, as long as this guy had a second on the clock, then we were supposed to win."

Such performances taught the quarterback of the future the value of patience. But just as the Montana-Young rivalry became the context for everything in San Francisco, the franchise was deeply shaken by another player strike.

Five years after the first significant work stoppage in NFL history, the Players Association once more threatened to strike if the owners failed to provide some sort of meaningful free agency. The owners refused, effectively calling the union's bluff. In a memorable showdown with Gene Upshaw, the NFLPA's executive director, Dallas Cowboys executive Tex Schramm lectured, "You're not going to get it in five years. You're not going to get it in ten years. You're not ever going to get it. Don't you see? You're the cattle. We're the ranchers!" Such condescension stirred the owners' resolve but did nothing to solve the impasse.

Even Keith Fahnhorst, the team's union representative, was riddled with doubts about the wisdom of a walkout, telling a reporter, "I was hoping that neither the management nor the union side would be stupid enough to get in this position again." The union leadership was determined to take a stand, and by a decisive 42–12 margin, the 49ers voted to join the strike, which began after the second week of the season, when the 49ers were 1–1. This time, however, the owners were much better prepared, announcing that the games would continue, featuring "replacement" players and any veterans willing to return to work. Like several other franchises, the 49ers had planned for such a contingency, trying out large numbers of former college players during training camp, filling their roster with athletes who relished the chance to earn the league minimum of $3,125 per week—while being harassed as "scabs" by picketing veterans.

The walkout divided every locker room across the league, none more bitterly than the 49ers. Montana attracted intense criticism from various teammates, including close friend Ronnie Lott, for crossing the picket line less than two weeks into the strike. They called him a scab. They called him worse. His presence among the replacement players—alongside several other veterans, including Roger Craig, Dwight Clark, and Russ Francis—was widely seen as undermining union solidarity.

Like many others who remained skeptical of the union's ability to win on the free agency issue, Montana believed the players were needlessly sacrificing their own financial security for a lost cause. "We aren't like steelworkers, who can make up lost wages over a thirty-year career," explained the man from steel country, who was losing more than $60,000 per week. "Most of us have about four years to make money. Why would anyone try to take that away?"

The decision was especially agonizing for Montana because he hailed from a place where union solidarity was so deeply embedded in the culture. He understood how it felt to see the world through a steelworker's eyes and appreciated the importance of taking a stand to achieve something meaningful. But this was different. As a man earning more than $1 million per year to play a game, he struggled to view the dispute through a blue-collar lens, with management as the enemy. After all, management was his good friend Eddie. He certainly didn't like the idea of alienating his teammates, but as he saw it, his primary responsibility was to his family and himself, so he went back to work. If this made him greedy, so be it. It was 1987, the year of Gordon Gekko and *Wall Street*. Greed was good.

Although the replacements won three straight games for the 49ers—including a 34–28 shoot-out victory over the St. Louis Cardinals, in which

Montana completed 31 of 39 passes for 321 yards—the games bombed with the public, as television ratings and stadium attendance plummeted. There was a good reason why most of the replacements had never played a snap in the NFL, and why most would never dart through a tunnel ever again. But as the owners dug in their heels and more high-profile players crossed the picket lines, the union's solid front crumbled. The replacement solution did not succeed in replicating the authentic NFL experience but it worked just well enough to break the strike. After twenty-four tense days, the membership voted to return to work without an agreement, handing the owners a clear victory—tempered by the significant damage inflicted once again on the NFL brand.

Among those who favored the work stoppage, many felt especially ambivalent because of their strong feelings for DeBartolo. No organization in the NFL negotiated the management-player divide quite like the 49ers. "Eddie DeBartolo has treated us well here," Fahnhorst felt compelled to say as the strike began. "It's certainly not the 49ers going on strike against him." When the paychecks stopped, causing widespread financial hardship across the team, Walsh, with DeBartolo's backing, began loaning money to various players. When the walkout ended, DeBartolo announced a bonus offer for making the playoffs that effectively wiped out the loans, a tremendous gesture of goodwill that struck a chord with his players but immediately drew the ire of the commissioner's office, which fined him $50,000 for violating the league's prohibitions regarding financial inducements. Upon hearing the news, a large group of players chipped in to pay DeBartolo's fine. Only in San Francisco.

Once the entire squad returned to work, tempers flared as the animosity generated by the strike shattered the unity that had helped make the 49ers such a powerful team. Reporters watched as Ronnie Lott and Russ Francis shouted at each other on the practice field, then saw Lott get in Bill Walsh's face. For several days, rumors, innuendo, and threats filled the air, causing once-close friends and colleagues to confront each other with suspicious eyes. *Did you really say that? About me?*

"I could feel the 49ers unraveling," Lott remembered. "The strike had turned us into people we weren't."

One particularly caustic rumor landed offensive lineman Bruce Collie in Walsh's office, where the boss asked, "Is it true you said you weren't going to block for Joe Montana?"

Collie swallowed hard.

"No way, Bill. I never said anything like that . . ."

Recalling the scene many years later, Collie said, "I didn't have any bad blood at all toward Joe Montana and the other guys who crossed the line. It was an excruciating decision for them. [The strike] was a disaster for everybody . . . The thought that I wouldn't block for Joe, that was just offensive . . . I think the rumors were started by the union."

As the players started the process of mending fences and the replacements faded into the history books, the real 49ers resumed their march to the playoffs. Once the strike was settled, the quarterback rivalry assumed center stage. Two relatively minor injuries, including a sprained index finger, sustained while holding the ball for a field goal attempt, caused Montana to miss three starts, giving Young an opening. He did not disappoint. Confounding defenses with his alacrity as a runner and his ability to quickly hit the open man, Young repeatedly made the most of his opportunities. Most impressive was his performance off the bench in a 41–0 rout of the Bears, when he tossed four touchdown passes and scrambled out of the pocket like vintage Fran Tarkenton, staking a claim as the most effective number-two quarterback in football. "To tell you the truth, I've always cringed at the word backup," Young told one reporter, straddling the fence between impatience and diplomacy. "But I'm learning from a living legend so I'll just continue to try to get better." The competition, in which both players saw significant playing time, was stoked by Walsh, who loved to talk about his new dynamic duo, drawing comparisons to the great QB combos in league history. He could not deny the reality that Young was good enough to start for many teams. "I've got one of those nice problems with my quarterbacks," he said. "Steve Young is not a second-string quarterback." Except, of course, on the depth chart. Because the rumors of Montana's demise were greatly exaggerated.

One play against the Cleveland Browns, featuring the league's third-ranked defense, demonstrated the power of Montana's mounting sophistication and maturity. Trailing 10–7 and facing third-and-long from the Browns' 30 yard line, the quarterback stood in the huddle and called a running play sent in by Walsh. But when he approached the line and recognized the Browns' two-deep zone, he quickly made the decision to audible, calling a play that sent Jerry Rice on a circuitous route across the middle.

The Montana-to-Rice passing battery was now deeply imbedded in the NFL experience, a potent force that provided a steady stream of highlights on *SportsCenter*—including a 51-yard strike in an easy victory over the Rams and a 57-yard, game-clinching bomb against the Packers—while also accomplishing Walsh's aim of spreading the defense. (The emergence of wide receiver John Taylor gave defenses still another threat to chase.) On his way to another outstanding season—65 catches for 1,078 yards and 22 touchdowns, in just 12 games—Rice would become the first receiver in the modern era to earn the league's Most Valuable Player award. The man who was supposedly too slow was now speeding his way toward the Hall of Fame.

When the quarterback pulled back from center, his favorite target sprinted into the distance.

"The only thing is," Montana explained later, "[Rice] has to make two breaks on the pattern, so you know you're most likely going to get hit. If I'd called it in the huddle I'd have told the line I was going to need a little extra time. But since it was an audible, I couldn't really stand up and yell, 'Hey, I need more time for this one.'"

Waiting just long enough to account for Rice's extended route, Montana held and held and held some more, releasing the ball an instant before he was leveled by Browns nose tackle Bob Golic. "May have been his greatest throw of the year," said quarterbacks coach Mike Holmgren. The pass landed softly in Rice's hands just as he crossed the goal line, demonstrating one way in which Montana was an even better quarterback in 1987 than he had been in 1981: He knew just when to overrule Bill Walsh and mustered the guts to do it.

After watching him complete 23 of 31 passes for 342 yards and four touchdowns to key the 38–24 victory, Browns head coach Marty Schottenheimer said, "He made it obvious why so many rank him the best quarterback around. We couldn't slow him down."

As the 49ers moved into December, Montana pulled a hamstring muscle, causing him to miss two starts. In the season finale against the Rams at Candlestick, Young led San Francisco to a 27–0 halftime lead, throwing for three touchdowns and 174 yards. Determined to get his starter ready for the playoffs, Walsh inserted Montana, who was still not fully healed, at the beginning of the second half. He was also impressive, throwing for two touchdowns and 107 yards as the 49ers completed a 48–0 drubbing of Los Angeles.

Asked to compare the two quarterbacks, Rams cornerback Mickey Sutton said, "Young or Montana? The way they were going tonight, it didn't make much difference."

As well as Young played, Montana remained several steps ahead, challenging the notion that he was over the hill by turning in one of the greatest seasons of his professional career while leading San Francisco to a 13–2 finish. The NFL's leading passer, he amassed the highest rating of his career (102.1), and led the NFL in completions (266) and completion percentage (66.8), while shattering John Brodie's team record for touchdown passes in a season (establishing a new mark of 31)—all while playing in just ten games. By the end of 1987, the dramatic image of him sprawled on the ground at the Meadowlands was starting to recede from San Francisco's collective consciousness.

He was even feeling better about his relationship with Walsh. The publication of Montana's autobiography the previous year had brought the tension out in the open, although the quarterback later said, "It was the wrong way to do it." No matter. It opened the lines of communication and now the men were making an effort to talk more frankly. Sometimes, however, they operated better with a buffer. Among his various contributions to the offense, Mike Holmgren, stationed in the press box during games, started communicating via phone with his quarterback between series. No longer did Joe feel the obligation to immediately head for Walsh on the sideline, providing a cooling off period that was often very helpful. "There are times," Montana said, "when he's upset and I'm upset. Maybe I didn't throw the ball well, and Bill hates to see the offense blunder." So he was able to get on the phone with Holmgren and vent, which sometimes led to a familiar refrain from the quarterbacks coach, in his best calming-down voice: "Could you just move the mouthpiece about four inches away from your mouth?"

When Montana took the field at Candlestick in early January for a first-round playoff game against Minnesota, he remained the 49ers' undisputed number-one quarterback, a player who was not merely holding on, desperately, against the ravages of time but forcefully pushing against the boundaries of his potential. But one game exposed his vulnerability and redefined his competition with Young.

Against the 8–7 Vikings, who had barely earned a wild card berth to the playoffs, heavily favored San Francisco struggled to give Montana enough time to pass. Bubba Paris, the left tackle who was primarily responsible for protecting the quarterback's blind side, proved no match for defensive end Chris Doleman, a ferocious player with tremendous speed and strength who repeatedly clawed his way into the 49ers' backfield, teaming with Keith Millard to terrorize Montana on nearly every snap. Across the line and in the clinch, Doleman started talking to the quarterback. "I'm killing Bubba!" "They're just letting me through!" Joe Cool said nothing, but Doleman could tell, "He didn't like getting hit a lot." It was not 1981 anymore, and the quarterback who was not quite as elusive as his younger self was unable to prevent the Vikings' menacing pass rush, working from an unusual four-man front, from harassing him. By early in the third quarter, with Minnesota leading 20–3 and Montana—a cold 12 of 26 for 109 yards—forced once more to give way to the punt team, the quarterback jogged off the field and was immediately collared by Walsh, who uttered a sentence reverberating with historic significance. "We're going with Steve."

Lingering nearby, Dwight Clark yelled, "That's bullshit!" loud enough for Walsh to hear.

The logic in the decision was difficult to argue. With Montana unable to deal with the pressure, Walsh concluded, while watching the Super Bowl slip away, that perhaps Young could use his superior running ability to penetrate the Vikings' smothering grip. But Montana was no ordinary quarterback, and this was not just another game. By benching Joe Cool in such a desperate situation, denying him the chance to pull out yet another miracle finish, Walsh was demonstrating a lack of faith in Montana that defied his immense stature and their own glittering history together. The symbolism was impossible to escape: Bill Walsh just told the world that Joe Montana isn't Joe Montana anymore.

The change very nearly worked. Young, often hailed by Walsh as an "explosive . . . spontaneous" runner, was able to move the football much more effectively than Montana, evading the rush and finding greater success throwing the football. But, in the end, he was unable to prevent Minnesota's 36–24 upset, one of the most crushing defeats in San Francisco history. It was the third straight year the 49ers had gone down in the first round of the playoffs, this time after posting the league's best regular-season record.

As the understudy took his place and scored the first of three touchdowns, trying to lead the 49ers out of a big hole, Montana could be seen on the sideline cheering, pumping his fist into the air, clapping for the man who wanted to take his job. "I was in a strange mood," he later conceded. He was a team man, and more than anything else, he wanted to win the football game. But he was also humiliated, drenched with the stench of doubt by a coach who had been instrumental in transforming him into a better version of himself. As Montana dressed and walked off into the night, no one knew how he would react to this unnerving development and what it meant to the future of the 49ers.

A decade into his professional football career, Montana faced a defining question: Was he willing to fight for his job?

Soon after Young arrived on the scene, sportswriters trying to read between Walsh's often cryptic lines began predicting Young's rise to the number-one position as early as 1988. Conventional thought held that by 1988, he would have enough time to master the offensive system and supplant an aging, fragile Montana weakened by diminishing skills.

As the 49ers approached the 1988 season, with the memory of the Minnesota debacle still fresh, this narrative appeared to be coming true. Sportswriters began to pronounce the end of the Montana age, casting his career in a past-tense haze. Mocking what he called the Bay Area's "provincialism" for embracing the idea that Montana was the greatest quarterback of all time, the *Chronicle*'s Glenn Dickey insisted, "Montana isn't even the best in his own time . . . I'm not even sure he's the best to play for the 49ers." Perhaps, Dickey said, Montana wasn't even better than Y. A. Tittle. In some quarters, this was blasphemy. But Joe Cool increasingly looked like yesterday's news. The belief that Montana was a better player than Young was no longer universal, and the competition quickly evolved from understudy chasing starter to two tenacious players battling as relative equals. On a trip to London for an exhibition game against the Miami Dolphins, Walsh unwittingly exacerbated the situation by telling reporters, "We may have a quarterback controversy." This sentence was like red meat to a press corps all too eager to put a negative spin on the competition, but the way Walsh handled some aspects of the battle added unnecessary tension that could not be ascribed to media hype.

No one watched the duel with more anxiety than the man who signed the checks. Infuriated by yet another playoff collapse, DeBartolo seriously considered firing the coach who had rescued the 49ers from the inept Joe Thomas days and built one of the most successful franchises in the game. That he survived was due in no small measure to the cool head of Carmen Policy, who satisfied DeBartolo by stripping Walsh of his title as president of the franchise, effectively ceding much of his administrative duties to DeBartolo, who in turn delegated them to Policy. Among other things, the demotion gave Walsh more time to wrestle with the quarterback dilemma, which was central to his burning desire to get back to the Super Bowl.

Prior to the 1988 season, the 49ers moved into a state-of-the-art, $10 million office complex and practice facility in Santa Clara, located farther down the peninsula from the old Redwood City headquarters, about fifty miles south of Candlestick. Especially compared to the antiquated compound it replaced, the Marie P. DeBartolo Sports Center—dedicated in

honor of DeBartolo's mother—was a palace, featuring three separate practice fields, a locker room several times larger than the old one, an entire
floor of private staff offices, a players' lounge with sofas and televisions,
and a marble-lined lobby that bespoke success and elegance.

The situation on the field was not quite as tidy.

After briefly flirting with the notion of trading Montana while he still
had enough value to warrant significant interest, Walsh appeared to be
treating the quarterback rivalry like the other competitions for starting
positions he managed through the years. But Montana's success and
popularity made this impossible. While the coach could orchestrate the
entrance of one linebacker and the exit of another with very little fanfare,
every syllable he uttered or even inferred about the quarterback situation
made news. After Walsh named Montana the number-one quarterback
heading into the season, Montana felt increasingly manipulated by the way
the coach moved Young in and out of the lineup, never allowing him to
feel comfortable.

"Walsh tried to play mind games with both of us," Montana recalled,
"sometimes indicating that Steve would be his starter even if I were healthy,
sometimes suggesting that my career might last longer and the team might
do better if I were the backup. I resented it at the time. I thought I had
earned Walsh's respect . . . and I couldn't understand why . . . he wasn't
giving it to me."

The resentment Montana felt toward Walsh on this matter was merely
one level of a complicated relationship, but his professional rivalry with
Young was largely devoid of subtlety. The two men shared a businesslike
rapport, apparently without a cross word, but in Montana's mind, when
he stepped onto the field, Young was the enemy. "Montana was pissed
that he was having to defend his position, after all he'd achieved," said
Art Spander, the longtime *Examiner* sports columnist. "It wasn't friendly
competition as far as Joe was concerned. Somebody was trying to take his
job and he wasn't going to give it up without a fight."

Examples of Young's impatience were never far from view. After one
game in which Montana started and played poorly, Young headed back
onto the field and began running wind sprints, up and down the field, in

full view of his teammates. The scene perfectly captured the feeling that the new man was a constant presence in Montana's life, lurking in the distance, waiting for his rival to falter, ready to take over. "Nothing drives me nuts more," he said, "than being on the sidelines."

For the vast majority of fans across the Bay Area and beyond who felt an emotional attachment to the man who led the 49ers to the promised land, the threat to his position was personal. Many saw Young as a Darth Vader character, trying to push Joe out before he was ready to go. Around the practice facility, the battle divided loyalties, but most players tried to stay above the fray, at least publicly. "We got questions from the media: Who do you want in there? Who's the best?" recalled offensive lineman Guy McIntyre. "We couldn't get into that. We had to go out and block for whoever was in there." Roger Craig, established as the league's best combination runner and receiving threat out of the backfield, walked the diplomatic line, telling one reporter, "They are two great quarterbacks. I just happen to be in the same backfield with them."

Amid the controversy, 1988 was a season of familiar magic. In the second game of the year, on the road against the New York Giants, Montana, nursing an injured elbow, stormed off the bench to lead one of the most stunning comebacks of his career. Trailing 17–13 with forty-two seconds left, he zipped a pass toward the sideline, into the opening created by a two-deep zone. "I threw the ball into the seam," he explained, "and the rest was all Jerry." As two defenders collided, Rice made a spectacular catch and raced into the distance for a 78-yard, game-winning touchdown.

By midseason, the competition neared a tipping point. Battling several nagging injuries, Montana performed poorly in a 10–9 loss to the Bears, prompting Walsh to start Young the following week against Minnesota, ostensibly to give Montana time to heal. *Joe Montana, benched.* That's all he heard when the word reached him through the media. Believing his coach had permanently flipped the order of the depth chart, convinced the man was trying to run him off, he lashed out, prompting Walsh to call him in for a private meeting to insist the reporters had twisted his words. On and on it went like this for weeks, contributing to the narrative that Montana was on his way out. Riddled with doubts, the quarterback found himself playing tentatively, hesitant to throw certain passes out of the fear that one mistake might cost him his job. Especially after the Niners, with Young at the controls, suffered a painful loss to the Arizona Cardinals, blowing a three-touchdown lead, the controversy swirled as San Francisco stumbled toward midseason 6–5 and every man on the coaching staff started fearing for his job, including Walsh. The quarterback situation was just one part of a team searching for identity. Montana? Young? One of the local papers even ran a readers' poll to determine who should be starting; naturally, Joe Cool won in a landslide. "At that point, it seemed the story had a life of its own," lamented Walsh, who insisted he was using Young only because Montana was ailing. But Montana assured reporters he was ready to play, coloring the drama with additional intrigue.

Montana slowly gathered strength, and as his elbow healed, he regained the zip in his passes. Returning to the starting lineup in week twelve against the Redskins, he tossed three touchdowns to lead a crucial 37–21 victory. San Francisco crawled out of the muck, with number 16 leading the way. Fighting for his job, Montana found his groove, leading the 49ers to four straight victories and a 10–6 finish, which earned a playoff rematch with the Minnesota Vikings.

A key change to the offensive line made Montana stronger. After watching Chris Doleman repeatedly blow past left tackle Bubba Paris in the '87 playoff game—significantly weakened by his inability to control his ballooning weight—Walsh benched him in favor of Steve Wallace. By the end of the season, the new man was clearly working out, possessed with the very peculiar skills necessary to provide a human barrier against each defense's best pass rusher. Standing six-foot-five and weighing 280 pounds, Wallace leveraged his body with great power and guile, mastering the application of his feet and hands to resist the assault of extremely gifted athletes intent on clobbering his quarterback.

In time, the man known to his teammates as "Sexy" would become one of the prototypes of the new-age left tackle, earning a record contract that paid him $465,000 per year, demonstrating his value to the 49ers and the growing importance of the position. In time, while protecting the quarterback from predators, including Lawrence Taylor, Richard Dent, and Dexter Manley, he would bathe in Jennifer Montana's eternal gratitude.

"When I first came [into the league], I honestly had no clue of the importance of the position," Wallace said many years later. "Part of that was because things were changing. The thinking was beginning to change. To be looked to by Joe in a valuable way . . . being part of his success . . . as that blind-side protector . . . that was just an awesome thing."

Like his teammates, Wallace entered 1988 burdened by the painful memory of the way Montana was manhandled the previous year by Chris Doleman and the rest of the Vikings. "They really got into Joe's head," he recalled. "He had no time, no room to breathe . . . he was looking over his shoulder the whole game."

By the time Minnesota returned to Candlestick on New Year's Day 1989, the high-and-mighty San Francisco 49ers had been eliminated in their first playoff game for three consecutive years. The Super Bowl days were fading fast and the Niners were developing a reputation for choking in the postseason, leaving the franchise open to ridicule. Phil Simms, who throttled two of the losses, famously mocked the 49ers for "laying down like dogs" in the playoffs. The inability of Montana to conjure his familiar magic was one reason for the slump. During the losses, he was an unimpressive 33 of 54 for 503 yards, without a single touchdown. No San Francisco fan needed to be reminded that their beloved hero had been forced to the sidelines in two of those devastating defeats, and the fear that Montana could be chased and replaced again hung in the air like a gathering fog rolling in off the bay.

Armed with the league's number-one ranked defense, and featuring Pro Bowl quarterback Wade Wilson, 11–5 Minnesota earned its way to San Francisco by knocking off the Rams in the NFC wild card game. The Vikings were a better football team than the one that had crushed the Niners the year before, and they arrived on the West Coast confident and hungry to take the next step in their own development, well aware that Walsh's team was teetering on a precarious edge.

After Minnesota kicked a field goal to take the early lead, Montana slowly seized control. Completing his first six passes and benefiting from excellent protection, he tossed three touchdowns to Jerry Rice to key a 21–3 halftime lead. Doleman was strangely silent as Steve Wallace dominated their decisive battle, skillfully turning his body into a fortress against one of the most feared rushers in football.

"We couldn't get the pressure in [Montana's] face," said Floyd Peters, the Vikings' defensive coordinator. "I had to blitz him to do it, and that leaves you vulnerable to the big plays. And when we got pressure on him, he was still zinging that ball . . . He was hot. That's as sharp as I've seen him."

After securing the enormously satisfying 34–9 victory, the San Francisco players were shocked to see Montana climb up on a locker room bench, drenched not in doubt but in vindication, and address his teammates for the first time in ten years. The usually quiet man made a little speech about how teams that win big games so often lose the next one, and then he assured them such a fate was not in their future. "We're gonna go to Chicago and kick their ass!" he thundered as the room reverberated with cheers. Watching from nearby, Mike Holmgren was struck by the player's assertiveness, understanding that gaining revenge against the Vikings was a proxy for something deeper. "I think a lot of the things that were said and written about Joe hurt him."

"That was so unusual for Joe," Wallace said. "You could tell it was a very emotional moment for him. And everybody in that room knew why."

In the triumphant glow, Montana's hold on the job grew stronger. "I'm proud to say I was one of the ones who helped put an end to the quarterback controversy," Wallace said.

Seizing the initiative, Montana called his coach to the center of the locker room and presented him with the game ball. In this emotionally charged moment, two professionals who greatly admired each other transcended the friction that so often produced sparks. It was Walsh's one hundredth victory with the 49ers, and no one knew how much longer the ride might last.

When the 49ers showed up in Chicago for the NFC Championship Game, it was hard to say which loomed as the bigger challenge: Mike Ditka's Bears, who had rampaged through the NFC Central with a 12–4 record, or the bitterly cold weather at storied Solider Field. The breeze whipping across Lake Michigan pushed the wind chill to twenty-two below at kickoff. In a concession to the brutal conditions, even Montana sported one glove to ward off frostbite—on his left hand. He kept his right hand warm with a steady forward motion against the vaunted Bears' defense, completing 17 of 27 for 288 yards and three touchdowns to lead a surprisingly easy 28–3 victory, the first by a road team in an NFC title game in nine years. "This could have been Joe's greatest game," Walsh said. "Under the conditions, and with so much to prove, it might have been his best ever." Then it was on to the Super Bowl, where Montana kept moving his own goalposts.

Six days before the San Francisco 49ers and Cincinnati Bengals convened at the new Joe Robbie Stadium in Miami for Super Bowl XXIII, a policeman shot and killed a speeding African-American motorcyclist in the city's predominantly black Overtown section. The incident sparked several days of bloody rioting, just blocks from the Bengals' hotel, where the flames from torched buildings cast an ominous glow across the night sky. Never before had the championship game of professional football— corporate America's most powerful conduit to the consumer culture— collided so forcefully with the problems of the inner city. "What's going on out there is life," Cincinnati quarterback Boomer Esiason remarked with a touch of sadness. "It makes you ask yourself, 'What does football really matter?'"

Against this unsettling backdrop, the hundreds of journalists who arrived to cover the game chased a variety of story lines, none more intriguing than the widespread speculation about Walsh's future. Feeling significant family pressures and burdened by the constant stress of his increasingly difficult relationship with DeBartolo, the Genius was moving toward a difficult decision. "The grind was getting to him," said his friend, the broadcaster Wayne Walker. "I know he still loved the game but he was getting burned out."

The questions about Walsh overshadowed some of the heat on Montana, who arrived in Miami like some modern-day Lazarus. In a rare moment of public introspection, he conceded, "This has been by far my toughest year, because of the constant uncertainty. When you are coming back from a physical thing, even back surgery, you know what is going on and how best to deal with it. But this year I felt like people were trying to count me out, and I didn't understand it."

Facing Paul Brown's Bengals once again allowed Walsh the opportunity to make a statement about the past and the present, but the game was a rematch of Super Bowl XIX in only the narrowest terms. Just six players from the 1982 title contest remained on the 49ers' roster: Montana, Ronnie Lott, Keena Turner, Randy Cross, Eric Wright, and Mike Wilson.

On the third play of the game, Montana faded into the pocket and was creamed, tumbling to the ground at the feet of Steve Wallace, his blind-side protector, who had planted his feet firmly into the loose, slippery turf, which caused problems for both teams throughout the night. The quarterback's helmet crashed onto Wallace's right ankle.

"I heard something pop," Wallace recalled. "Three pops. *Pop. Pop. Pop.* And I thought, man, somebody's really hurt bad. And it winded up being me!"

Devastated to be forced out of the Super Bowl with shattered ligaments, Wallace would always remember the way Montana spent the next several months apologizing to him. "Every time he saw me limping around [on crutches], he'd say, 'Steve, I'm so sorry!' I'm thinking, wait, you're the quarterback. You got hit. You had nothing to do with this. I mean, this is a guy that's a legend. Was constantly apologizing. How could you not like a guy like that?"

The night before the game, Jerry Rice was restless. He always spent significant time visualizing his plays, imagining the approaching arc of Montana's various passes and exactly where and how he would snatch them out of the air. Around four o'clock Sunday morning, the twelve-time Pro Bowler and two-time NFC Offensive Player of the Year bolted out of bed, wide awake, and began pacing around his room with anticipation, "playing the game over and over in my head."

After four years in the league, Rice was on his way to widespread acclaim as the greatest receiver ever to play the game. His pairing with

Montana resulted in 353 regular-season receptions, 6,121 yards, and 55 touchdowns over a six-year span, according to the Elias Sports Bureau, ranking among the most potent batteries in league history. Montana's uncanny knack for delivering a pass at just the right time—first noticed by his basketball teammates back at Ringgold—was an asset with all of his receivers through the years, especially the gifted Rice, who could make a slight adjustment to his route, to find a seam in the defense, without throwing off the quarterback's timing. The moves he made with a ball in his hand became the stuff of legend. "No one else can make things happen the way he can after catching the ball," Montana once said.

Sometimes Montana and Rice seemed to be in each other's head, and on the night of January 22, 1989, the connection was especially strong.

For nearly three quarters, the San Francisco–Cincinnati showdown ranked among the biggest yawners in Super Bowl history. The half ended in a 3–3 tie, thanks to two 49ers drives that stalled in the red zone— including one that negated a one-handed Rice catch and run, covering 30 yards, down to the two—and with less than a minute remaining in the third quarter, it was a nail-biting 6–6, a score befitting leather helmets and buzz cuts. Then the fireworks began: Stanford Jennings returned a kickoff 93 yards for a Cincinnati touchdown; Montana led the Niners on an 85-yard march, culminating with a 15-yard pass to Rice, who made a marvelous catch while falling out of bounds; and Esiason, who abandoned the no-huddle, quick-count offense that had been the focus of intense pregame attention, began driving the Bengals toward a go-ahead score.

Around the middle of the fourth quarter, an agitated DeBartolo stormed into the 49ers' training room, where he found Steve Wallace propped up on a table, crippled by his ankle injury. "Get your ass over here," the owner said, motioning to a nearby television in the locker room. "We're watching this game! Joe's done it before and he'll do it again!"

As the owner and the tackle reminisced about the various comebacks engineered through the years by Joe Cool, the Cincinnati drive stalled, forcing the Bengals to settle for a 40-yard field goal, which staked the AFC champions to a 16–13 lead with 3:10 remaining in the game. Even then, DeBartolo refused to consider the possibility of anything but another storybook ending—at least out loud. "[Eddie] never backed down one second," Wallace recalled. "No doubt whatsoever [in his mind] that we're gonna win the game, and that we had the right guy to do it."

Thirty-one times in his professional career, empowered by what Atlanta sports columnist Furman Bisher called "an economical respect for time," Montana led his team back from a fourth-quarter deficit, conditioning teammates and fans to the art of the possible, even in the most dire circumstances—pulling out stunning victories that defied the odds while bathing him in a mythical glow. But no situation had ever mattered so much, to his team or to his own legend.

After a penalty was assessed following the kickoff, the ball rested on the eight-yard line when the San Francisco offense jogged onto the field, facing a situation nearly identical to the game-winning drive against the Dallas Cowboys in the 1981 NFC Championship Game. This time, Montana had even less time—one minute, forty-four seconds less—to pull off another miracle, setting the stage for the most dramatic finish in Super Bowl history.

On the Cincinnati sideline, a teammate approached wide receiver Cris Collinsworth with a gleeful expression, smelling victory. "We've got 'em now!"

The former Florida Gator was incredulous. "Have you taken a look at who's quarterbacking the San Francisco 49ers?" Even opponents appreciated Montana's capacity for miracles.

When the Niners huddled near their own goal line, right guard Guy McIntyre focused on the task at hand: "I'm gonna block my man. I'm not gonna be the one giving up a sack."

Nonchalantly taking the measure of his team as pulses quickened all across America, Montana noticed the anxiety in right tackle Harris Barton's eyes. Barton, in his second year out of North Carolina, was a good player who worked diligently on his sets. But he was also, in the words of McIntyre, "our Nervous Nellie." Every San Francisco fan of a certain age knows what happened next. The moment quickly became deeply embedded in the Montana legend. About the time he noticed that Barton, perhaps more than anyone else, needed to be distracted, the quarterback happened to see a familiar face in the distant stands. "Look! Isn't that John Candy?" Sure enough, there he was, the rotund comic actor known worldwide for films, including *Planes, Trains and Automobiles*.

"He just gave me one of those looks," Montana remembered. "Don't you understand where we are and what we're doing?"

Indeed he did.

The athletes feeding off Joe Cool's icy demeanor could not help smiling at such an unexpected comment at the most pressure-packed moment of their professional lives. "That was so Joe, and it broke the tension," recalled center Randy Cross, playing the final game of his outstanding career. Recalling the scene, McIntyre said, "Stuff like that [is] what made him such a great leader. He didn't let the moment overwhelm him." The detachment that Montana was somehow able to achieve in such situations defied explanation, but Cross may have come closest when he said Joe Cool played football "in the third person."

After years of observing his friend from the sidelines, Huey Lewis had developed a theory. "It's kind of a reverse metabolism somehow," he said. "When the stuff gets real frantic, and there's not much time left, he just chills . . . Pressure relaxes him somehow." Like many other fans, the rock star watched the unfolding drama with frazzled nerves, fully invested in Montana's ability to produce another miracle ending.

Instead of going straight for the jugular, Walsh decided to attack the Bengals with a rather standard mix of short passing routes and runs, which Montana executed to near perfection. The series that soon would become known as The Drive in San Francisco lore began with an eight-yard completion to Roger Craig, the NFC's Offensive Player of the Year; followed by a seven-yarder across the middle to tight end John Frank; a seven-yarder to Rice; and two straight runs by Craig, which gained a net of five.

Well-schooled by Walsh's frequent two-minute drills, Montana was calling two plays at once in the huddle to save time. "Because Montana is so cool under pressure and because we had practiced it so often . . . it was almost second nature," Walsh said.

In the stands, Theresa Montana flashed back to the brutally cold day in Dallas all those years before, feeling a similar energy, even as many of

Montana's old Notre Dame teammates, scattered across the country, watched with admiration and hope. "You just had a feeling Joe would pull it out, somehow," Steve Orsini said. All those years after the story began with a little boy waiting on the doorstep, Joe and Theresa remained a central part of their son's life. After watching him endure a very difficult period, they understood how much it meant for him to reach such a moment.

Except for one incomplete pass, which he purposely threw out of bounds when he was hyperventilating, the quarterback led the 49ers down the field flawlessly: making one good decision after another, putting the ball right on the money time after time, and filling the unit with a sense of radiating inevitability.

"The second we took the field . . . I knew we had the game won," said Rice, Montana's most powerful weapon.

More than fifteen hours after he climbed out of bed with excitement, the San Francisco receiver was playing one of the greatest games of his life, catching 11 Montana passes for a Super Bowl record 215 yards, which won him the game's Most Valuable Player award. Three of the grabs came on the final drive, including a 17-yarder down the right sideline that pushed the Niners into Cincinnati territory, and a 27-yarder across the middle, featuring a highlight-reel move to avoid three defenders, that gave San Francisco a first down at the 18.

As the clock ticked below the one-minute mark, Montana broke the huddle at the Bengals' 10. The call was 20 Halfback Curl X-Up, but when Roger Craig and Tom Rathman lined up incorrectly, the quarterback quickly realized he was vulnerable. "If they'd blitzed from the right, I never would've seen them coming," recalled Montana, who completed 23 of 36 for a Super Bowl record 357 yards.

But there was no blitz. Using Rice as a decoy, the quarterback patiently pulled back from center, waited for the play to develop, and hit John Taylor perfectly in stride for the touchdown, giving San Francisco and Montana their third Super Bowl championship in eight years. Thirty-four seconds remained on the clock. The number soon was tattooed on Sam Wyche's soul. "Thirty-four seconds," he lamented in the dejected Cincinnati locker room. "We're not going to forget that."

After witnessing one of the defining moments of Montana's career—a 92-yard, 11-play drive that ranked among the most consequential in NFL history—the Bengals' Collinsworth told reporters, "Montana is not human. I don't want to call him a god, but he's definitely somewhere in between. I have never seen a guy . . . that every single time he's had the chips down and people are counting him out, he comes back."

As dozens of sportswriters prepared to wax glowingly about a man many had written off only months earlier, Ronnie Lott said, "I've seen him do this time and time and time again. It's sad that people have questioned his ability, but you can't question his heart. You can't question his desire. Without a doubt, he has to be one of the greatest quarterbacks ever to play."

On his way out of the 49ers' dressing room for the final time, Cross said, "As far as Joe Montana's concerned, I hope people will finally stop saying they rate him with the best. He is *the* best. There's never been a better big-game quarterback."

While Montana took a step into the football stratosphere by becoming only the second quarterback to win three Super Bowls—leaving him one short of Pittsburgh's Terry Bradshaw—and the most accurate passer in the history of the big game with a 65.6 cumulative completion percentage, the season that culminated in Miami demonstrated something far more universal: Forcing a man to fight for his job can lift him to unimagined heights.

The arrival of Steve Young stirred something deep inside Montana, empowering him to churn resentment into determination. The presence of a talented rival breathing down his neck, ready to step in at any moment, was just what he needed to propel him toward a whole new level.

"That was a very tough time for Joe but, in the long run, I think the competition actually benefited him," Cross said many years later. "Steve Young pushed him and made him better."

Two years after back surgery, Montana was enjoying the greatest period of his remarkable career. No one knew how long it would last—especially an increasingly frustrated Steve Young.

The question was asked by a reporter as he stood in the locker room, surrounded by his celebrating players, surrounded by his success. Bill Walsh did not answer. He was too emotional. Precisely when he decided to resign from the 49ers was not known for certain, but after informing Eddie three days after the Super Bowl, he made the official announcement at a news conference the day after that, when George Seifert was introduced as his chosen successor.

Despite the rampant speculation concerning his departure, the news shook San Francisco like an earthquake. For a decade, he had cast a dominant shadow across the Bay Area's sporting landscape, transforming a moribund franchise into the most successful club in the National Football League. In the process, he had reinvented himself. The man who could not convince an NFL team to take a chance on him as a head coach became the standard by which every head coach for the foreseeable future would be judged.

His record of accomplishment ranked him among the giant figures in professional football history. While leading the 49ers to three Super Bowls in eight years, he approached the run enjoyed by Chuck Noll, who won four in six years with the Pittsburgh Steelers. The three league championship trophies tied him with his mentor, Cleveland's Paul Brown (Washington's Joe Gibbs would soon join this elite club), trailing only Chicago's George Halas and Green Bay's Curly Lambeau (six titles each), Vince Lombardi (five), and Chuck Noll (four).

The debate—was it the system or Montana?—would continue among San Francisco fans for years to come. By the time Walsh stepped away, the quarterback was still dealing with a certain amount of bitterness about the way he was treated and perceived. But in the years ahead, as Walsh became an analyst for NBC Sports and then returned to the field for a brief, unsuccessful tenure at Stanford, followed by a stint in the 49ers' front office, and finally back to Stanford as assistant athletic director, the teacher and the pupil grew considerably closer. They played golf and laughed and shared stories about the old days. They had always admired each other, but in those final years, liberated from the circumstances that had allowed them to lift each other to unimagined professional heights but also prevented a genuine friendship, they grew to like each other, too.

In 2007, after Walsh learned he was dying of cancer, he meticulously planned his memorial service, which concluded with a few words from the quarterback who would be linked with him forever. As tears gathered on his cheeks and his voice broke, Montana spoke of his admiration and affection for the coach who had touched his life so profoundly. "Outside of my dad," the old quarterback said, "he was probably the most influential person in my life."

The sky was Bruce Collie's sanctuary. When he was sailing through the clouds high above Northern California in his twin-engine Beechcraft Duchess, the man who spent his days violently slamming into defensive linemen to protect Joe Montana from harm felt a peace he could never adequately express. "There's nothing quite like being up there, looking down on the world," he said.

Owning a pilot's license and a small plane also endeared him to his teammates.

During training camp, the 49ers continued to prepare for the season at Sierra College in Rocklin, north of Sacramento, which, with traffic, could be a five-hour drive back to the Bay Area. Unless you happened to own a pilot's license and a plane. "I would go out there and hop in my plane and be in Palo Alto in thirty-five minutes," Collie recalled.

Several days into camp in 1989, when new head coach George Seifert gave the team twenty-four hours off and Collie mentioned that he was planning to fly home, several teammates asked if they could hitch a ride. Soon the six-seat aircraft was fully loaded, including Joe Montana and Steve Young, and off they flew to Palo Alto, enjoying their day off with family and friends, and returning to Rocklin the next day.

News of the air taxi somehow reached Seifert, who called Collie into his office with a sneer.

"You can take either Steve or Joe but you can't take both my starting quarterbacks in that goddamned airplane!" he thundered, going on and on about the potential for franchise-shattering calamity.

Collie nodded, then asked, "What about your starting guard?"

"We don't care about you!"

By stepping into Bill Walsh's enormous shoes, Seifert faced one of the toughest assignments in NFL history, knowing that everything he did would be judged against the standard set by Walsh. As the 49ers prepared to defend their Super Bowl title with a team largely intact, Seifert benefited from an offense loaded with talent and experience: Joe Montana, Jerry Rice, John Taylor, Roger Craig, and Tom Rathman. Seifert knew little about the intricacies of Walsh's scheme, allowing newly promoted offensive coordinator Mike Holmgren to operate, at least in the beginning, with a free hand.

Soon after taking over, Seifert publicly declared Montana his starting quarterback, striking a clear distinction from the way Walsh handled the situation during the muddled 1988 season. "Confidence-wise, it helps," Montana said. "Mentally, it relieves a little pressure." The league's most closely watched quarterback rivalry continued, as the two players pushed each other on a daily basis, but Montana's hold on the position was now unquestioned. The job was his until he lost it, and in 1989, his career was still on an upward trajectory, headed for rarefied air.

After opening the season with narrow victories over the Indianapolis Colts and the Tampa Bay Buccaneers—in which Montana completed a combined 40 of 65 for 519 yards—San Francisco fell into a ditch against the Philadelphia Eagles, one of the NFC's strongest teams. The quarterback took an especially hard pounding from Reggie White and one of the most feared defensive fronts in football. Nearly the entire game, the Eagles dominated the Niners' offensive line, knocking the quarterback down fourteen times and recording eight sacks. His ribs ached. His elbow throbbed with pain. Still, Montana led San Francisco back from the dead with one of the gutsiest performances anyone around the franchise had ever witnessed.

Trailing 21–10 early in the fourth quarter, he rallied the 49ers for four touchdowns in the final twelve minutes—hitting 11 of 12 passes for 227 yards and scrambling for another 19—to pull out a stunning 38–28 victory. After sustaining one especially vicious hit from White, lineman Harris Barton recalled, "I was just amazed he could line up at all." On the winning drive—culminated with a 33-yard pass to Jerry Rice—Eagles defender Ron Heller remembered thinking, " 'We're not going to stop him. We can't stop him.' It was just that will."

Montana was shocked when Bobb McKittrick, the 49ers' offensive line coach, took the unusual step of apologizing to the quarterback on behalf of his players—in front of the entire squad.

Week after week, Montana methodically throttled an offense that proved incredibly difficult to stop, piling up some of the biggest numbers of his age, including nine games in which the 49ers generated more than 400 yards in total offense. His effectiveness in the red zone was off the charts. With Montana, Roger Craig, Jerry Rice, and John Taylor all near the peak of their abilities, Bill Walsh's invention hummed without him, even as he watched from a distance, understanding full well that Montana was driven by one thought: He wanted to show the world he could be a great quarterback *without* Bill Walsh.

"He found a freedom without Bill [and played] with a level of confidence that was just incredible," Steve Wallace said. "He was absolutely flawless on the field."

While leading the 49ers to a league-best 14–2 regular season—including a memorable rally to beat the Rams, when he threw for a franchise-record 458 yards—Montana crept still closer to perfection, completing a league-record 70.2 percent of his passes and finishing with the highest single-season passer rating in league history (112.4). Enjoying the greatest season of his career while leading one of the best teams ever assembled, he took a step out of Walsh's imposing shadow, causing all who watched to wonder if he had received enough credit for San Francisco's dominant decade.

While the enormous pressure of 1988 unquestionably lit a fire, causing Montana to perform at a high level to withstand the challenge from Young, what happened in 1989 proved that he could also thrive in an environment without such motivating tension. No longer was his mind cluttered by off-the-field drama. He still felt Young's presence, knowing the understudy was ready and able to take his job, but the way Seifert handled the situation unquestionably worked to his advantage. At a time when everyone recognized that he was at the top of his game, he somehow flipped a switch and found a new gear. "I think he is playing kind of relaxed," Holmgren said toward the end of the year, echoing a sentiment expressed by many of his teammates. In a game of grizzled professionals driven by some combination of money, fame, and self-preservation, Montana had always played with a certain youthful exuberance that was closely tied to many of the characteristics that made him successful. Now more than ever, he looked like a little boy having fun. "He got this twinkle in his eyes and you just sort of knew . . . he was playing with such joy," Collie said.

In the years before he moved on to Green Bay as head coach, where he would produce two Super Bowl teams led by Brett Favre, Holmgren tweaked the offense at the margins to maximize his quarterback's skills. After preparing a reel of his ninety-nine career interceptions heading into the '89 season, Holmgren discovered that about one-third of those picks had resulted from two pass routes. Presented with such evidence, Walsh might have worked with Montana to improve his mechanics on those two passes, but Holmgren, unburdened by the stubbornness that can result from inventing a system, simply eliminated the problem plays. This was a small, virtually unnoticed change, but it helped Montana dramatically reduce his errant throws—to eight, for a career-best 2.1 interception percentage—while tossing 26 touchdown passes.

One of the greatest seasons in the history of the 49ers took shape against a painful autumn for the Bay Area. On October 17, with millions of baseball fans across the country tuned to the ABC network to watch the third game of the World Series between the San Francisco Giants and the Oakland A's, which was just about to start, Candlestick began to shake violently. A massive earthquake, centered in a remote area along the San Andreas Fault and measuring 6.9 on the Richter scale, was under way, live and in living color. The Loma Prieta quake caused sixty-three deaths, several thousand injuries, and an estimated $6 billion in property damage, devastating Northern California like no national disaster in modern history. Aging Candlestick withstood the shock surprisingly well. Joe and Jennifer Montana happened to be at the game with their infant son, Nathaniel. After the tremor subsided, Jennifer wanted to leave immediately but Montana insisted on staying to see the game. Only after the event was postponed and the crowd instructed to evacuate the stadium did the Montanas head for the parking lot, where, like thousands of others, they wound up trapped for hours in a massive traffic jam. The roller coaster of anxiety and relief they felt concerning the safety of their two young girls, who were staying with a babysitter and made it through safe and sound, was shared by parents across the region.

Although Candlestick suffered only minor damage, the 49ers' next home game was shifted to Stanford Stadium in Palo Alto, to prevent complications with the ongoing cleanup effort. San Francisco knocked off the New England Patriots, 37–20, as Young came off the bench to throw three touchdown passes.

While Montana enjoyed a special season, Young played often and usually very well in a backup role. When speaking to the media, he was always complimentary of the man ahead of him on the depth chart, praising his unique ability to "do things under pressure that most human beings or quarterbacks can't do." He said he was learning from Montana and sounded sincere. But he was increasingly impatient, consumed with the question of how long he would have to wait for Montana to retire or falter.

Largely unnoticed in the roster shuffling heading into 1989 was San Francisco's acquisition of running back Spencer Tillman from the Houston Oilers. Tillman, a former University of Oklahoma star, was a special teams terror known for delivering devastating tackles while also battling for playing time against deeply entrenched Roger Craig, who was responsible for 1,527 yards of offense. Tillman soon realized his presence served an additional purpose.

"I wasn't there to unseat Roger Craig. That wasn't going to happen," Tillman said. "It was leadership that brought me to San Francisco."

In the carefully organized 49ers locker room, Tillman found himself placed between Montana and Young by Dr. Harry Edwards, the widely admired University of California sociology professor who had been hired by Walsh to mentor the players. The relationship he witnessed between the two quarterbacks was civil but distant. "They were professional," he said. "I never saw them falling all over each other but they would engage with each other and laugh."

Three years removed from the Tampa Bay debacle, Young was still not the Hall of Fame player he would become. His tendency to rely too heavily on his scrambling ability sometimes caused him to bail out of the pocket too quickly, and his decision making still lacked the speed and sophistication of his rival. But everyone associated with the 49ers realized he was a better athlete than Montana in several respects. Clearly he had demonstrated he was an outstanding quarterback capable of starting and winning in the NFL.

"More than anything else," Tillman said, "Steve Young needed an example . . . of how to go out and compete and not let being behind a legend bother you."

Tillman, who went out day after day knowing he did not have a prayer of unseating Craig, provided such an example, frequently discussing his mental approach to the situation with Young and even convincing him to join a Tuesday night Bible study at the home of tight end Brent Jones. For Tillman, the competition, like everything else in his life, took place in the context of his strong Christian faith. During those Tuesday nights, the direct descendent of Mormon Church leader Brigham Young found himself caught up in deep philosophical discussions about the Bible that offered lessons about his own struggle, including the parable of David versus Goliath. "We weren't evangelizing folks," Tillman recalled. "We were looking for practical solutions" to problems of everyday life. Out of this process, Tillman saw Young develop a deeper perspective about his rivalry with Montana, perhaps realizing in a more profound sense that ultimately he was competing with the man in the mirror.

Keeping Montana in his sights proved increasingly difficult.

When the New York Giants arrived at Candlestick to renew their bitter rivalry in November, Montana tossed three touchdowns and just six incomplete passes to lead a 34–24 victory. But it was Joe Cool's block on linebacker Carl Banks—who outweighed him by more than thirty-five pounds—to spring Jerry Rice's reverse that made the most powerful statement. In this game, even the *quarterbacks* hit hard. "I got in Banks's way, just long enough for Jerry to get away," he explained, apparently unaware that fragile, aging, washed-up quarterbacks with spine problems and sore ribs aren't supposed to pick fights with linebackers.

During playoff routs of the Minnesota Vikings (41–3) and Los Angeles Rams (30–3), he completed 79.6 percent of his passes for 503 yards and six touchdowns. By the time the 49ers arrived at the Superdome in New Orleans to face the Denver Broncos, the talk of Montana as perhaps the greatest quarterback of all time filled newspaper columns and occupied conversations across the country. As the new decade dawned, his blue eyes beamed from the cover of *The Sporting News*, which selected him as its Man of the Year, joining a chorus of cheers that included unanimous acclaim as the NFL's Most Valuable Player, Athlete of the Year by the Associated Press, and selection to the Pro Bowl for the sixth time. Football people struggled to describe the depth of his achievement, including Seifert, who said, "Montana has everyone in the NFL shaking their heads in awe."

The quarterback who led the Broncos to New Orleans was also on the road to the Hall of Fame, a master of comebacks with a powerful arm, but in Super Bowl XXIV, John Elway proved to be little more than a spectator in the demonstrative culmination of Montana's most amazing season. While a clawing defense led by Kevin Fagan, Tim McKyer, and Ronnie Lott hammered Elway into submission, Montana, benefiting from an offensive line that wrapped him in a blanket of protection, methodically led the greatest offensive explosion in Super Bowl history, shattering seven game records. Completing 22 of 29 passes for 297 yards and a Super Bowl–record five touchdowns—giving him a stunning 78.3 percent completion percentage for the 1989 postseason, with 11 touchdowns and no interceptions—he piloted a 55–10 destruction of the Broncos that ranked as the most lopsided championship game since the NFL began counting in Roman numerals. For the third time, he was named the game's

MVP, more than any other player. Linebacker Matt Millen, traded from the Raiders to the 49ers prior to the season, said, "There's not an adjective made to describe what Montana did."

The blowout began to take shape quickly. After Denver running back Bobby Humphrey fumbled into the arms of 49ers safety Chet Brooks, Montana led a 10-play, 54-yard march, culminated by his seven-yard pass in the flat to Brent Jones. Two passes across the middle to Jerry Rice moved the chains and set the tone for the whole game, the quarterback skillfully taking advantage of a soft zone and virtually no pressure to distribute the ball at will. "I saw Joe's little smile and I knew we were okay," Rice, who caught a record three touchdowns, told reporters. "It's kind of a sneaky grin, and I know he's on. It's like, 'Everything's under control.'"

Evidence of Montana's mastery in the pocket could be seen in the closing moments of the first half, when he sent Rice on a post pattern. Leaning on his preparation, which revealed that the Broncos tended to overplay based on where the quarterback trained his eyes, he faked to John Taylor, who was running a slant, freezing the safety just long enough to give Rice a wide alley to the end zone. One flick of the wrist later, Rice caught the ball in stride and outran the defense for a 38-yard touchdown, giving the 49ers a 27–3 halftime lead.

"The way Montana was playing," Denver defensive coordinator Wade Phillips said, "we could've dropped eleven guys and rushed eleven and it wouldn't have mattered. Not at all . . . We tried everything, and nothing worked."

Prior to the game, Montana decorated his Superdome locker with a picture of his three children, each sporting one of his Super Bowl rings. The inscription read, "Okay, Daddy, the next one's for you." As his career surged, the quarterback could see all the pieces of his life coming together. He was a proud father who could not wait to show off the latest pictures to his teammates. "Off the field, I've never seen him happier," said Dwight Clark, who by this time had moved into the 49ers' front office.

Most players dreamed of one precious band of gold, glistening in the sun, gleaming in the heart. The family man was now closing in on a handful of Roman numeral–denominated jewelry. As the leader of the undisputed team of the 1980s, with four Super Bowl victories in nine years, Montana pulled even with the Pittsburgh Steelers' Terry Bradshaw. In the all-time championship rankings, the two men trailed only Bart Starr, who led the Green Bay Packers to five NFL championships in seven years, including three in the pre–Super Bowl era.

"Yeah, I think we can say we're a dynasty now," Roger Craig told reporters. "This is the most focused bunch of guys I've ever been around . . . We just keep going."

Talk of joining Vince Lombardi's Packers in the history books by winning three consecutive titles—the elusive threepeat—filled the air, tantalizing no one more than the quarterback, who quickly waved off retirement and gravitated to a new goal.

Later in the evening, inside a suite at the Hilton Riverside, with the champagne flowing and the room service pizza and Cajun wings going fast, a small gathering of Montana's family and friends mingled while a replay of the game filled the television screen. Theresa and Joe Sr. looked happy—even as grandpa sprawled baby Nathaniel across the couch to change his dirty diaper. The hero, dressed in a white shirt and tie, chatted casually about the game, wearing the contented smile of a man who knew the singular pleasure of proving so many people so terribly wrong.

Several weeks later, in the glow of the 49ers' fourth Super Bowl victory, DeBartolo rewarded the entire team with a trip to Hawaii. Everything was first-class, from the accommodations to the entertainment. When the players and their significant others gathered for a special meal together, the presentation of rings was followed by a private concert featuring Huey Lewis and the News. Several songs into the set, Montana yelled out a request. "Would you do 'It's Alright'?"

By this time, Lewis had learned to appreciate Montana's musical tastes. The quarterback had heard the group warming up to an a cappella version of the R&B classic made famous by Curtis Mayfield and The Impressions, but he was not prepared for Lewis's response.

"Sure, but you gotta sing with me on it!"

A chill ran up Joe Cool's spine.

*Me?*

*On stage?*

*In front of all these people?*

"We embarrassed him into doing it," Lewis said.

As Montana reluctantly joined Lewis at the mic and moved through the lyrics with a tortured wail—eventually watching his buddy back away and turn the duet into a solo—the scene opened a window into the dichotomy of his personality. Even surrounded by a group of teammates, he was terrified. "Scared out of his mind!" Lewis said. "Nobody's ever seen the eyes of Joe Montana like I have. Linebackers look at him and all they see is cool. When I looked at Joe that night, one foot away, it wasn't cool."

Later in the evening, when he had regained his composure, Montana told Lewis and the guys, "You should record that song. It would be a big hit for you."

Lewis laughed off the suggestion, but several months later, when Mayfield was paralyzed during a live performance in Brooklyn, by the impact of lighting equipment falling on him, a group of his friends began organizing a tribute album to commemorate his career. One thing led to another, the News recorded the a cappella version of "It's Alright" for 1993's *People Get Ready,* and it indeed became a hit, reaching number seven on Billboard's adult contemporary chart.

Eight months after the Super Bowl, Montana was back in New Orleans, in deep trouble. As millions of fans stayed up late to watch another *Monday Night Football* thriller, the 49ers trailed the Saints, 12–10, with 1:30 remaining. The ball rested on San Francisco's eight yard line. Underdog New Orleans had played a marvelous defensive game, led by linebacker Rickey Jackson, who recorded two quarterback sacks and landed several other hits on Montana, who was still stinging from all the personal attention. So deafening was the noise in the Superdome that the quarterback's voice was now a screech.

As Montana convened yet another huddle needing to drive a long way in a short time, he turned to tackle Steve Wallace, who was having an especially difficult time hearing his cadence. Four times, Wallace had jumped offsides. Now the seconds and yards were too precious and the quarterback knew he could not afford another five-yard penalty. Turning to Wallace, he said calmly, "Steve, if you can find a way to stay onsides, I swear we'll find a way to win this game."

Recalling the scene many years later, Wallace said, "That's the type of quarterback he was. You knew the only thing you had to do was your job. Shoot, I found a way."

Cue the heroic rally. Three plays after a 25-yard completion to John Taylor, Montana faced third-and-six from the San Francisco 48 with thirty-nine seconds left. He hit Roger Craig for 11 yards and then found Jerry Rice for 20 and bounced the ball to stop the clock at twelve seconds, making time for Mike Cofer to save the day with a 38-yard field goal, which gave the defending Super Bowl champions a 13–12 victory, the first of ten consecutive wins to start the 1990 season. "We had the world's best team beat and we just couldn't pull it out," lamented Jackson, who spoke for a generation of frustrated defenders victimized by Montana's clutch performances.

As the thirty-four-year-old quarterback signed a four-year, $14-million contract—working out the details with DeBartolo over a lunch of tuna salad—and moved into his twelfth NFL season, even casual fans understood the way to derail the San Francisco express: *Hammer Montana. Get in his face. Disrupt his decision making. Put him on his rear end. Make him worry about your next visit. Get in his head. Make him hurt.* Of course, this sounded easy on paper but proved much more difficult to pull off against one of the league's best offensive fronts. When predators found a way to him, often landing vicious hits that caused teammates to cringe, he almost always climbed off the turf and went back to work. In a preseason game against the San Diego Chargers, after lofting a touchdown pass to Jerry Rice, the quarterback was clobbered by defensive end Lee Williams, who later confessed, "I tried to bury Montana's butt! I thought he wasn't going to get up. I thought it was a decapitated shoulder. You know, like, 'There's your arm right there, pick it up.'"

The Ringgold High School star sometimes visited moonlighting teacher Steve Russell. (Courtesy of Steve Russell)

Montana's basketball skills attracted several college scholarship offers. (Courtesy of Don Devore)

As a junior, Montana played on a Ringgold basketball team that won the Western Pennsylvania Interscholastic League (WPIL) championship. (Courtesy of Don Devore)

Dan Devine doubted Montana—until he led Notre Dame to the 1977 national championship. (Courtesy of Getty)

In a virtually deserted Cotton Bowl, Montana led a furious rally despite an ailing body. (Courtesy of Getty)

Dwight Clark's leaping catch to beat the Cowboys demonstrated Montana's perfect touch. (Courtesy of Getty)

In his first full year as the 49ers' starter, Joe Cool brought San Francisco a Super Bowl championship. (Courtesy of Getty)

Bill Walsh's system proved a perfect fit for a quarterback who entered the NFL surrounded by low expectations. (Courtesy of Getty)

Despite modest arm strength, Montana proved incredibly accurate, consistent, and able to hit the open man. (Courtesy of Getty)

The rivalry with Steve Young pushed Montana to new heights—but eventually forced him to leave San Francisco. (Courtesy of Getty)

The quarterback's marriage to onetime model Jennifer Wallace brought him longtime happiness. (Courtesy of Getty)

Montana's battery with Jerry Rice produced a long list of thrilling moments. (Courtesy of Getty)

Defenders learned to respect the way Joe Cool took punishment and kept performing. (Courtesy of Getty)

The sight of Montana's arms aloft helped define an age in the NFL. (Courtesy of Getty)

After moving to Kansas City, Montana suffered a concussion against Buffalo that left him dazed. (Courtesy of Getty)

Years of tension related to former coach Chuck Abramski being bothered by what he thought of as Joe's lack of commitment to football faded when Montana returned to Monongahela for a reunion organized by a group that included former teammate Don Devore (left) and Chuck Abramski himself. (Courtesy of Getty)

No team hit harder, or wanted to neutralize Montana more, than the New York Giants, who understood that the road to the Super Bowl led through San Francisco. The memory of Jim Burt's ambulance-necessitating hit lingered, and the various machinations required to protect Joe Cool from Lawrence Taylor infused the series with the uneasy tension of a heavyweight prize fight, the greatest offensive player of the age squaring off against the greatest defensive player of the age, each man looking for his own version of a knockout punch.

A measure of their rivalry and the quarterback's icy demeanor could be seen after Taylor once crushed him to the ground with a mighty thud. "Glad you got here," Montana yelled out with a grin, while pulling himself off the ground. "I was beginning to wonder if you were in the game!"

As the two teams, who combined for six Super Bowl titles over a ten-year period, took turns frustrating each other's ambitions—the 49ers owned a 9–4 edge during Montana's tenure. "We couldn't wait to get on the field," said Leonard Marshall, who relished the chance to "prove himself" against the 49ers. Bill Parcells often stoked the rivalry with his macho chest-beating. When the NFC Championship once more led through San Francisco, and he noticed Huey Lewis on hand to once again sing the national anthem, Parcells stirred his team with a pregame rant detailing how much he *hated* San Francisco . . . how much he *hated* the 49ers . . . how much he *hated* Candlestick. The Big Tuna was on fire, filling the room with his seething disdain for the Bay Area and everyone associated with the Golden Gate region, building to a dramatic conclusion to send the Giants bursting through the locker room door with a vengeful fury. "And I hate Huey Fucking Lewis!" he roared. (Several years later, when Parcells stepped off the sidelines and began a career in television, ESPN's Chris Berman formally introduced the coach and the rock star prior to taping a promotional spot at the cable channel's Connecticut headquarters. "Oh, I know you," the now-cordial Parcells greeted him with a wink. "You're Huey Fucking Lewis!" The moniker stuck, becoming a running joke with many of the Giants, especially those who happened to be News fans.)

Except for the 49–3 blowout in the first round of the 1986 playoffs, which figured so prominently in Montana's career, the games in the yardstick series typically turned on one or two crucial plays. "In order to win a game like this," New York linebacker Carl Banks once said, "you've got to outhit your opponent." If you loved football, it was impossible not to enjoy the way those two teams attacked each other, battling on every snap not just to win but to dominate, to crush the other into physical and psychological capitulation. Charges of late hits and cheap shots frequently heightened the intensity, as did the raging gamesmanship of players on both sides.

When the *Monday Night Football* crew convened in San Francisco four days after Thanksgiving in 1990 for a widely anticipated showdown of 10–1 division leaders, Montana was just weeks away from winning his second straight league MVP award as well as being named *Sports Illustrated*'s Sportsman of the Year, joining a list of luminaries including Roger Bannister, Stan Musial, Muhammad Ali, and Jack Nicklaus. An injury to Roger Craig's knee significantly hampered the Niners' running game, which put more pressure on the quarterback, but as his completion percentage dipped to a still-sterling 61.7, he tossed 26 touchdowns, including a record six in a 45–35 victory over Atlanta. As the quarterback of the 1980s entered the 1990s near the top of his game, San Francisco fans could smell a third straight Super Bowl.

With a huge crowd of 66,092 elbowing into Candlestick and a record audience estimated at 41 million watching on ABC, the Giants and 49ers spent the evening proving why they were the two best teams in football, trading one jarring tackle after another in one of the most memorable defensive struggles of the modern era. The way Bill Belichick's top-ranked defense stifled Montana—who completed just 12 of 29 for 152 yards—was a thing of beauty: LT and Leonard Marshall applying the pressure up front, Mark Collins and Greg Jackson clogging the passing lanes. It was a brilliant performance, except for one play.

Midway through the second quarter, armed with good field position thanks to a 30-yard kickoff return by Spencer Tillman, Montana scrambled, faked to Jerry Rice and, quickly recognizing defensive confusion, drilled a 23-yard touchdown pass to John Taylor, which staked San Francisco to a 7–3 lead.

"The only way Montana could beat us on that play was with an ad lib, which he did," said onetime Cowboy Everson Walls, who took the fall for the breakdown, nine years after losing the jump ball to Dwight Clark high above the same end zone.

Chris Berman spent much of the night walking the sidelines with Huey Lewis, and as the game moved into the final minutes, Simms drove the Giants toward a winning touchdown. The game came down to a brilliant goal line stand by the 49ers, who stopped New York on four stabs from inside the nine. When Simms's fourth-down pass was knocked to the ground by Darryl Pollard, an emotional Ronnie Lott, playing through a knee injury, charged over to Simms. Hours before kickoff, the leader of the San Francisco defense had been worked into a frenzy when teammate— and former Giant—Jim Burt told him that Simms was saying the All-Pro cornerback was "overrated." Lott needed no extra motivation to get up for the Giants, but on a day when he delivered several bone-rattling licks and demanded to play despite a hobbled leg, the gamesmanship helped pump him to a fever pitch. Mimicking the arm thrust the quarterback typically displayed when celebrating a score, Lott started taunting Simms. Soon, the two men were face mask to face mask, yelling obscenities at each other. "The atmosphere was so charged," Berman recalled. "You could feel the tension of the moment." Before things got out of hand, Montana helped pull Lott away from trouble.

The 7–3 loss was like a punch in the gut for the Giants, a wound still festering six weeks later when the teams collided at Candlestick in the NFC Championship Game.

With less than six minutes remaining in another stirring defensive battle, San Francisco controlled the ball and led New York 13–12. The three-peat was close enough to touch. Then, it slipped away. Once dependable Roger Craig fumbled, never to play another down for the 49ers, and the Giants drove close enough for Matt Bahr's fifth field goal of the day as time expired. New York 15, San Francisco 13.

The chain of victory was inexorably linked to the fumble and the kick, but the game also turned on two thunderous hits.

Two years after being acquired by the 49ers, Jim Burt was still able to deliver a jarring tackle. Early in the fourth quarter, with Phil Simms out with an injury, Burt slammed into New York quarterback Jeff Hostetler, forcing him out of the game with a hyperextended knee.

Minutes later, Montana went back to pass and was creamed from his blind side by Leonard Marshall. Marshall had fallen to the turf but got up and went looking for the quarterback, who had been flushed out of the pocket. The force of the collision made an impression on all who witnessed it. "When I hit him," the defender later acknowledged, "I heard him cringe," Carl Banks remembered. "We thought he killed [Montana]." As he tumbled to the ground, the ball popped out, eventually to be recovered by the 49ers. The powerful collision shattered a bone on his right hand and bruised his sternum, forcing him to the sidelines for the rest of the game, to be replaced by Steve Young.

The fumble and the kick sent the Giants to Super Bowl XXV, where they would hand the Buffalo Bills the first of four straight losses, but the decisive blow may have been delivered by Marshall, who single-handedly prevented the possibility of another Montana miracle. "He's like magic to them," Marshall remarked as the importance of the hit began to sink in. "Today we pulled out a little bit of our own magic."

Several days later, after surgeons inserted two screws into the fractured fifth metacarpal of his passing hand and every deep breath he took produced tremendous pain, Montana told reporters he was satisfied that he suffered a clean hit. "At the time, my stomach hurt so bad I didn't even know anything was wrong with my hand until I got to the sideline," he said. Joe Cool was never one to complain about vicious hits, but several years later, he remained bitter about what apparently happened after the whistle: "He grabbed my hand on the way down, and after we hit the ground, he snapped it back and broke it."

Pressed on the issue after arriving in Tampa for the Super Bowl, Marshall insisted he was not retaliating for Hostetler's injury. "It was a big play, and it gave us momentum," he said. "But because of the situation and the way things have happened with Joe physically, I'm not comfortable."

In the fifty months since he returned from back surgery, Montana had led the San Francisco 49ers on an emotional, frustrating, satisfying, and ultimately historic journey back to the summit of professional football. Only in retrospect, only after the darkness gave way to the light, would his decision to ignore Dr. Arthur White's advice be understood for what it was: the fulcrum on which his legend pivoted. The chain of events that followed led him down the path to greatness. It took the combination of Steve Young pushing him, Bill Walsh manipulating him, and George Seifert liberating him to produce the most remarkable second act in football history. The truth of the rivalry's impact may have been best captured by offensive lineman Keith Fahnhorst, who said, "Before Steve arrived, Joe was the best in the league. After Steve arrived, Joe was the best ever." It took those last two Super Bowls, and the smell of the third, slipping just beyond his grasp, to lift him to the pantheon. It took the struggle and triumph of 1986–90 to make him Joe Montana.

Four years after Burt knocked him out cold, Marshall's tackle lacked the shock value of the previous hit. It did not require flashing lights or a team of doctors and nurses monitoring vital signs into the wee hours. But the life of a football player is measured in accumulated trauma, and even as the quarterback vowed to return good as new in 1991, he was starting to feel the weight of his thirty-four years. Marshall had not simply knocked Montana out of a game and prevented the threepeat. He had placed a period at the end of an era.

# CHAPTER NINE

# Elbowed

FOR SPENCER TILLMAN, THE TRANSFORMATION can be reduced to two private moments. The first happened soon after he joined the 49ers in 1989, while walking off the practice field at the new DeBartolo Center alongside his quarterback. Adjacent to the artificial turf field was a basketball court, and on their way across the hard surface, headed for the locker room, he watched as Montana casually picked up a basketball and forcefully took it to the hoop, slam-dunking the ball through the iron effortlessly. He did this the way a mere mortal might thrust a wadded up piece of paper into an office trash can. "Like it was no big deal," Tillman recalled. "He was that athletic." Joe Cool was headed toward his greatest season, a man at the top of his game, and even after sustaining a long list of injuries, his body remained strong, every part of it firmly within his control.

Flash forward two years, to training camp in 1991. The 49ers' special teams captain was icing down his knee on the practice field when the quarterback casually approached. "Hey, Spence, let me get that bag from you." Tillman gladly shared his ice and Montana applied it to his sore right elbow. This moment would strike Tillman as meaningful only in retrospect, only after he learned that Montana had torn a tendon in his right elbow, as the resilient body that had sustained all those devastating hits started to fail without meaningful contact. One little piece of connective tissue, torn asunder, and the magic began to unravel. Only later would Tillman look back on the passing of the ice pack as the beginning of the end of Montana's career with the San Francisco 49ers. "That was the inflection point when the transition was starting to take place," Tillman recalled. "Joe never really recovered after that point."

By the time the players arrived in Rocklin, Montana was fully healed from the broken finger and bruised sternum sustained in his collision with Leonard Marshall. After a busy off-season, which included a vacation to France with the family; taping commercials for Diet Pepsi and LA Gear; charity work for the Make a Wish foundation and a local homeless shelter; and lending his likeness to a new Sega video game, *Joe Montana Football*, the quarterback approached his thirteenth NFL season eager to lead the 49ers back from the devastating loss to the Giants. "There's no reason why we shouldn't play to a level that we have played [to] in the last few years," he said.

The quarterback's playful side came out when he interrupted a reporter's chat with Jerry Rice, turning his right hand into a make-believe microphone. "Can I get in on this interview, too? I need to hear what he's got to say about this."

The serious business of keeping San Francisco competitive had prompted some difficult off-season decisions by the front office, prompting the departure of Ronnie Lott and Roger Craig, for years pillars of the franchise. Both signed with the Raiders, freeing up roster space and budget for younger men. Several other veterans retired or were released, including Keena Turner, Bubba Paris, Matt Millen, and Jim Burt, leaving Montana as the last active player from the 1981 Super Bowl team. "The transitions are hard to take," Montana said. "But that's all part of the game."

When his own transition period arrived, his elbow started aching and he was unable to throw without intense pain. Doctors diagnosed the condition as tendinitis and he was placed on the injured reserve list. The deactivation was initially expected to last for four weeks, and so anticipated was his return to active practice in early October that journalists from across the country showed up to watch him test the elbow. "There was a little bit of tightness, but I didn't feel any soreness when I threw," Montana reported. Soon, however, the pain returned with a vengeance and he was advised to stop throwing.

When it became clear that he would not be able to play in 1991, Montana, who had missed just ten starts scattered across the previous eleven seasons, opted for a solution that offered him the chance to play again: surgery to repair the common flexor tendon, which was detached from the bone. Without the operation, the prospects of him returning to action were, at best, cloudy. With it, he at least had a reasonable shot to negotiate yet another comeback. Dr. Michael Dillingham deemed the ninety-minute operation a "technical success," but offered no guarantees that Montana would be able to play in 1992—or ever again. "Not to be too cocky or arrogant . . . but I think there's a good chance he'll be able to return."

As the curtain lifted on the long-awaited Steve Young era in San Francisco, Montana endured the most miserable autumn of his life, spending his Sundays standing on the sidelines in street clothes while another man took his job. The relationship between the two had grown even frostier prior to the season when Young, while negotiating a two-year, $4-million contract, pushed for guaranteed playing time, a bizarre concept that reflected the unusual nature of the most scrutinized quarterback rivalry in NFL history. The point was now moot. Although he played very well in 1991, leading the league in passing efficiency, the 49ers stumbled to a 2–3 start. They finished 10–6 but missed the playoffs for the first time since the strike-shortened season of 1982, which filled Montana with ambivalence as he counted down the days until he could start throwing a football again.

Perhaps no player understood his torment quite like former Steelers quarterback Terry Bradshaw, who sustained the same injury in 1982. "I couldn't stand to stand on the sidelines and watch Cliff Stoudt throwing passes and taking the team up and down the field with the fans cheering. That was ripping my heart out," recalled Bradshaw, who rushed his recovery and, as a result, was forced into a premature retirement. In a story by 49ers beat writer Ira Miller in the *San Francisco Examiner*, Bradshaw sounded like he was speaking directly to Montana: "Don't come back too soon . . . Don't let the performance of Steve Young make you do something that will cost you a career."

As cards and letters of support arrived from fans across the country, the quarterback exploited the attention to join tennis star Jimmy Connors in a series of television commercials for pain reliever Nuprin. "I'm hurting, Jimmy," Montana says to Connors in the spot. "I'm talking football pain."

While Montana dedicated himself to a grueling rehabilitation schedule, including whirlpool treatments, ultrasound, and electrical stimulation, updates on the condition of his elbow generated significant media attention in San Francisco and beyond in late 1991 and early '92, competing for ink and air time with the contentious confirmation hearings for Supreme Court nominee Clarence Thomas and the salacious allegations against a former Arkansas governor bidding for the Democratic presidential nomination.

Because the prospect of an aging athlete attempting to deal with a debilitating injury was so deeply engrained in the fabric of professional sports, Montana began the road back facing a wave of understandable skepticism. Soon he would be thirty-six years old, and the sobering reality that the Comeback Kid would eventually run out of miracles confronted every football fan who thought about the situation logically. Still, they wanted to believe. The fans who looked back on The Catch and The Drive as defining moments in the life of their city anxiously scoured the newspapers for every word about their man's recovery. They wanted to believe he would come back good as new, beating this problem just as he had conquered an ailing spine and all those other obstacles on the way to the history books, on the way into their hearts. They wanted to believe, because they didn't want to let go.

For Montana, the same quality that fortified him when facing a desperate situation on the field caused him to keep fighting back against yet another instance of anatomical distress. Sometimes it seemed as though his entire career had been one long two-minute drill, animated by dropped balls and sacks and linemen jumping offsides. Time after time, he kept making the big play to move the chains. Now he was facing yet another third-and-long as the seconds ticked away, and the only way he knew how to deal with such a situation was to plot a course for the first-down marker. Jennifer, who was pregnant with their fourth child, told reporters, "Everyone knows their limit, and Joe's awfully in tune with his body. He knows he's fighting time but he feels he's not finished yet."

When Montana told *The Washington Post* he feared the 49ers were planning to phase him out, positioning him to become Young's backup, DeBartolo felt compelled to call Ira Miller and offer his unequivocal support for Montana as the 49ers' starter once he recovered. "I think he's got a lot of football left, I really do," DeBartolo said. "[The thought of pushing Montana out] has never crossed my mind."

Several weeks later, the same sportswriter advanced the story by getting Montana to open up in a way that sounded like a warning to the 49ers: "If I still feel my ability's 100 percent or close to it, then I'm not the kind of guy that's going to sit there and say, 'Yeah, here, it's my job, take it.' That's not me."

When Montana, with all the time in the world to let his mind race, said he would not be surprised if the 49ers decided to place him on the Plan B free agency list, Carmen Policy assured, "You don't put the franchise quarterback on Plan B."

By the spring, he was throwing again, several weeks ahead of schedule. All signs looked good, even after going under the knife for an unrelated, minor knee surgery. After pausing for ten days, he was cleared to begin tossing footballs again during the team's minicamp, drawing a crowd of print, television, and radio reporters to the 49ers' complex, including one from Japan. "It's like learning to walk again," he said after playing catch with backup quarterback Steve Bono and throwing some deep routes to a free agent trying to make the team. With each passing day, he felt stronger. Watching the old man's new motion, Seifert expressed the opinion that he was throwing better than ever.

The coaching staff and the front office acted like Montana was the presumed starter heading into the season, but refusing to consider trading either Young or Bono reflected understandable caution. The 49ers were hedging their bets, waiting to see if the world's most famous elbow could negotiate a full recovery . . . whether Joe Cool could still conjure the magic after a year away from contact. "For a long time I made disbelievers out of people," he told one reporter, "and that's the way I'm approaching this."

Now more than ever, surrounded by so many supporters who wanted to see him return, Montana reached for a source of motivation that had helped propel him to greatness: other peoples' doubts.

But two months later, in training camp, under the strain of a full-scale workout, the arm faltered. The doctor advised him to throw no more than forty passes in a day, which rendered him little more than Mr. Handoff. A visit to Dr. Frank Jobe, the man who invented the so-called Tommy John surgery, which revolutionized baseball, convinced Montana that all he needed was additional rest. Perhaps he had rushed his recovery, just as Terry Bradshaw and others warned. "Sometimes I want to kick myself for coming out and throwing too early after surgery," he told reporters as the season approached.

Eventually, swelling in the elbow required another surgery, forcing him to miss the first half of the 1992 season. When he was finally cleared to play, it was too late. Steve Young had taken his team.

As Young put together a sensational season, completing 66.3 percent of his passes and rushing for eight yards per carry en route to league MVP honors, the 49ers finished 14–2, clinching their ninth NFC West title in twelve years. Somewhere along the way, Seifert gave up on Montana. The decision was awash in pragmatism. The 49ers could not wait forever for a player to recover—not even the man most responsible for four Super Bowl victories—and benching the hottest quarterback in the league for a man who hadn't played a down in nearly two years is not the way to keep your job or get to the Super Bowl.

"That was one of the most painful things any coach could have to endure," Spencer Tillman said. "How do you choose between two such great players in such a difficult circumstance?"

The harsh realities of football confronted every man on the roster, coloring the quarterback controversy in a ruthless hue. Football is a bottom-line business; not even Montana could escape the imperatives of a zero-sum game. "[Seifert's choice] was one of those things where you had to just sort of let that part of the game be that part of the game," said offensive lineman Guy McIntyre. "You know there's a business side of the game, and it can be pretty tough. There are very few guys who walk out the door on their own terms, like Jim Brown."

Unwilling to upset the chemistry of a team that was clearly responding to Young, Seifert made sure that when Montana began throwing again, he did so away from the practice facility. He wanted to avoid the tangible distraction of the old man zipping perfect spirals within view of the new model—and the media, which needed no excuse to find the tension in a situation slathered in conflict. Eager to turn the page and distance himself from Bill Walsh's menacing legend, which Montana represented, Seifert saw in Young the face of his own new era. He was determined to avoid a new quarterback controversy, even if this stance meant turning his back on a player who was capable of beating Young in an open competition for the job. Ultimately, one of the greatest competitors in the history of football was denied the chance to regain his position because Seifert decided competition was, in this case, too risky.

Addressing the situation the following year, after he had moved on, Montana said, "There should have been no qualms about him competing with me and no worry about how it would affect him mentally. If he can't handle the pressure of competing, he certainly isn't going to handle the pressure later on."

While determined to strengthen Young's position with the team, fans, and in his own head, Seifert unwittingly undermined it. By pushing the real-life Montana to the margins, he forced Young to contend even more directly with the Montana myth. Young might have been able to best a battered, aging Joe Cool on the field, but he was no match for the glittering legend whose intimidating shadow confronted him at every turn.

Even as Young led the 49ers into the playoffs, offensive tackle Harris Barton, his onetime roommate, said, "I don't think this team will ever be anybody's team like it was for Joe Montana. He was really responsible for putting four Super Bowl rings on a lot of fingers."

For several weeks, a healthy Montana waited to be activated, privately seething as Seifert ignored him. (The prize for most clever headline went to some editor at the *New York Post*: "Montana Elbowed Aside.") "Sure he's been miserable without football," Policy told one reporter. "How would Picasso feel if he couldn't paint?"

Toward the end of the year, a familiar face returned to the 49ers' locker room. Bruce Collie, who had played a large role in protecting Montana in the late '80s, was nearing the end. Cut by Philadelphia, he was acquired on a short-term contract by his old team, which allowed him to retire as a 49er. Even as he struggled to deal with the inevitable demise of his own career, surrounded by the suddenly unfamiliar faces that demonstrated how football teams must constantly reinvent themselves in order to stay competitive, Collie was struck by his former teammate's burning desire to defy the calendar. "Talking with Joe, he was pretty frustrated the way Steve got the job," he said. "But I know he felt like he wasn't done."

Prior to the last game of the regular season, Seifert told Montana to get ready. The call came at the start of the second half against the Detroit Lions. When he entered the game, the Candlestick crowd gave him a rousing ovation, many no doubt believing they were seeing their beloved icon for the last time. It was a moment fraught with emotion. It was a moment loaded with pressure. After missing two full seasons, Montana confronted what he would later describe as "the most difficult situation I ever faced on a football field," but soon found the groove, looking very much like his old self. Passing for two touchdowns as San Francisco knocked off the Lions, 24–6, Montana proved he could still play. After the game, the quarterback walked around the locker room and thanked many of his teammates, caught in a bittersweet moment, trapped somewhere between euphoria and sadness, because he knew the performance meant absolutely nothing, at least in terms of the quarterback hierarchy in San Francisco. It was a highlight reel for some team willing to roll the dice. Nothing more. By refusing to use him in the playoffs, as the 49ers defeated Washington and lost to Dallas in the NFC title game, Seifert sent a clear signal.

The greatest player in the history of the San Francisco 49ers had been discarded, like an old pair of cleats.

Because he was under contract for another year, Montana entered 1993 feeling trapped. If he stayed in San Francisco, he appeared permanently stuck behind Young, without an opportunity to win his job back. Seifert was taking a beating from many fans who couldn't understand his reluctance to use Montana in the playoffs, but the boss had made his choice, leaving Joe Cool with two viable options: retire or ask for a trade.

The easiest option, of course, was simply to walk away from the game. Next stop, Canton. But he still wanted to play, and even after the two-year layoff, he was convinced he still could perform at a high level, which the last half of the Lions game appeared to confirm.

On the day his request to have his contract voided by Commissioner Paul Tagliabue was denied—a Hail Mary attempt to become a free agent—Montana was attending a benefit in Baltimore, where he insisted, "We're trying to stay in San Francisco. The fans have just been unbelievable to me over the years. I would really hate to go someplace else." But soon after this, Montana convinced DeBartolo to let him start shopping for a new team. Partly out of good faith, partly out of a desire to unload him while he still had some value, the 49ers extended him unprecedented leeway in exploring his options elsewhere. "I'm just looking for an opportunity to play, and that isn't going to be the case [in San Francisco]," he told Kansas City television station KMBC. "That's all right as long as I can find a home somewhere and get on the field."

For those with memories reaching into the seventies, the situation was buffeted by a gathering fear: the painful image of Joe Namath, claimed on waivers by the Los Angeles Rams, looking like a statue on a rainy night in Chicago. No one wanted to see Joe Cool wind up like Broadway Joe, a shadow of his once-great self at the age of thirty-five, struggling to hit receivers as a pall descended across *Monday Night Football*. No one wanted to watch Montana humiliate himself.

Montana still thought he could play. They all do. Even Namath. Especially Namath. No one really knew how long Montana had left, but more than anything else, he was filled with a resolve to prove to the 49ers management they were wrong to throw him away.

Several franchises expressed interest in Montana, including the Arizona Cardinals, who showed Montana and Jennifer around Phoenix and talked a good game. Bill Bidwell was willing to pay San Francisco's asking price, but the Kansas City Chiefs quickly emerged as his best option, offering him the opportunity to play on grass (thanks to a recent sodding of Arrowhead Stadium) for a winning team capable of making a run at the Super Bowl. Even before he entered the picture, Montana had influenced Kansas City's offensive direction: Head coach Marty Schottenheimer had already made the decision to abandon his run-oriented scheme for the West Coast Offense—yet another tangible example of the Walsh philosophy filtering through the game. The presence of new offensive coordinator Paul Hackett, the onetime 49ers quarterbacks coach, gave Montana a level of comfort no other team could match.

The Chiefs began their existence in 1960 as the Dallas Texans, one of the original teams in the American Football League, owned by AFL founder Lamar Hunt, one of the true visionaries in professional football history. After moving to Kansas City in 1963, the newly christened Chiefs, coached by Hank Stram and featuring quarterback Len Dawson and defensive end Buck Buchanan, remained one of the upstart league's best teams. The franchise earned a second AFL championship in 1966, before losing to the Green Bay Packers in Super Bowl I, and a third in 1969, after which the Chiefs knocked off the heavily favored Minnesota Vikings in Super Bowl IV, the last before the merger of the rival leagues.

By the time Schottenheimer, the former Cleveland Browns' coach, took over the team in 1989, Kansas City had qualified for the playoffs just once in fifteen years, falling behind the Denver Broncos and Oakland Raiders in the AFC West. Martyball quickly reversed the Chiefs' fortunes. Featuring an intimidating defense led by Hall of Fame linebacker Derrick Thomas, Kansas City made three straight playoff appearances from 1990–92 but was unable to advance past the second round. One reason was uninspired quarterback play. The club had been searching for a long-term quarterback since Dawson retired, drafting ten different hopefuls over a seventeen-year period. No one lasted for very long. Kansas City experimented with journeyman Steve DeBerg, Montana's onetime rival, as well as former Eagle Ron Jaworski and former Seahawk Dave Krieg, the presumptive starter heading toward the 1993 season. To get over the hump, the Chiefs desperately needed a big-time quarterback, one capable of running the 49ers style offense Paul Hackett was installing. The first man to suggest Montana, even before he was officially available, was player personnel director Lynn Stiles, who told team president and general manager Carl Peterson, "You don't have to build a new rocket. All you need to do is get Joe Montana." By early April, Peterson was prepared to place a large bet on Joe Montana.

"We were looking at risk and reward," recalled Peterson, one of the league's shrewdest deal makers. "How many real productive years could we get out of this guy? And what would we have to give in return?"

The haggling with Carmen Policy went on for more than two weeks. With both sides feeling pressure to finalize the deal before the draft, the offers and counteroffers flew back and forth over long-distance telephone lines, the quarterback's future resting on a game of high-stakes poker.

"Carl, I'm Sicilian and this is the minimum I'm gonna take."

"Carmen, I'm Swedish and I can be as stubborn as you. This is the maximum I'm gonna give."

Reluctantly, the miserly Peterson finally agreed to trade a first-round draft pick, number eighteen overall, for Montana—meeting the Cardinals' bid—but told Policy, "I need something back."

"What do you need?"

"I need another player and a draft choice."

San Francisco's side of the deal included a third-round draft pick as well as safety David Whitmore.

After Peterson negotiated a three-year, $10-million contract with Montana, believing he had already secured a deal with the 49ers, Policy pushed the pause button. DeBartolo was lining up for a Hail Mary pass of his own.

Because he had moved to the San Francisco front office, Dwight Clark wound up in the middle of the negotiations leading to his old buddy's departure, which estranged him from Montana for several years. The Catch was forever, but the lingering residue of this legendary moment was not strong enough to save their friendship.

"There was a period when there was some tension because it was such a bad scene when he left," Clark said. "It was a difficult time for everyone and I don't think either one of us knew how to handle it."

Now determined to go, and feeling betrayed, Montana flew to Youngstown to meet with DeBartolo face-to-face, to tell him he was ready to move on and to remind his good friend that the 49ers had pledged to trade him to the team of his choosing. DeBartolo loved him like a brother and was willing to try anything to keep him, and when Montana arrived, he made one last-ditch effort: If he stayed, Joe would enter training camp as the team's "designated starter," presumably with the opportunity to compete directly with Young. Nobody could say with any certainty what "designated starter" meant, and while the offer officially came from Seifert, it smelled of DeBartolo's influence. At the very least, the new position seemed difficult to reconcile with the last few months of franchise behavior. On this, Policy tried to explain: "It took George some time to reverse his field." The gambit was manipulative and insulting, the equivalent of an old girlfriend who ditched you showing up at the church on the day of your wedding. Montana was already gone, with a deal in hand, and DeBartolo was still trying to play Monte Hall.

"It didn't make Joe happy," Peterson said, "because he's thinking, where were you when I really wanted to stay? By then, he had already made the decision to leave [San Francisco], which you know was so very tough to do . . . He was already down the road mentally."

Several years later, when the damage was done, Policy conceded, "It was a farce. George was willing to name Joe the starter only because he knew Steve would eventually beat him out. We should have done it a lot more cleanly."

The news hit the papers while Montana was in Youngstown. Surprised by the sudden development, the quarterback said he would think it over. "[Joe] has a deep heart and a lot of decisions to make," DeBartolo said after arriving back in San Francisco. The situation was further complicated by the fact that Young's contract had expired, giving the team leverage against him as well as the Chiefs. Seeking a deal in the range of $5 million per year while his client was busy studying for law school finals at Brigham Young, agent Leigh Steinberg said, "Steve is comfortable in his role as quarterback of the 49ers and is confident in retaining that. He will not stand in the way of any happy resolution between Montana and the 49ers." In other words: Bring it, Joe.

After Montana declined the offer to stay, DeBartolo waved his hand and did right by his friend, telling Policy to make the deal.

When the news hit, a feeling of loss descended across San Francisco like a fog rolling in off the Bay. Secretaries at the Santa Clara facility could be seen wiping back tears. Bars all across the Bay Area were filled with patrons drowning their sorrows and cursing 49ers management.

Steve Wallace heard in a telephone call from a teammate. Soon, his phone was ringing incessantly. Everybody wanted to talk about Montana. And Young. And what this meant to the rest of the team.

"Once guys started calling around, all the butt holes got very tight," Wallace said with a laugh. "Because the word was, if they'll get rid of Joe Montana, they surely will get rid of your ass! Man, it was tight around there after that."

Four days later, the quarterback stood before a packed news conference in Kansas City, wearing a bright smile. Several local television and radio stations preempted regular programming to broadcast live from the scene, reflecting the unmistakable buzz wafting across the Midwestern metropolis. Joe Montana coming to town was big news.

"There is a big desire to prove I can still play, just to prove to myself," Montana said.

*Two years.*

This was the thought running through Carl Peterson's mind, as he listened to his new quarterback take questions.

*Three years with Joe Montana would be wonderful, but I'll take two and count myself lucky.*

While Montana was busy plotting his exit, an earthquake was just starting to rattle the foundation of the NFL. Prodded by the threat of a lawsuit, which was working its way through the federal judicial system, the owners agreed to a new system in which players achieved unrestricted free agency after four years in the league, coupled with a salary cap, which guaranteed the athletes 65 percent of gross revenues. The new order, which took effect in 1993, altered the dynamics of building and maintaining a successful franchise, transferring enormous power to the players by giving them a new level of mobility and a once-unimagined stake in the enterprise of professional football. Suddenly veterans who played through their contracts were able to offer their services to the highest bidder, pitting teams against each other in a high-stakes game, undermining the ability of a team like the 49ers to keep a star like Montana for such a long period of time. A new age had begun, and the adjustment was difficult for many owners to negotiate.

Not only were executives like Peterson able to more accurately budget for player compensation, they could "immediately address the deficiencies on their football teams" by countering the inverse effects of the college draft, which was designed to punish success and reward failure. Free agency proved to be an advantage for competitive teams who were willing to spend freely to chase success, including the Chiefs, who moved quickly to sign a player who could make their offense even stronger.

Aging Marcus Allen had been one of the premier running backs in the league, and after his relationship with Al Davis soured, the former Heisman Trophy winner from Southern Cal desperately wanted out of Los Angeles. Suddenly one of the most coveted of the new free agents, he was pursued by several teams, including the Chiefs. The day after Peterson signed Montana, he received a phone call from Allen. "That does it for me," he said. "I want to be a Chief." The player who had already rushed for 8,545 career yards and scored 79 touchdowns offered two reasons: "One, I've always wanted to play with Joe Montana. Two, I want to play against Mr. Davis twice a year."

The switch to the West Coast Offense was facilitated by Paul Hackett's firing the previous year as the University of Pittsburgh's head coach, pulling him back to the NFL at a fortuitous time. "The heart of what I'm doing is from Bill Walsh," he explained. "It's exactly the 49er attack. We may even pull out some old game plans."

By the time the Chiefs opened training camp in River Falls, Wisconsin, three months later, Joe Montana fever was running wild. A billboard heading into town proclaimed, "Welcome Joe Montana and the Kansas City Chiefs." Wearing a number 19 jersey—his familiar 16, once donned by the great Len Dawson, was retired—the man from Monongahela was the main attraction for thousands of fans who descended on the small college town to peer impatiently from behind a security fence. When draft pick Chip Hilleary, trying in vain to make the team, led one offensive series, a dissatisfied fan shouted, "We're not here to watch some rookie. We're here to see Joe Montana!"

Unfailingly polite and accommodating to autograph seekers, Montana was clearly a little embarrassed by all the attention—and, at times, a bit unnerved. While having dinner with some of his teammates after practice at a nearby pizza place, a woman came up and snatched the beer can out of his hand, fleeing the scene with a rather unique souvenir. "Sometimes it gets carried away," Montana said. "But you just take it in stride and hope that other times, like when you're out with your family, people will understand and leave you alone."

The frenzy was especially overwhelming during Kansas City's exhibition season trip to Tokyo in 1994, where the players enjoyed mocking their leader's larger-than-life celebrity with the American-loving Japanese: "Bigger than Budda! Bigger than Godzilla! It's Joe!"

Back in Kansas City, as the Chiefs felt compelled to hire six additional security guards to handle the crush, the impact of Montana's migration was already being felt in sales of tickets and merchandise, especially across the vast American heartland that Hunt and his staff saw as their extended market. "Joe was like a rock star," Peterson said. "Fans just clamored to him . . . the whole [franchise] just sort of exploded." As part of a promotion for a Kansas City radio station, residents in the tiny hamlet of Ismay, Montana agreed to rename their town. *Joe, Montana*. As a reward for this gesture of civic flexibility, twenty-two locals were flown to KC and given the first-class treatment, including meeting the man himself. As many San Francisco fans suddenly felt divided loyalties, the Chiefs' radio network even picked up two affiliates in Northern California.

In suburban Atlanta, a pretty blond woman in her late twenties illustrated the phenomenon. For years she had planned her Sundays around watching the 49ers games, at least those available in her area, proudly wearing her red number 16 San Francisco jersey and cheering at the television set. She admired the way Montana played, the way he always led the Niners back. She liked his blue eyes. Now she felt compelled to go out and buy a number 19 Kansas City jersey, which draped across her tiny body like a skirt as she yelled at the TV. She was a Chiefs fan now, as long as her Joe was a Chief.

As the more delirious fans dared to utter *Chiefs* and *Super Bowl* in the same sentence, Marty Schottenheimer tried to tamp down expectations. "This is not now, never has been, nor will it ever be a one-man game," he said. Of course, he was simply doing what head coaches do. Nobody was more excited to have Joe Cool around than the man whose job was largely dependent on his success, well aware of the fine line between winning and losing, well aware of the impact one extraordinary individual could exert.

Without a Jerry Rice, and maneuvering behind an offensive line that gave up 48 sacks in 1992, Montana was playing with a weaker hand. But he made the Chiefs a much better football team, sparking an 11–5 regular season while completing 60.7 percent of his passes and throwing 13 touchdowns.

"There was something about Joe," said kicker Nick Lowery. "He brought the glue to the whole team. Looking down the sideline and seeing a guy who had been to Super Bowls, it changes your team confidence when you've had years of mediocrity."

Working with him for the first time since 1985, Hackett noticed that his foot speed had diminished somewhat but saw him putting "more zip on the ball" than his 49ers days.

Any lingering doubts about Montana's recovery were quickly dispelled in a 27–3 road victory over Tampa Bay to open the season, as he completed his first nine passes and tossed three touchdowns, earning AFC Offensive Player of the Week honors.

Injuries to his wrist, thumb, and hamstring forced him to the sidelines several times during the season, to be replaced by the demoted Dave Krieg, who was still trying to master his third offensive system in three years. Each of Montana's ailments offered a reminder of his age and medical history. "It's aggravating to me, one little thing after another," he said. The hamstring kept taking longer to heal, a clear sign of the creeping calendar.

Still, he kept performing. In a game against the Chargers, the hamstring had him hobbling but he limped back onto the field to direct a game-winning 80-yard touchdown drive in the final minutes.

The fear of a career-ending injury hung in the air every time he was rocked, which was often. One such collision came in the home opener, a 15–7 victory over the Denver Broncos, as a capacity crowd filled Arrowhead with a pulsating energy not seen in many years. Simon Fletcher crushed the new hero like a soft drink can. "I just got squashed sideways," Montana said. "It knocked the breath out of me." During a midseason victory over the Raiders, he was clobbered on his way out of bounds by Aaron Wallace. He said nothing but the hit drew the ire of several Chiefs, including defensive lineman Neil Smith, who called it "a real cheap shot."

Toward the end of the season, as a massive winter storm approached from the west, Schottenheimer sent the team home early to avoid the worst of the travel conditions. Later in the afternoon, on a well-manicured street in the Hallbrook subdivision, adjacent to a golf course in the suburban Kansas town of Leawood, a group of boys started a snowball fight. The white powder was flying left and right, direct hits on wet toboggans and near misses landing harmlessly after a timely duck. One of the boys wasn't so young, and the neighbor kids noticed he had a pretty powerful arm.

"I haven't had that much fun since I was a kid back in Pennsylvania," the quarterback said several days later, while vividly painting the scene for Peterson, his face animated with a boyish glow.

Laughing about the image many years later, the Chiefs' executive said, "The whole time he's telling me how much fun he had out there with his boys [who were two and four then] . . . throwing at the neighbor boys and having the neighbor boys throw back . . . all I can think is, I'm glad nobody had a rock to hit my expensive quarterback in the head!"

The scene demonstrated one of the qualities that remained central to Montana's success. Even at the age of thirty-seven, there was still deep inside him the heart of a young boy. He played football with the same childlike joy and enthusiasm he displayed in the big snowball fight. Moving to Kansas City did not simply allow him to extend his football career. It gave him a chance to feel alive again, in a way he hadn't during those final two years in San Francisco.

"He had a real fire in himself," recalled Hackett. "A fire that was similar to the early years: 'Hey, I can still do this.'"

The goal that drove him to keep pushing himself was returning to the Super Bowl, and after winning a wild card berth to the playoffs, he was impressive in the first two games. Trailing the Pittsburgh Steelers by a touchdown with less than four minutes left, he drove the Chiefs into the red zone but faced a fourth-and-goal from the seven yard line with 1:48 remaining. The Cinderella story could have stopped there, but it didn't. With primary receiver J. J. Birden covered, his pass to little-used Tim Barnett sent the game into overtime, where Nick Lowery's 32-yard field goal sealed a 27–24 victory.

Afterward, in a jubilant Chiefs locker room, a reporter asked, "Did you realize it was fourth down on that pass to Barnett?"

The quarterback flashed an incredulous look. "Really? Was it fourth down?"

The Kansas City media was still learning his sense of humor, which often featured tongue planted firmly in cheek.

The following week, Montana rallied the Chiefs for three fourth-quarter touchdowns for a hard-fought 28–20 road win over the Houston Oilers, coached by old nemesis Buddy Ryan, which propelled the Chiefs to the AFC Championship Game for the first time since the merger. Suddenly the old warrior emerged as a sentimental favorite. Who could possibly pull against Joe Cool as he stood just one victory away from a record fifth Super Bowl?

During the early 1990s, roughly spanning the period from Saddam Hussein's invasion of Kuwait through the attack on Olympic skater Nancy Kerrigan, the Buffalo Bills owned the AFC, rolling up a cumulative record of 49 wins and 15 losses. Four straight years, Marv Levy's Bills advanced to the Super Bowl, carrying the banner of AFC pride, and promptly lost to superior NFC champions. Not even Denver swooned with such dependability. Featuring quarterback Jim Kelly, running back Thurman Thomas, and a swarming defense led by Bruce Smith, the team's all-time sack leader, Buffalo played host to Kansas City at Rich Stadium on a miserably cold, rainy, and windy January day. The breeze pushed the wind chill to 12 degrees.

From the start, Montana struggled. To grip the ball. To hit receivers. To stay vertical. And ultimately, to remember anything about the game he was playing.

Many of his passes wobbled erratically, way off target, as he completed just 9 of 23 attempts for 125 yards and one interception.

"I don't know if it was so much the wind as it was me," he said. "There were times I had guys open and I couldn't get the ball to them."

On the opening series of the third quarter, with the Bills leading 20–6, Montana faded back to pass. As the coverage disintegrated, he was slammed almost simultaneously by three different Bills: Bruce Smith from the left, and Phil Hansen and Jeff Wright from behind. As he tumbled to the ground, his head landed violently against the artificial surface.

Smith looked down and immediately knew he was hurt. "I asked him if he was okay. He didn't comprehend what I asked."

Once again, the disturbing sight of Montana sprawled across a football field caused fans across America to cringe.

Needing help to leave the field, he had suffered a concussion that cast the entire day in a fog. He was unable to remember the score or how the Bills amassed those 20 points.

"Everything went white," he explained when the grogginess began to wear off after Buffalo's 30–13 victory, which sent the Bills back to the Super Bowl. "They said it was more from the turf than from the hit, but I don't know. I just know that as soon as I landed everything went white, and I had a severe pain in my head."

The throbbing in his head would eventually subside, but the agony of falling one step short of a fifth Super Bowl may linger in his mind forever. He had escaped San Francisco and led a new team to the brink, reviving his career when many people thought he should have walked off into the sunset. By getting this far, he had proven he was not washed up. That he could still lead a team to within sight of the mountaintop. That he could still take the punishment and keep battling. But getting close was no consolation. Failure was a kind of torture, especially to be thirty-seven and know the clock was rapidly ticking to zero.

"I'm not sure how satisfying it is when you almost make it," Montana said many years later. "It hurts more when you almost make it than when you go home early."

On an electric evening at Mile High Stadium in October 1994, John Elway and Joe Montana traded blow after blow in one of the most memorable duels ever seen on *Monday Night Football*. It was like Ali versus Frazier. Magic versus Bird. McEnroe versus Borg. The midseason showdown of AFC West rivals featured two legendary quarterbacks with reputations for clutch performances, battling to 14–14 at the half and 21–21 entering the fourth quarter.

Late in the fourth, Elway, who engineered a record 35 fourth-quarter comebacks in his professional career, passed the Broncos into scoring position, then surprised the Chiefs with a perfectly timed quarterback draw, giving Denver a 28–24 lead. But Elway made one fateful error. He scored too quickly, leaving his rival one minute and twenty-nine seconds to pull off another miracle.

Carefully working the clock, Montana drove the Chiefs 75 yards in nine plays, completing 7 of 8 passes.

"We thought they'd concede some things, play deep, so we took the short gains," he said. "We did that and kept moving. We talked about it on the sideline: just be smart with the ball underneath."

In this climactic moment, it felt like Bill Walsh was right there with him, and of course, in a way, he was. His ethos was now synonymous with Montana, and every time Joe Cool led the Chiefs downfield with those short and intermediate routes, the idea behind the West Coast Offense was melded deeper into the fabric of professional football.

The game-winner came on a five-yard toss to Willie Davis, who caught the ball near the goal line and slipped just inside the right pylon with eight seconds left, giving Kansas City a dramatic 31–28 victory. It was the Chiefs' first win in Denver since 1983.

At the age of thirty-eight, Montana was still capable of unquestioned brilliance. No longer bothered by the hamstring that caused such problems in 1993, he appeared more nimble in fleeing the pocket while leading a roller coaster 9–7 season that earned the Chiefs another wild card bid to the playoffs. His 16 touchdowns remained below his statistical average in San Francisco, but he still completed 60.6 percent of his passes, spreading the ball among a capable group including wide receivers J. J. Birden and Willie Davis and running backs Marcus Allen and Kimble Anders.

By now, the living legend was one of the boys around the Chiefs' locker room, reverting to some of his old practical joking and absorbing grief about his fragile-looking physique and his scrambling. "He's out there trying to high-step but he looks like a big frog," teased center Tim Grunhard. "That's why we hold our breath when a pass doesn't get off in three seconds. We start thinking, 'Oh, no, he's gonna run! Throw it away, Joe, throw it away!'"

The mood was not quite so jovial heading into the second game of the season. Seventeen months after leaving San Francisco, Montana faced his old rival as the 49ers came to town. The bitterness lingered, despite the quarterback's attempt to downplay the showdown, which he insisted was merely "one of sixteen games on the schedule."

The man who took his job had led the league in passing for a second straight year in 1993, but after losing to the Cowboys in the NFC Championship Game once again, he remained trapped in Montana's enormous shadow. Steve Young owned the keys to the offense, but he was still trying to acquire the hearts and minds of San Francisco fans who longed for Joe Cool.

"I don't know if any quarterback can really say, 'You did it all,' unless you take a team to the Super Bowl," Young conceded. "There's no doubt as I line up this year, that's the number-one thing I hope to do."

The enormous buildup for the game suggested the possibility of a Super Bowl preview, but it was difficult to see beyond the very personal clash of two outstanding players, both headed for Canton, who were now forever linked. Young wanted to show he could best the man who kept tormenting him from afar. Montana wanted to prove he never should have been forced to take his act out of town.

Trying to wave off the media fascination, Young said, "You get on the field, it's still just reading defenses and blocking and everything else. All you can do is perform and let everything else take care of itself."

On this Montana would agree, but no game ever churned his emotions quite like Kansas City's 24–17 victory over San Francisco. While completing 19 of 31 with two touchdowns—including a rare tackle eligible pass and the Chiefs' first two-point conversion since the AFL days—he made a clear and unambiguous statement about his playing abilities against one of the best teams in the league.

"It was like playing your brother or your best friend," he said many years later. "And you always want to beat them worse than anybody."

Several weeks later, during a regular-season game in Buffalo, Bruce Smith and his punishing friends chased Montana all day, repeatedly knocking him to the same turf that had resulted in his concussion. After one violent slam, he pulled himself off the ground and walked up to Smith, much in the same way he had once approached Too Tall Jones during the cocky splendor of youth. But he was a different man now. He no longer had anything left to prove; he was starting to dread going off to work in the morning; and his rapidly aging body was beginning to overrule his heart.

"I'm too old for this," he said.

After missing two late-season games with a foot injury, the old man returned in time for a wild card game in Miami, where he dueled Dan Marino like it was 1984. The two Pennsylvania boys lit up the South Florida sky with nearly identical numbers while battling to a 17–17 halftime tie. "Like the Doublemint Twins in helmets and shoulder pads," surmised Tony Kornheiser of *The Washington Post*. Playing one of his most inspired games as a Chief, Montana completed 26 of 37 for 314 yards and two touchdowns, including a remarkable 12 of 15 in the first half, when he led Kansas City to two touchdowns and a field goal in three drives.

Trailing 27–17 in the fourth quarter, Montana piloted a long drive from deep in his own territory to the Miami five. It all looked very familiar, and millions of fans from coast to coast sat on the edge of their seats, invested once more in another comeback led by the immortal Joe Cool. Then he threw an interception. At the five yard line. In the playoffs.

The moment was jarring for a man who so often struck lightning in the clutch. It was sad. It was humbling. It was painful. Endings are often all of these things.

Several weeks later, he stopped by to see Carl Peterson. The quarterback began to express how much he loved Kansas City and how much he appreciated the opportunity the Chiefs had given him. Then he started explaining why he thought it was time for him to retire. Several times in recent years, he had talked about walking away, so much so that Jennifer had grown accustomed to the off-season dance. But he always reinvigorated. Now it felt different. Now he was talking about his lagging enthusiasm for the game, and his desire to spend more time with his young children.

By this point, Montana realized the Chiefs were a long shot for the Super Bowl, and the chance at a record fifth ring was the only real goal he had left in football. ("We are struggling," safety David Whitmore said around this time. "When a guy gets to the point in his career Joe's reached, he's not playing for anything but championships.") Peterson listened patiently, flashing back to the thought that had rattled around in his head on the day Montana arrived. *Two years.* He had squeezed two terrific years from a man who was supposedly over the hill, achieving a modern-day high-water mark for the franchise. (As of 2014, the Chiefs were still look-ing for their first playoff victory since 1993.) He counted himself and the Chiefs lucky.

"Joe, you know what? Lord, would I love to keep you here for another year! You've done so much for this organization . . ."

In his heart, Peterson sensed Montana was doing the right thing. He liked Joe and admired him. Deep down, he feared if the quarterback kept playing, it was only a matter of time before he sustained a hit that chased him to the sidelines for good. He didn't want to be the man to have to place an aging Montana on injured reserve, when he could no longer play. It was better this way.

"If you ask me, I think you've probably already retired in your mind."

Indeed. He was gone now as surely as he had departed San Francisco even before DeBartolo's Hail Mary.

Peterson advised him to think it over for a few days and call him back. When the phone rang and he heard the quarterback's voice, he knew. An era was over.

When his decision was announced, sportscasts across the country as-sumed a melancholy tone and sportswriters colored his various career obit-uaries with a widespread opinion: The greatest quarterback ever to play the game had just stepped off the stage.

Unlike so many other giants, including Joe Namath and Johnny Uni-tas, Montana walked away before he was pushed—not at the top of his game but still able to harness the furies, as his electric performance against the Dolphins demonstrated. His body was starting to wither, but it was his diminishing desire that prompted the decision. Playing football was starting to feel less like a game and more like a job. "I didn't think I would ever lose that passion for the game," he said. "I have lost the drive, more or less, to want to do what is necessary to compete in the NFL. It wasn't as much fun. I wasn't looking forward to it as much."

This decision may have been the greatest audible of his life. It protected his legacy. It prevented him from becoming Joe Namath.

In the spring of 1995, Jeff Petrucci arrived home from work and stopped at the mailbox. Walking into his house, Montana's onetime quarterbacks coach at Ringgold High School started flipping through his mail. One envelope caught his eye, and he ripped it open.

"You're not going to believe this," he yelled out to his wife, Melanie. "Jennifer just sent us an invitation to Joey's retirement party."

By this time, Petrucci had moved into administration after a successful coaching career. Even as the estrangement from Chuck Abramski deepened through the years, Montana stayed in close contact with Petrucci, who played a central role in his early development.

"I was in the right place at the right time," Petrucci said. "He's always given me credit, for whatever reason. I'm not exactly sure what I taught him. But he's never been too big for me. He's always remembered."

Many times through the years, the Montanas shared their important moments with the Petruccis, including San Francisco's first Super Bowl. Now Jennifer was planning a supersecret surprise party for her husband, and she knew he would want Jeff to be there.

"We really couldn't afford to go," Petrucci recalled. "But we couldn't afford not to go."

Not long after the invitations dropped in the mail for the private party, the city of San Francisco honored its greatest sports legend with "Joe Montana Day," complete with an outdoor ceremony at Justin Herman Plaza, attended by an estimated 30,000 screaming fans and emceed by Bill Walsh, who called his onetime pupil "the greatest football player of our time, most probably of all time."

When the program started, Carmen Policy stepped to the podium and introduced Carl Peterson as "the man who stole Joe Montana from San Francisco!"

Assaulted by a torrent of boos, the Chiefs' president felt like Lawrence Taylor strutting into Candlestick. Walking to the microphone, he looked out over the crowd, into the sea of fans dressed in number 16 San Francisco jerseys, waving signs proclaiming We LOVE YOU JOE and SAY IT AIN'T SO JOE. It was, truth be told, a throng larger than the 49ers drew for many home games when the quarterback first arrived all those years before. But now? Now was different. As Wayne Walker once remarked, "Who says this isn't a sports town?"

Staring out into this pulsating testimonial of eternal affection, Peterson decided to audible, slightly deviating from his brief prepared remarks. "We want to thank the city of San Francisco and the San Francisco 49ers for letting us *borrow* the greatest export of this wonderful city on the Bay! Joe Montana!"

As the place erupted in cheers, Peterson quickly returned to his seat, next to his wife, who leaned in and whispered, "Man, you got out of that one!"

"I never let Carmen forget that," Peterson said many years later. "I said, 'You son of a gun! You set me up so bad!' He said, 'I wanted to get you one more time for working me so hard on that trade.'"

The celebration came less than three months after the San Francisco 49ers defeated the San Diego Chargers, 49–26, in Super Bowl XXIX, extending the franchise's dominant run to five championships over a fourteen-year period. Steve Young passed for six touchdowns—breaking Montana's record—en route to the game's Most Valuable Player award. With each year, he placed a bit more distance between himself and the quarterback controversy, making the job his own, earning a reputation as one of the leading quarterbacks in the game while spending a total of thirteen years in San Francisco. He would throw more balls to Jerry Rice than his rival ever did. He would finish with a higher career passer rating. He would be inducted into the Pro Football Hall of Fame in 2005. But he would win just one Super Bowl, and he would never be as beloved as Joe Montana.

When the time arrived for the man of the hour to speak, he was a bundle of nerves. This sort of spotlight was difficult for him, and he dreaded it. He would have preferred to simply disappear from view, like some white-hat cowboy riding off into the sunset, but Joe Montana couldn't just slip away. His public needed him to show up and be adored, and when it was over, he would be glad. He would be glad he had taken the opportunity to say good-bye to all the fans who made him feel so appreciated.

"My career was like living a dream," he said as the crowd bathed him in thunderous applause and cheers. "Like all dreams, I woke up. It's time to move on."

Somehow, Jennifer kept the private party secret, inviting a large group of teammates, coaches, celebrities, and friends and tricking the guest of honor into thinking he was headed to a family function with the De-Bartolos.

Joe Sr. and Theresa insisted that the Petruccis ride to the party in their limo, and when they showed up at the the Flood Mansion, Jeff found himself surrounded by football royalty: Ronnie Lott, Jerry Rice, Jim Plunkett, Sam Wyche, John Taylor, Dwight Clark. He also spotted Huey Lewis and some people from Hollywood. He was a bit starstruck. He wished they were all wearing jerseys with names on the back, because some faces didn't quite register but he knew they were important.

After all the guests arrived, Jennifer and the DeBartolos showed up with Joe, who was completely blown away by all the friends who had flown in from across the country to celebrate his retirement. He looked happy. He looked genuinely touched by the gesture.

"Joe walked in and he had no clue whatsoever," Petrucci said. "Jennifer did a great job keeping the secret. He was really stunned."

When somebody introduced him to George Seifert, the two coaches talked shop for a while. Petrucci couldn't resist. He just had to ask the 49ers' boss *the* question: Was Steve Young really that much better of an athlete than Joe? Seifert did not hesitate: "Absolutely not." He would always remember the definitive answer. He would always remember the serious look on Seifert's face.

# CHAPTER TEN

# Homeward Bound

THE IDEA ORIGINATED WITH Don Devore, who was always the peacemaker in the group. He was out to dinner one night at the Eat'n Park on Main Street in Monongahela and happened to run into an old Ringgold teammate, Chuck Smith, a local businessman who was on the school board. The high school had relocated to a modern building on the outskirts of town, adjacent to the 43 turnpike, and the Ringgold Rams now played next door in a $1.8 million, 5,500-seat stadium with a FieldTurf surface. For several years, various citizens and former Rams had floated the notion of dedicating the football stadium in honor of the school's most illustrious alumnus.

"It's time to do it," Devore said to his old friend.

"You think so?"

"Yes. Why wait any longer?"

Joe Montana Stadium had a nice ring to it, but both men understood the issue was much more complicated than erecting a new sign.

More than thirty years after Montana started his march toward immortality with the Ringgold Rams, many of his old teammates remained embittered by the rift that could be traced to the off-season weight-training program. "There was always that animosity," Devore said. From time to time, the quarterback returned to the Mon City to see relatives, especially his beloved aunt Elinor, who owned, at the time of her death in 2012, what was believed to be the largest single collection of memorabilia and clippings concerning his career. If you lived in the area and desperately wanted Joe's autograph on a helmet or a football or a picture, sweet Elinor was always happy to handle the logistics. But most of the old Rams never saw him. Montana never called them to have a beer or share a meal, probably because he felt unwelcome, which deepened the feelings of disconnection. "Estrangement would be the right word," Devore said.

For Paul Timko, the grudge was especially personal. He never quite got over losing his job to Montana. "I had a hard time letting go of what happened," he said.

Like his rival, Timko envisioned playing quarterback for a big-time college program. But once Montana supplanted him, the trajectory of his life forever changed.

Even after they formed a powerful passing battery and became friendly, the resentment boiled below the surface. Early in his career at Notre Dame, Montana came home for the weekend and bumped into Timko at a local nightspot. They spent a few minutes catching up, two high school teammates sharing war stories about college. When Joe started expressing his frustrations about Dan Devine benching him for another player, Timko nodded and held his tongue. "I didn't say, 'Well, how does it feel?' Because that's exactly what happened to me. But I was thinking it," he recalled many years later.

Two lives pivoted on the position battle. Timko's dream of playing professional football never materialized, and while Montana became one of the greatest quarterbacks in football history, his high school rival became a carpet installer in Pittsburgh.

"Everything worked with Joe," Timko said. "He had not only the talent but many other things that it takes to get to the NFL [including] the ability not to question what his dad was doing. Everything just fell into place."

The way Chuck Abramski reacted to Montana's success exacerbated the tension. The repeated shots he took at his former quarterback in the media baffled many of his players, including Devore. "One time Coach Abramski was looking for something from Joe and he didn't have time for him or whatever, and it got ugly," he said. "He said, 'I'll never do that again. You guys are more important than him.' Well, we didn't want to hear that, 'cause everybody's important."

While Smith and a committee from the Rams Club, a Ringgold booster organization, began working through the school board to sell the stadium rededication politically, Devore and several others started trying to mend fences. The onetime offensive lineman had been pushing his old teammates for years to forgive and forget. "Why would Joe want to come back if nobody was going to be here for him?" Devore said.

The key was securing Abramski's participation. In his initial telephone call with his former coach, who was retired and living in New Castle, Abramski said he wouldn't attend the ceremony. He was still carrying a grudge. The thought of honoring Montana without Abramski was unacceptable to all those who were planning the event, including his aunt, Elinor Johnson, and former neighbor Bonnie Polonoli Kosh. Undeterred, Devore organized a small group of players and arranged to take Abramski out to dinner at Chuck Tanner's steak house in Pittsburgh. Soon after the delegation from Ringgold took their seats in a private dining room, Timko started razzing his old coach.

"Coach, do you know you changed history?" Timko said with a mischievous smile.

"How's that?"

"If you'd started me instead of Joe Montana, don't you realize how much history that would've changed?"

Abramski glared at him. "After thirty years, Timko, give it the fuck up!"

The table roared. Several other times during the night, Timko kept coming back to the same sore subject, good-naturedly needling his old coach as the boys told stories about the old days and enjoyed one another's company.

During a lull in the conversation, Devore started telling Abramski about the festivities they were planning for Montana and several other former Ringgold stars, finally looking him squarely in the eyes and insisting, "In order to make this work, we need you."

The eating and drinking lasted until the wee hours of the morning, and by the time the aging athletes dropped off their old coach, he was so happy, he agreed to attend the Ringgold Hall of Fame Weekend. The schmoozing worked. What happened when the two men were finally face-to-face, no one could reliably predict.

For a man who stiff-armed retirement so zealously for so long, Montana glided with apparent ease into the life of former athlete. After three years away from the sport, he told a reporter, "I miss the excitement of the game. I don't miss all the other stuff that went along with it—the work every day, traveling, training camps." He missed the camaraderie with the guys. He missed the adrenaline rush of third-and-long with a deficit on the scoreboard and a ticking clock. But he felt peace in the decision to walk away when he did, embracing his new life with enthusiasm. And he did not miss the glare of the spotlight. "What makes him comfortable is his home and kids and everyday life," Jennifer explained. "Not being put on a pedestal, not being called a hero every five minutes."

Toward the end of his playing career, Jennifer decorated their front lawn for Halloween with a skeleton she jokingly dubbed, "The Ghost of Joe Montana," because he was so frequently away from home. Now he was able to spend more time with his four children, who were all under ten when he retired, relishing the chance to catch up on all the things he had missed, sharing his daughters' interest in show horses and his sons' in football and other sports.

The primacy of family concerns surged to the forefront in 2006, when Montana became embroiled in a controversy with the league. After he turned down an invitation to participate in a ceremony featuring former Super Bowl MVPs prior to the fortieth anniversary game, a published source accused him of demanding a $100,000 appearance fee, which the NFL refused. Pointing out that he had been in Detroit for several days prior to the game representing a sponsor, he insisted he had never planned to stay for the game because of a conflict with his sons' athletic schedule. "I wasn't going to stay there for another three days," he said. "For what? To walk out on the field with a bunch of other once-weres for a few seconds of applause? I don't need that. I'd rather be at my boys' basketball games. The NFL wasn't happy with that. But that's okay. My boys were happy." During this period, he also took the NFL to court seeking workman's compensation for his various injuries—apparently motivated more by the principle at stake than the money, which he did not need—contributing to a tension that lingered for several years.

Moving into middle age, the old quarterback played a lot of golf with friends, including Huey Lewis and Bill Walsh, and indulged various other passions: Buying a winery in the Napa Valley, where he eventually began producing his own Montagna vintage; a single-engine airplane, which, once he obtained his pilot's license, allowed him to find a thrill above the clouds; and a piece of the Chip Ganassi racing team on the Indy racing circuit, which fueled his need to compete.

"I don't like looking back or living in the past," he said during this period. "I'd rather be doing something than watching somebody do something, so I try to find things that I can do."

The search for meaning led him to television, where he enjoyed a brief career as a football studio analyst for NBC Sports. But he never quite felt comfortable as a commentator who was expected to criticize athletes. He put his name and money to work in a series of businesses, including a beer distributorship in Kansas City, a venture capital firm in San Francisco (joining former teammates Ronnie Lott and Harris Barton), and several real estate deals, building a portfolio that would eventually produce a retail development adjacent to the Bay Area's new football stadium early in the twenty-first century. He continued to exploit his image to advertise various consumer products, including one especially close to his heart. After discovering he suffered from high blood pressure and high cholesterol, the self-described "junk-food junkie" signed on as a spokesman for the drug Lotrel and a healthy-eating campaign backed by Novartis Pharmaceuticals, maker of the medication. The thought that Joe Cool could have high blood pressure was hard for many baby boomers to fathom, sort of like Broadway Joe promoting Depends. The spots made everyone who had watched him on the field with such vicarious thrill feel a bit older. And many no doubt felt compelled to go see their doctor. His effectiveness as a pitchman would keep him in the advertising spotlight well into the second decade of the twenty-first century, including a series of spots for AT&T.

Once the initial retirement buzz faded and he began to get on with life after football, the first major milestone in the hardening of the Montana legend took place on an electric Monday night at Candlestick in December 1997, when he became the eighth 49er to have his jersey retired. The ceremony brought him back to the old stadium for the first time since the Niners traded him to Kansas City, generating a predictably loud and long ovation from a crowd starting to grow restless with the franchise's still-gathering downward spiral. The old quarterback appreciated the gesture and the warm reception, but confessed to a reporter, "I can't wait 'til it's over." Now more than ever, the adulation made him uncomfortable.

Even as he faded from public view, Montana still found it difficult to go anywhere without causing a stir. He and Jennifer still chose their dinner destinations carefully, and several years after his playing career ended, they were having a meal at a popular San Francisco restaurant called The Boulevard when old friends Sylvia and Wayne Walker walked through the front door. While the Walkers waited for a table at a little nook in the bar, Joe came over and visited—while kneeling on the floor. "There was no place for Joe to sit, and so he just got down on his knees and talked to us for at least ten minutes," Sylvia recalled. "He didn't care that there was no seat for him. Now, some celebrity athletes, that would be a big deal. Not Joe. God love him."

Many years after his last touchdown pass, Montana remained the most popular player in his ancestral homeland of Italy. One-time Cotton Bowl hero Kris Haines saw it in the faces of the players he coached in a European semipro league, especially after he told them Joe Cool was coming to tutor them. "The guys didn't believe he was coming," Haines said. "It seemed impossible to them, that the great Joe Montana was actually going to spend some time with them." The old Notre Dame teammates had a blast, and even though Haines understood that his friend was content to walk away from the game, he could see, in the way he interacted with the Italian players, Montana still loved the sport, and he could not help wondering what he might have been able to achieve as a coach. "His knowledge is just incredible. He'd be a great coach, if he had the desire to do that."

In July 2000, the quarterback faced yet another pressurized situation with little time left on the clock. He was headed out the door for one of the preinduction events at the Pro Football Hall of Fame when he discovered one of his children had drenched his necktie—the one Jennifer picked out to match the distinctive gold blazer presented to inductees— with water. A wet tie just wouldn't do. "Thankfully, there was a dryer in my room, and we got it all taken care of," he told the assembled media, Joe Cool coming through once more in the clutch.

Each new Hall of Famer chooses the person to induct him, and Montana's decision to anoint Eddie DeBartolo Jr. was a nod to their longtime friendship, which had endured even after his painful departure from San Francisco. Within three years, DeBartolo, implicated in a bribery ring involving Louisiana governor Edwin Edwards, would be forced to transfer control of the team to his sister, ending one of the most successful ownership periods in professional sports history. "Joe Montana, simply stated, was the greatest quarterback ever to play the game," DeBartolo said in his emotional introduction. "And I don't think we'll see the likes of him again."

Immortalized on the same day as his teammate Ronnie Lott as well as former 49ers defensive tackle Dave Wilcox (who played for San Francisco from 1964 to '74), Oakland Raiders' linebacker Howie Long, and Pittsburgh Steelers' executive Dan Rooney, Montana stepped to the podium as a record crowd of more than 18,000 leaped to their feet. Many wore red 16s. Looking a bit nervous, he cracked a couple of self-deprecating jokes and said something nice about every one of his fellow inductees, including special mention of Lott, whose friendship had never wavered, despite their disagreement concerning the 1987 players' strike. The forty-four-year-old legend joked that he initially had a difficult time believing the induction was for real, feeling "like I'm in my grave, in my coffin, alive . . . and they're . . . throwing dirt on me, and I can feel it, and I'm trying to get out."

Then he began to explain an epiphany he had experienced during the middle of the previous night, causing him to fumble for pen and paper after waking from a fitful sleep. "I've now seen the light," he said. "This is not an ending point . . . This is the beginning of the rest of my life, post-career, with a new team . . ."

Once more watching the clock with the pressure on, determined to keep his remarks under the prescribed eight minutes, he took the time to acknowledge a long list of people who had been influential on his career and his life, including Bill Walsh, his parents, his wife, his teammates, Carl Crawley, Jeff Petrucci, Sam Wyche, Eddie DeBartolo . . .

He even thanked Chuck Abramski.


Like his father, Chuck Smith planned to become a man of steel. The elder Smith spent thirty-five years in the mills, earning a good living and supporting a family in a place rife with opportunity. Everyone thought those days would last forever, including Chuck, who envisioned himself staying in Monongahela and following his old man's career path. "Steel was sort of the family business," he said. His brother and brother-in-law eventually embraced the employment legacy, planning their lives around the steady demand that stoked Pennsylvania's robust economic engine.

Football took Chuck in an entirely different direction. After he grew into a six-foot-four, 240-pound bruiser who dominated the line for the Ringgold Rams, Smith attracted 135 different scholarship offers, eventually choosing the University of West Virginia, where he starred for Bobby Bowden's Mountaineers while earning two degrees. "Football," he said, "was very good to me." In fact, football saved him from tripping into the trap of the family business. Following a brief career with the NFL's Cleveland Browns, Smith put his education to work with a white-collar job as a safety engineer in the chemical industry, migrating far from the Mon Valley, like so many others of his generation, as the steel mills entered the death spiral that eventually forced his brother and brother-in-law to the unemployment line.

Eager to spend more time with his wife and four young boys, Smith stepped off the corporate fast track in 1989. "I was traveling all the time for my job and I really wanted to do something else," he said. "What it came down to was, my family was more important than money."

More than fifteen years after leaving for college, Smith returned to his once-vibrant hometown, where the large number of vacant houses and storefronts told a story all too familiar across the vast Rust Belt.

"Chuck came back at a time when a lot of people were leaving," said Don Devore. The loss of thousands of steel and coal jobs—and thousands more in the various sectors that supported those heavy industrial workers—forced many people with deep roots in western Pennsylvania to seek opportunity elsewhere, including Devore's two children. Those who were determined to stay needed to reinvent themselves, against the battered relief of an area grappling for relevance in the postindustrial age. The despair swallowed many lives whole. "Some of my classmates, they've been looking for work for thirty years," Devore said.

In this difficult climate, Smith emerged as one of the leaders of a new era in the community's slow comeback, putting his money and expertise to work in launching a series of small businesses—including a transportation firm, a mobile home sales and rental agency, a mobile home park, and a restaurant—that provided jobs for his laid-off brother and brother-in-law, who eventually became his partners. Soon, he began a twenty-year tenure on the school board, dealing with the lingering effects of a decimated tax base, an aging infrastructure, and a dramatically transformed culture buffeted by the rise of single-parent households and latch-key children.

As the once-steady pulse of young boys playing football in backyards and vacant lots gradually faded—the younger generation no longer conditioned to see the sport as a defining measure of toughness, no longer imbued with the same impulse to compete—and Main Street evolved from a bustling center of commerce to a rather sleepy strip of antique shops and law offices, Devore presided over a critical link to Monongahela's past. Once the immediate area had provided ample business for seven different independent hardware stores. By the turn of the new millennia, only Devore Hardware remained, moving into its second century with the feel of a cultural relic, surviving and prospering by focusing on the kind of personal service difficult to find in the big-box stores located in the modern shopping centers up and down the big river. On any given day, the little shop stacked to the ceiling with hammers and nails and batteries and locks—where the owner answered the telephone and manned the cash register—was alive with conversation about their little corner of the world, much of it stoked by old-timers who slipped in the back door, poured a cup of coffee, and engaged Devore about the news of the day. Embedded in this scene was the heartbeat of a community battered but not broken, pulsing with the hopes and dreams of a new generation of parents who were determined to reach beyond the industrial decay to forge a new era of opportunity and aspiration for their children.

The conversation frequently turned to the Rams Club, a group of concerned citizens who found creative ways to supplement Ringgold's frequent budget shortfalls by raising nearly $1 million over a ten-year period for a wide range of needs: computers, microscopes, art supplies, a mentoring program, and after-school sports for at-risk teens.

"We let the teachers and administrators tell us what the needs are, especially for those kids who might be falling through the cracks of the system, and then we try to raise the money to make it happen," said Smith, who became one of the leaders of the effort.

Identifying eighty prominent Ringgold alumni—including Stan Musial, Ken Griffey Sr., and retired U.S. Army General Carl E. Vuono—the Rams Club began to leverage their success. One of the first to sign on to the campaign was Montana, who allowed the group to auction a long list of autographed items that generated thousands of dollars for his old school. When the bidding for a signed helmet reached $1,500, the quarterback graciously agreed to provide another for the fan who lost the auction—doubling the club's take with the stroke of a pen.

"Joe has bent over backward to help the youth of where he came from," Smith said.

Still, the tension was high when the Rams Club organized the community to honor Montana and three other legends prior to Labor Day in 2006 because no one knew what fireworks might transpire between the old quarterback and his old coach.

The Hall of Fame Weekend featured a banquet celebrating Montana, Musial, Griffey, and former NFL kicker Fred Cox, who played in four Super Bowls with the Minnesota Vikings, as well as the dedication of the Ringgold football field as Joe Montana Stadium, adorned with a giant sign featuring the quarterback in his most ubiquitous pose: wearing a 49ers uniform, arms extended triumphantly to the sky.

A big part of the motivation was infusing the current Ringgold students with a sense of possibility. "Show them, if you work hard, this is what you could be," Smith said.

More than a decade after taking his last snap, fifty-year-old Montana returned to his old school as an inspirational figure, a legend whose celebrity gave Ringgold students unmistakable pride, but for the members of the student body who crowded into the gymnasium and blanketed him in cheers, he was a largely abstract icon ripped from an aging highlight video. The youngest seniors had still been in diapers when Joe Cool captured the last of his four Super Bowls, and most knew him from his television commercials, not his on-the-field heroics. He was a man from the past, old enough to be their father, animated by their parents' breathless storytelling, and the lack of personal memories left the teenagers grappling to fully appreciate his journey from Monongahela to the history books.

Prior to a football game against nearby rival Indiana, after the new signage was unveiled and a burst of fireworks and blue and gold balloons filled the dusky sky, the quarterback told the large crowd: "Sometimes in a lifetime, something happens that goes beyond your wildest dreams and your wildest imagination. And that's what's happening here tonight."

Before the ceremony, a black stretch limousine pulled up to the stadium. Out walked Eddie DeBartolo, who soon slipped one of the organizers a check for $40,000, the biggest single donation in the history of the Rams Club. "Mr. DeBartolo offered to help with anything we needed," Devore said, calling the former 49ers owner a "very, very generous man." Because the hospitality tent was erected on school property, the bar served only nonalcoholic drinks, in observance of a strictly enforced policy. But DeBartolo was the sort of man for whom people made exceptions. When the visitor from Youngstown asked for a glass of wine to toast his friend,

Devore took matters into his own hands, sending one of the club members off in the limo to procure a bottle.

At a private gathering of the old Rams, inside the local fire hall, the bar was open and fully stocked. As the onetime teammates mingled, laughing and sharing stories, a photographer interrupted the festivities long enough to line everyone up for a group picture. All those years after he had initiated Montana into the starting quarterback's job with a bone-crunching sack, Chuck Smith, whose six-four frame now carried more than 330 pounds, playfully positioned himself in front of the man of the hour, eclipsing him completely. "Now take it!" he said with a laugh, before moving out of the way so they could all have a keepsake from a memorable evening.

Something profound happened that night. Everyone felt it. The tension wrought by the inevitable collision of competition, hurt feelings, jealousy, and tangled friendships dissipated into the cool September air, uniting the Rams in sober middle age in a way that had proved elusive during the stubborn days of youth. "We all felt good," Devore recalled. "Even Paul."

"We could never get Paul to even talk about [the animosity]," said Devore, one of his closest friends. "But that night . . ."

The two old rivals could be seen chatting casually. Determined to bust Montana's chops, Timko asked him, "When you wake up in the morning, do you have pain . . . ?"

"Yeah, I sure do . . ."

Timko knew the answer before he asked the question, and he flashed a sly grin. "You know what? I don't." Then he laughed, and Montana laughed, the price of fame and fortune reduced to something tangible for a couple of old athletes beginning to feel the weight of the creeping calendar. In this moment, the most destructive thought to rattle any middle-aged mind— *what might have been?*—began to lose its power over the man who was pushed aside to make way for Joe Cool. He began to make peace with Montana for winning. He began to make peace with himself for losing.

"If you can stretch yourself out of your selfishness, it really benefits you," a newly philosophical Timko explained several years later, trying to dissect the rivalry that he eventually described, in the wake of the reunion, as a friendship. "And back then, I didn't have that ability. Looking back, doing it all over again, I would've liked to have changed that. But I was too young to really understand . . ."

When Montana and Abramski found themselves alone in a corner of the room, many eyes darted nervously in their direction.

A measure of Montana's decency had been seen on the day of his induction into the Pro Football Hall of Fame six years earlier, when he lauded Abramski for doing "a tremendous, tremendous job . . . preparing kids not just for football but for later in life." This comment made its way into his prepared remarks despite the fact that the quarterback had been repeatedly blindsided by his coach in the media, for reasons that even Abramski's defenders struggled to explain. Now, as they met face-to-face for the first time in many years, the ether crackled with the echoes of all that swirling bitterness.

"Chuck loved Joe," Chuck Smith insisted. "I know he did. We talked about it. He wanted to make Joe a great football player, and there was always this disappointment in the way things happened."

What started out as a struggle between Montana's desire to be a multisport athlete and Abramski's insistence on making him 100 percent football player somehow metastasized into a conflict that undermined Montana's standing in his hometown.

"Joe'd bite his lip when he heard those things," said Jeff Petrucci. "He has to have ill feelings. If he doesn't, he's not normal. But he always went out of his way to not respond to that stuff."

As the rich, beloved, happily married father of four moved into the second half of his life, hailed far and wide as a Mount Olympus figure in the history of professional football, Chuck Abramski was not simply a disgruntled old coach. He was the last piece of unfinished business from Montana's football career.

The quarterback was unaware of the prodding it took to convince Abramski to attend the festivities, but when the two men began to talk, the players standing nearby could see them smiling and enjoying each other, acting "like gentlemen" in the words of Devore. "I heard them thank each other," Smith said.

More than 100 million people had watched each of Montana's four Super Bowl victories, but on an emotional night in 2006, in the back room of a fire hall not far from the big river, fewer than thirty witnessed one of the greatest moments of the old quarterback's life. When Chuck Abramski embraced him, hugging him like a son, every single man in the room felt the power of their reconciliation. The man from Monongahela had not merely returned to western Pennsylvania to take another bow. He had made peace with his past. He had found his way home.

Several years after Montana retired, a San Francisco television station aired one of the first segments to offer a glimpse into the next generation's budding athleticism. Young Nathaniel and Nicholas could be seen playing a game with their famous father, who eventually proclaimed, "Good going, guys, but Daddy wins again!"

Much like his own father, Montana encouraged a competitive environment with all of his children. When his boys gravitated to football, he and Jennifer made sure they enjoyed all of the opportunities a prosperous family could afford, without pushing them to contend with a legend's menacing shadow. Both Nathaniel and Nicholas starred as quarterbacks at De La Salle High School in the first decade of the twenty-first century and won major college scholarships.

On a bright autumn afternoon in 2012, Jeff and Melanie Petrucci were running a few minutes late. They had driven from Pennsylvania to West Virginia to watch Nate Montana play quarterback for Division II West Virginia Wesleyan. Kickoff had been moved up by half an hour, and by the time the Petruccis arrived, the game was under way and Joe and Jennifer Montana were lost somewhere in the crowd of perhaps five hundred who gathered to experience college football in its purest form. It was halftime when the couples finally found each other.

"I got to see a whole new side of Joe that day," Petrucci remembered. "He was this proud father, so into the game his son was playing. Just soaking up the joy of watching his son competing."

Highly recruited coming out of high school, Nate originally signed with Notre Dame and transferred to the University of Montana before winding up at West Virginia Wesleyan, where he impressed his father's old coach by passing for more than 400 yards, showing flashes of the old Montana touch. Around this time, younger brother Nick was working his way up the depth chart at Tulane, where he would eventually become the starting quarterback. It was impossible for the two players to separate themselves from their famous name, which proved to be both a blessing and a curse, but neither man would approach the athletic achievements of their iconic father.

Over dinner with the Montanas at a local hotel, Petrucci enjoyed talking X's and O's with the young quarterback. They spoke about favorite plays and the thrill of victory, and one thing Petrucci especially wanted to know: "How old were you when you realized who your father was?"

Nate flashed a puzzled expression, and the coach tried to explain.

"I mean, your dad is the standard by which everybody is measured for your position. How old were you when you figured out who your dad really was?"

Nate thought about the question for a moment and finally said, "Probably a sophomore in high school."

Petrucci smiled and nodded, pressing the moment into his memory.

"Kind of threw him a curveball," he recalled. "He really didn't know what to say, because to him, Joe wasn't this great quarterback we all watched. He wasn't this legendary figure. He was just Dad."

The debate will rage for as long as the game is played. Many knowledgeable observers insist Montana was the greatest quarterback who ever lived, while others prefer to make a case for Johnny Unitas, Tom Brady, Bart Starr, Otto Graham, or some other high-achieving passer from the sport's past. Ultimately, the argument rests on the definition one confers on the title, which makes determining the greatest quarterback of all time as fruitless as proclaiming the greatest hamburger or the greatest actor.

Even before Montana retired, some of the most high-achieving men to ever play the position repeatedly anointed him as the greatest in football history.

"I'm just an average Joe compared to him," Joe Namath said. "He's absolutely the best I've ever seen."

Bart Starr: "Vince Lombardi would have loved this guy . . . I think Montana's the best ever."

Roger Staubach: "Overall, Joe Montana has played the position better than anybody else ever has."

Fran Tarkenton: "There hasn't been a quarterback in my lifetime who has played so well for so long."

In the first two decades after he gathered his last snap, Joe Cool's place among the football immortals was repeatedly validated by various media institutions, including *The Sporting News,* which ranked him as the third-greatest player, regardless of position, in professional history, and the NFL Network, which rated him fourth all-time. *Sports Illustrated* named him the greatest clutch quarterback ever. ESPN proclaimed him the twenty-fifth greatest athlete—and top quarterback—of the twentieth century.

"If you ask me, in 2014, who's the greatest quarterback of all time, I won't even hesitate on the answer," said ESPN's Chris Berman. "It was Joe Montana. I don't even have to think about it."

Empirical evidence on the subject can be both demonstrative and irrelevant.

His four Super Bowl titles, just one short of Bart Starr's five overall league championships, testified to a level of team achievement matched only by Terry Bradshaw in the half century since the league started counting in Roman numerals. For a quarterback, nothing matters more than victories and championships, and no quarterback ever owned the Super Bowl like Joe Cool. It was his stage. In four trips to the big game, he completed 68 percent of passes for 11 touchdowns—without a single interception—compiling a gaudy passer rating of 127.8, which remained untouched two decades later.

Yet, as the aerial game grew more sophisticated because of the very forces he unleashed, making historical comparisons difficult to accurately calibrate, the man who approached the final years of his career with the highest passer rating in the history of the sport (92.3, weighted heavily by a once-astounding 63.2 completion percentage), slipped further and further down the list, eclipsed by a long list of outstanding players who followed behind his blocking, including Aaron Rodgers, Peyton Manning, and Tony Romo. Through 2014, he ranked tenth all-time in passing efficiency, far above many of the leading quarterbacks from the so-called dead-ball era, including Otto Graham (sixteenth), Roger Staubach (thirty-fourth), Bart Starr (fifty-sixth), and Johnny Unitas (seventy-sixth).

Like many of his old teammates, Steve Wallace saw flashes of Montana in Tom Brady, who grew up cheering for the 49ers before becoming the most coolly efficient quarterback of his time. While watching him lead the New England Patriots to three Super Bowl championships in four years in the first decade of the new century, Wallace found himself torn. "I have so much respect for Tom Brady," he said. "But I will not pull for him because I do not want him to break one of Joe Montana's records. Just can't do it."

But records are made to be broken, and Brady made a case for his own greatness in 2014 by winning his fourth Super Bowl, pulling even with Montana and Bradshaw, and shattering one of Montana's most enduring records: his forty-five career postseason touchdowns. (Serious Montana fans will point out that Brady needed four more playoff games to set a new standard.)

As the ethos at the heart of the West Coast Offense began to filter through the sport, and the passing game moved to the forefront, Montana became the standard for a new type of quarterback. The ability to make quick reads, get rid of the ball fast, exploit every inch of the field, audible aggressively, and throw with tremendous accuracy became valuable currency, pushing completion percentages to new heights and fostering a much more offensively oriented sport. As the precision needed to consistently complete a seven-yard pass became more important than the power to stand in the pocket and drill a 50-yard bomb, it was a measure of his undeniable influence. As every offense in the league began to flood the field with eligible receivers, placing a new premium on distributing the ball wisely, his fingerprints were easy to see. As teams began making wide receivers out of the kind of big, tall, strong athletes who might have played professional basketball a generation ago, it was a change inexorably linked to the revolution he helped to unleash.

"Fifty years ago," noted Dan Fouts, "if you completed half your passes, that was good. And if you threw the same amount of interceptions as you did touchdowns, that was okay. Now if you did either one of those things, you'd never play. Joe's success played a big part in creating a new emphasis on accuracy. Suddenly the old standards weren't good enough anymore."

By breaking the mold and injecting his DNA into a long list of quarterbacks from Peyton Manning to Drew Brees, Montana helped usher in a new age, administered by a new group of gatekeepers applying a different set of empirical tests, each one of them, consciously or not, looking for the next Joe Cool.

But Montana's ultimate legacy to the sport was something far more visceral, something everyone who invested the game with such meaning could instinctively understand. It was the reason we watched with a quivering pulse in the closing moments of a tight game. It was the thought his name conjured in even the most dire circumstances. Every time he led a team back from certain defeat, he reinforced a larger truth that connects football to life itself: As long as the scoreboard glows, anything is possible. Sometimes magic can happen. By harnessing a power to lead all those improbable comebacks, he did not simply make us appreciate Joe Montana. He reminded us why we loved the game.

For as long as the memories endure, Joe Montana will be the man who won the Cotton Bowl with hypothermia . . . the man who engineered The Catch against all odds by sending Dwight Clark into the clouds . . . the man who returned from back surgery in fifty-five days . . . the man who withstood the challenge of a younger, stronger man to write the most remarkable chapter of his career. He was not just a winner; he was a man who repeatedly overcame tremendous obstacles in order to achieve victory. The championships made him one of the most significant figures in football history. The struggle made him Joe Montana.

# Acknowledgments

Whenever you spend four years on a project, as I have with this book, the list of accumulated debts is inescapably long.

First and foremost, I want to acknowledge the significant role David Black, my long-time literary agent, played in bringing this book to life. Thanks for everything, David.

This is my fourth book with the Thomas Dunne Books imprint of St. Martin's Press, and my latest collaboration with TDB's executive editor / associate publisher Pete Wolverton, whose guiding hand was crucial in making this book hit all the right notes. Thanks also to assistant editor Emma Stein and all the great folks at St. Martin's Press, including publicity director Joseph Rinaldi.

I am especially grateful to a long list of Montana's teammates, coaches, friends, and rivals who agreed to be interviewed, including Don Devore (who was my go-to go in Monongahela on various things—thanks so much Don!), Jeff Petrucci, Paul Timko, Carl Crawley, Ulice Payne, Craig Gary, Tom Caudill, Steve Russell, Alan Veliky, Chuck Smith, Ara Parseghian, Steve Orsini, Ken MacAfee, Vagas Ferguson, Daniel "Rudy" Ruettiger, Kris Haines, Ross Browner, Bob Crable, Dan Fouts, Steve Bartkowski, Zeke Bratkowski, Terry Donahue, Don McNeal, Earl Cooper, Eason Ramson, Randy Cross, Johnny Davis, Wayne Walker, Huey

Lewis, Sylvia Walker, Spencer Tillman, Guy McIntyre, Bruce Collie, Steve Wallace, and Carl Peterson.

Thanks also to several media colleagues who helped in various ways, including my friend Ron Barr, the San Francisco–based radio host who played a crucial role in bringing Montana and Walsh together, as well as *Sports Illustrated*'s Douglas S. Looney, the *San Francisco Examiner*'s Art Spander, ESPN's Chris Berman, long-time Notre Dame announcer Paul Hornung, San Francisco-based author Steve Travers, and two friends from *The Kansas City Star*: Blair Kirkhoff and Randy Covitz.

The narrative owes a debt to a lengthy list of books that informed my knowledge of Montana, Walsh, the San Francisco 49ers, the NFL, and the larger culture of the time. This includes two autobiographies: *Audibles*, which Montana coauthored with Bob Raissman, and *Montana*, which Montana coauthored with Dick Schaap.

Among the various books that have been written about San Francisco's NFL franchise, I found *Glenn Dickey's 49ers* particularly authoritative. Dickey, who covered the Montana years and beyond for the *San Francisco Chronicle*, brings an insider's knowledge to the subject that I found very compelling, and extremely helpful in developing a sense of Montana's rise.

My understanding of Walsh was bolstered by two very good books: *The Genius*, David Harris' definitive biography of the coach, as well as *Building a Champion*, which Walsh coauthored with Glenn Dickey.

Gary Myers' *The Catch*, which focused on the San Francisco-Dallas showdown in January 1982, is full of wonderful detail and insights, which allowed me to better understand a turning point in NFL history.

Other books that proved helpful included *Total Impact* by Ronnie Lott and Jill Lieber; *Rice* by Jerry Rice and Michael Silver; *America's Game* by Michael MacCambridge; *Simply Devine* by Dan Devine and Michael R. Steele; *The Blind Side* by Michael Lewis; *Season of the Witch* by David Talbot; *Best of Rivals* by Adam Lazarus; *Parcells* by Bill Parcells and Nunyo Demasio; *Steve Jobs* by Walter Isaacson; *The League* by David Harris; and *Resurrection* by Jim Dent.

In writing history books, I stand on the shoulders of many sportswriters who performed their jobs so capably decades ago. Specific quotations appear in the source notes, but I also want to take this opportunity to acknowledge my gratitude to the *San Francisco Chronicle, San Francisco Examiner, San Jose Mercury News, The New York Times, Sports Illustrated, USA TODAY, The Kansas City Star,* and the *South Bend Tribune.* The detailed game accounts, news coverage and analysis left behind by these news organizations and various others all those years ago provided a great road map concerning Montana's career.

Several excellent magazine features proved invaluable in my attempt to understand and explain the arc of Montana's life, including "You've Got It Made, JoeMontana," by Curry Kirkpatrick in *Sports Illustrated*; "What Price Glory?" by Bob Raissman in *Inside Sports*; "State of the Art" by Irvin Muchnick in *The New York Times Magazine*; "Born to be a Quarterback" by Paul Zimmerman in *Sports Illustrated*; "Montana Fading Out" by Tom Junod in *GQ*; "Montana's Cool Days and Hot Nights" by Glenn Dickey in *Inside Sports*; and "An American Dream" by Leigh Montville in *Sports Illustrated*.

The good folks at the University of Notre Dame have my sincere thanks, especially John Heisler and Carol Copley, who helped me track down former players.

Once again, my job was made much easier by the outstanding archival operation at the Pro Football Hall of Fame, where Jon Kendle went out of his way to help me in numerous ways. Thanks also to the Elias Sports Bureau for help in verifying several key statistics.

Last but not least, thanks to my family and friends scattered across the country who helped me in various ways as *Montana* negotiated several possession downs and kept moving toward the endzone.

# Notes

Unless otherwise indicated, all direct quotes were taken from interviews conducted by the author.

## ONE: THE FIRST CRACK

3 "When I was a kid": *Sports Illustrated,* August 6, 1990.

4 "He used to wreck his crib": *Sports Illustrated,* August 6, 1990.

5 "Grabbed . . . pushed . . . [and] threw": Joe Montana and Dick Schaap, *Montana* (Atlanta: Turner Publishing, 1995).

5 "Joe thrives on competition": *The Plain Dealer,* January 18, 1982.

7 "I was really concentrating": Joe Montana and Dick Schaap, *Montana* (Atlanta: Turner Publishing, 1995).

8 "I think that was": *The Plain Dealer,* January 18, 1982.

14 "The players on the teams": Joe Montana and Dick Schaap, *Montana* (Atlanta: Turner Publishing, 1995).

20 "Every day he just beat": *Sports Illustrated,* August 6, 1990.

23 "Once he walked on the field": ESPN SportsCentury documentary, July 30, 1999.

23 "If you didn't know Joe": *Sports Illustrated,* September 4, 1985.

25 "The combination": *The Daily Herald,* October 2, 1972.

25 "A moral victory": *The Daily Herald,* October 2, 1972.

26 "Joe was very coachable": *Observer-Reporter,* February 4, 1989.

28 "The next Joe Namath": *Pittsburgh Post-Gazette,* September 7, 1973.

28 "Let's put it this way": *Pittsburgh Post-Gazette,* September 7, 1973.

28 "We have to stop Montana": *Pittsburgh Post-Gazette,* September 8, 1873.

## TWO: GREEN JERSEYS

35 "Play varsity as a freshman": *The Daily Herald,* March 7, 1974.

36 "No one cared": Joe Montana and Bob Raissman, *Audibles: My Life in Football* (New York: William Morrow, 1986).

36 "I am emotionally and physically": *South Bend Tribune,* December 16, 1974.

37 "I was pretty rough": Dan Devine with Michael R. Steele, *Simply Devine* (Champaign, Illinois: Sports Publishing, 2000).

39 "I saw that the cornerback": *South Bend Tribune,* October 12, 1975.

39 "My biggest victory": *South Bend Tribune,* October 12, 1975.

40 "I'd hate to single out Joe": *South Bend Tribune,* October 19, 1975.

41 "Sure, I'd like to start": *South Bend Tribune,* October 19, 1975.

43 "He looks like a parish priest": *Los Angeles Times,* October 23, 1977.

44 "I feel bad for Joe": *South Bend Tribune,* September 2, 1976.

44 "At the time": *Sports Illustrated,* August 6, 1990.

46 "When you come off": *South Bend Tribune,* September 23, 1977.

49 "I'll be dreaming": *South Bend Tribune,* September 23, 1977.

51 "A great psychological lift": *South Bend Tribune,* October 23, 1977.

51 "Go and kick some butt": Football history section, und.com.

53 "We were a high-profile": Pamela Ryckman, *Stiletto Network* (New York: Amazon, 2013).

53 "Rushed into": Joe Montana and Bob Raissman, *Audibles: My Life in Football* (New York: William Morrow, 1986).

56 "Everything just went perfect": *South Bend Tribune,* January 2, 1978.

57 "I usually try to hold": *South Bend Tribune,* January 3, 1978.

57 "It's not how you start": Football history section, und.com.

## THREE: CHICKEN SOUP

61 "If you are living near": *The Tuscaloosa News*/Associated Press, January 1, 1979.

62 "We are defending": *South Bend Tribune,* September 1, 1978.

63 "I needed to have the time": *South Bend Tribune,* October 15, 1978.

63 "You give a passer like Montana": *South Bend Tribune,* October 15, 1978.

63 "We might have been too": *South Bend Tribune,* November 26, 1978.

63 "It was a remarkable comeback": *South Bend Tribune,* November 26, 1978.

65 "Garbage": *Sports Illustrated,* January 8, 1979.

66  "I felt like I was sitting": Joe Montana and Dick Schaap, *Montana* (Atlanta: Turner Publishing, 1995).

69  "I wanted to get back": Joe Montana and Dick Schaap, *Montana* (Atlanta: Turner Publishing, 1995).

69  "Extreme chilling": CBS television broadcast, January 1, 1979.

70  "Right then our whole bench": *South Bend Tribune,* January 2, 1979.

73  "I didn't have second thoughts": *The New York Times,* January 2, 1979.

74  "You get in a certain mode": *Inside Sports,* August 1991.

74  "So it all comes down": CBS television broadcast, January 1, 1979.

74  "Do you want to get in two": Dan Devine with Michael R. Steele, *Simply Devine* (Champaign, Illinois: Sports Publishing, 2000).

75  "Joe, let's run a 91": Dan Devine with Michael R. Steele, *Simply Devine* (Champaign, Illinois: Sports Publishing, 2000).

75  "If your first pass": Dan Devine with Michael R. Steele, *Simply Devine* (Champaign, Illinois: Sports Publishing, 2000).

76  "I went to the short side": *South Bend Tribune,* January 2, 1979.

77  "Every kicker fantasizes": *The New York Times,* January 2, 1979.

77  "These players have done it": *The New York Times,* January 2, 1979.

78  "At the time": *The Dallas Morning News,* January 10, 1982.

78  "Suffering a cold": *The New York Times,* January 2, 1979.

78  "Unbelievable!": CBS television broadcast, January 1, 1979.

## FOUR: NUMBER EIGHTY-TWO

81  "What happened in Cincinnati": David Harris, *The Genius* (New York: Random House, 2008).

84  "I knew I had to lay it": *The New York Times,* June 19, 2012.

92  "Most of the stuff we did": Joe Montana and Bob Raissman, *Audibles: My Life in Football* (New York: William Morrow, 1986).

93  "He was quick": David Harris, *The Genius* (New York: Random House, 2008).

93  "I knew of his inconsistency": *Sports Illustrated,* September 4, 1985.

96  "I learned more football": Bill Walsh with Glenn Dickey, *Building a Champion* (New York: St. Martin's Press, 1990).

97  "Are you with the 49ers?": Gary Myers, *The Catch* (New York: Three Rivers Press 2009).

98  "Joe was wonderful": David Harris, *The Genius* (New York: Random House, 2008).

99  "Keep your knees bent": David Harris, *The Genius* (New York: Random House, 2008).

99  "Every drop-back I did": Joe Montana and Bob Raissman, *Audibles: My Life in Football* (New York: William Morrow, 1986).

99 "Credibility that gained him": Bill Walsh with Glenn Dickey, *Building a Champion* (New York: St. Martin's Press, 1990).

101 "As soon as you made a mistake": *The New York Times,* October. 15, 1981.


## FIVE: THE CATCH

107 "It's very hard to go back": *Sports Illustrated,* September 4, 1985.

107 "A lot of people in Monongahela": *Baltimore Sun,* January 22, 1990.

107 "I never knew a thing about it": *Sports Illustrated,* August 6, 1990.

107 "Joe broke my heart": *The Plain Dealer, Baltimore Sun,* January 22, 1990.

108 "If I was in a war": *Baltimore Sun,* January 22, 1990.

109 "Jonestown released a poison cloud": David Talbot, *Season of the Witch* (New York: Free Press, 2012).

112 "We're still not where I'd like": *The Christian Science Monitor,* November 3, 1981.

112 "Bill told me I was going to be": Joe Montana and Bob Raissman, *Audibles: My Life in Football* (New York: William Morrow, 1986).

113 "I admired [DeBerg]": Joe Montana and Dick Schaap, *Montana* (Atlanta: Turner Publishing, 1995).

113 "I never thought about downing": *Philadelphia Inquirer,* September 21, 1981.

115 "The idea is": *Inside Sports,* August 1989.

116 "I want them saying over and over": David Harris, *The Genius* (New York Random House, 2008).

116 "There has been a metamorphosis": *Football Digest,* January 1982.

116 "As an instinctive player": *Philadelphia Inquirer,* January 23, 1982.

118 "Taylor is a super football player": New York *Daily News,* January 6, 1982.

120 "A cross between the Pope": Skip Bayless, *God's Coach* (New York: Simon Schwfer, 1990).

121 "They didn't beat the real": Gary Myers, *The Catch* (New York: Three Rivers Press, 2009).

121 "All you have to do": Gary Myers, *The Catch* (New York: Three Rivers Press, 2009).

122 "A fairy tale": Joe Montana and Bob Raissman, *Audibles: My Life in Football* (New York: William Morrow, 1986).

122 "[Clark's] ability was the key": Joe Montana and Bob Raissman, *Audibles: My Life in Football* (New York: William Morrow, 1986).

124 "The Cowboys were just": *San Francisco 49ers: The Complete History* (NFL Films DVD, 2006).

125 "Handled himself": *Cleveland Plain Dealer,* December 24, 1984.

125 "Joe spearheaded a confidence": ESPN SportsCentury documentary, July 30, 1999.

125 "I thought that was the": *San Francisco Examiner,* January 11, 1982.

126 "The word 'choke' kept passing": Joe Montana and Bob Raissman, *Audibles: My Life in Football* (New York: William Morrow, 1986).

126 "As soon as you see": *San Francisco 49ers: The Complete History* (NFL Flims DVD, 2006).

127 "When I saw it": ESPN.com, December 5, 2013.

127 "Instead of floating": ESPN SportsCentury documentary, July 30, 1999.

127 "History was just made": ESPN SportsCentury documentary, July 30, 1999.

127 "I knew Dwight had it": *Football Digest*, April 1991.

127 "It ended up being": *San Francisco 49ers; The Complete History* (NFL Films DVD, 2006).

128 "I'm so proud": *San Francisco 49ers; The Complete History* (NFL Films DVD, 2006).

129 "I've got the radio on": *Sports Illustrated*, January 26, 1996.

129 "The most resourceful": *The Christian Science Monitor*, January 12, 1982.

130 "This is it!" Bill Walsh with Glenn Dickey, *Building a Champion* (New York: St. Martin's Press, 1990).

132 "He's one of the coolest": *Football Digest*, May/June 1982.

133 "The whole experience": Ronnie Lott with Jill Lieber, *Total Impact* (New York: Doubleday, 1991).

133 "Seeing the outpouring": David Talbot, *Season of the Witch* (New York: Free Press, 2012).

## SIX: THE ART OF REINVENTION

135 "What Joe had": Bill Walsh and Glenn Dickey, Building a Champion (New York: St. Martin's Press, 1990).

135 "What do we have": Bill Walsh with Glenn Dickey, *Building a Champion* (New York: St. Martin's Press, 1990).

135 "It helped our players": Michael MacCambridge, *America's Game* (New York: Anchor Books, 2004).

136 "The almost clinical atmosphere": Bill Walsh with Glenn Dickey, *Building a Champion* (New York: St. Martin's Press, 1990).

141 "There's no magic": *The Argus-Press*, January 24, 1994.

142 "If the 49ers are wearing": Joe Montana and Bob Raissman, *Audibles: My Life in Football* (New York: William Morrow, 1986).

144 "Joe's mechanics": *San Francisco Chronicle*, July 25, 2000.

144 "Sometimes Joe": *Newsday*, February 14, 1989.

144 "Find something when": *Sports Illustrated*, November 22, 1988.

144 "Montana is the guy": *The Atlanta Journal*, January 14, 1985.

144 "Joe Montana stretches": *Sports Illustrated*, September 4, 1985.

144 "Montana's eyes are so fast": *The New York Times*, Nov. 12, 1990.

146 "Joe could be in the most": *San Francisco Chronicle*, July 25, 2000.

146 "We knew he was the guy": *Sports Illustrated*, August 13, 1990.

146 "I don't go seeking pressure": *Sport*, July 1990.

146 "It wasn't that I played": *Sports Illustrated*, January 22, 1996.

146 "Like watching a seminar": Bill Walsh with Glenn Dickey, *Building a Champion* (New York: St. Martin's Press, 1990).

147 "My husband hasn't had many": *Inside Sports*, August 1982.

147 "Joe Montana, have you": *Inside Sports*, August 1982.

147 "Successes": *Inside Sports*, August 1982.

147 "But you know": *Inside Sports*, August 1982.

148 "I've done everything": *Inside Sports*, August 1982.

149 "What you have to understand": David Harris, *The League* (New York, Banton, 1986).

151 "There were some bitter feelings": *Los Angeles Times*, September 23, 1987.

152 "There was anger": *Sport*, October 1985.

152 "A lot of bad-mouthing": Joe Montana and Bob Raissman, *Audibles: My Life in Football* (New York: William Morrow, 1986).

153 "When it's third-and-six": *Gameday*, volume XIV, number no. 9, 1983.

153 "It's taking away": Glenn Dickey, *Glenn Dickey's 49ers* (Roseville, California: Prima Publishing, 2000).

154 "Joe is a coach's ideal": Bill Walsh with Glenn Dickey, *Building a Champion* (New York: St. Martin's Press, 1990).

155 "They're both very competitive": *San Francisco Chronicle*, December 28, 1987.

156 "Offensively, we sputtered": *Philadelphia Inquirer*, September 4, 1983.

157 "The best I've ever": *Sports Illustrated*, October 3, 1983.

157 "I'm just in awe": *Philadelphia Daily News*, October 17, 1983.

158 "It was just a reflex": Associated Press, October 24, 1983.

158 "To come back": *Lexington Herald-Leader*/Associated Press, October 24, 1983.

158 "[The defense] confused me": David Harris, *The Genius* (New York: Random House, 2008).

159 "The defense kept us": *Miami Herald*/Associated Press, January 1, 1984.

160 "They have different": *The Miami Herald*, January 1, 1984.

160 "Montana is": Associated Press, January 2, 1984.

160 "No one": *Miami Herald*, January 6, 1984.

160 "Like riding on a twisting": Ronnie Lott with Jill Lieber, *Total Impact* (New York: Doubleday, 1991).

161 "I thought we could set": *Miami Herald*, January 9, 1984.

161 "I went outside": *Miami Herald*, January 9, 1984.

162 "It's my fault": *Miami Herald*, January 9, 1984.

162 "They're trying": *Miami Herald*, January 9, 1984.

163 "That's the kind of gesture": *Inside Sports*, August 1989.

165 "Football is a game": *San Diego Union*, January 21, 1985.

165 "They take the four": (Torrance) *Daily Breeze,* October 29, 1984.

165 "The way our offense": (Torrance) *Daily Breeze,* October 29, 1984.

165 "Out of my system": *Sport,* October 1985.

165 "Man for man": Joe Montana and Bob Raissman, *Audibles: My Life in Football* (New York: William Morrow, 1986).

165 "We were going to do": Joe Montana and Bob Raissman, *Audibles: My Life in Football* (New York: William Morrow, 1986).

166 "Even when we were": Bill Parcells and Nunyo Demasio, *Parcells* (New York: Crown, 2014).

168 "The quickest arm": *The Philadelphia Inquirer,* November 7, 1984.

168 "Phenomenal": *The Philadelphia Inquirer,* November 7, 1984.

168 "Scary": *The Philadelphia Inquirer,* November 7, 1984.

169 "I don't remember": *Lexington Herald-Leader*/Associated Press, November 5, 1984.

170 "They took us to school": *Sacramento Bee,* December 24, 1984.

170 "He has surprised": *Sacramento Bee,* December 24, 1984.

170 "There is a lot of talk:" *Sacramento Bee,* December 29, 1984.

170 "Sometimes our offense": *Lexington Herald-Leader*/Associated Press, December 30, 1984.

171 "As artistic as we'd like": *Lexington Herald-Leader*/Associated Press, December 30, 1984.

173 "We speeded up": Bill Walsh with Glenn Dickey, *Building a Champion* (New York: St. Martin's Press, 1990).

174 "That's why Joe Montana": *San Francisco Examiner,* January 15, 1985.

174 "I'm just an ordinary Joe": *The Dallas Morning News,* January 18, 1985.

175 "Joe's very confident": *The Dallas Morning News,* January 18, 1985.

177 "About as perfect a game": *San Diego Union,* January 21, 1985.

178 "They drilled us": *San Diego Union,* January 21, 1985.

178 "Almost perfect": David Harris, *The Genius* (New York: Random House, 2008).

178 "We felt like we were": Bill Walsh with Glenn Dickey, *Building a Champion* (New York: St. Martin's Press, 1990).

178 "The 49ers looked better": New York *Daily News,* January 21, 1985.

178 "[Montana] was outstanding": *Los Angeles Times,* January 21, 1985.

178 "Marino is a great": Associated Press, January 21, 1985.

179 "All week, all we heard": *Los Angeles Times,* January 21, 1985.

179 "I'm sure it motivated": *Los Angeles Times,* January 21, 1985.

## SEVEN: NO PAIN, NO FAME

182 "There ought to be a bigger": ABC broadcast, Super Bowl XIX, January 20, 1985.

183 "Are you kidding": *Gameday,* September 1982.

185 "The hardest part": *Gameday,* September 1982.

185 "My football career could end": *San Jose Mercury News,* January 20, 1991.

185 "Relax. The sheriff always": *Inside Sports,* January 1985

186 "I felt like a mother": *Inside Sports,* January 1985.

186 "The best show": *San Francisco Chronicle,* August 12, 1984.

187 "This image of the athlete": *Sports Illustrated,* September 4, 1985.

187 "One morning in the summer": *Sports Illustrated,* September 4, 1985.

187 "To dodge the light": *Team NFL* magazine, September 1991.

190 "[Montana] didn't say it": Jerry Rice and Michael Silver, *Rice* (New York: St. Martin's Griffin, 1996).

190 "He was trying": Jerry Rice and Michael Silver, *Rice* (New York: St. Martin's Griffin, 1996).

191 "I've taken one": *Los Angeles Times,* November 14, 1985.

191 "Joe Montana sightings": *Los Angeles Times,* November 14, 1985.

191 "I wish there was": *USA Today,* November 14, 1985.

191 "I can categorically say": *The Washington Times,* November 14, 1985.

191 "I think by confronting": Bill Walsh with Glenn Dickey, *Building a Champion* (New York: St. Martin's Press, 1990).

192 "Wasn't the end of": Joe Montana and Dick Schaap, *Montana* (Atlanta: Turner Publishing, 1995).

192 "Everyone wants a piece": *Sports Illustrated,* September 4, 1985.

192 "I am two different people": *San Francisco Chronicle,* December 28, 1987.

192 "It reached the point": *Team NFL* magazine, September 1991.

193 "I just sat there thinking", *Sports Illustrated,* August 6, 1990.

195 "When he was getting up": *Pittsburgh Press,* December 3, 1985.

195 "What do you think": Bill Parcells and Nunyo Demasio, *Parcells* (New York: Crown, 2014).

195 "You could knock": ESPN SportsCentury, July 30, 1999.

196 "I knew this time": *Sports Illustrated,* November 17, 1986.

196 "I was real scared": *The Sporting News,* December 8, 1986.

196 "We'll have to wait": *USA Today,* September 15, 1986.

196 "We expect to face": *Cleveland Plain Dealer/*Associated Press, Sept.ember 18, 1986.

196 "It was hard to tell which": *The Sporting News,* September 29, 1986.

198 "The most difficult task": Associated Press, November 8, 1986.

198 "You don't replace a Joe Montana": *49ers Report,* September 28, 1986.

198 "My legs were wobbly": *49ers Report,* October 5, 1986.

198 "He looked and acted": *The Sporting News,* December 8, 1986.

198 "Watching him stumble" *Sports Illustrated,* November 17, 1986.

199 "You're physically able": *The Sporting News,* December 8, 1986.

200 "The underlying basis": Joe Montana and Bob Raissman, *Audibles: My Life in Football* (New York: William Morrow, 1986).

200 "All we're doing": *Cleveland Plain Dealer/*Associated Press, August 17, 1986.

200 "I know there's a campaign": *The Sporting News,* November 10, 1986.

201 "An electric chill": *San Francisco Chronicle,* November 10, 1986.

201 "We're all crazy": *Cleveland Plain Dealer*/Associated Press, November 11, 1986.

202 "You're a helluva man": *Sports Illustrated,* November 13, 1986.

202 "He's like Lazarus": *Sports Illustrated,* September 19, 1994.

202 "He's a tough": *The Sporting News,* November 17, 1986.

202 "The greatest comeback": *Los Angeles Times,* August 9, 1987.

203 "I didn't want to hurt": Associated Press, January 4, 1987.

204 "I wanted to jump": *The Sporting News,* April 24, 1995.

## EIGHT: THE OTHER MAN

206 "Fred, don't you": *The Sporting News,* April 24, 1995.

208 "This really is": *The Repository* (Canton, Ohio), November 27, 1987.

208 "He's clearly on": *San Francisco Chronicle,* March 12, 1987.

211 "Most coaches": Bill Walsh with Glenn Dickey, *Building a Champion* (New York: St. Martin's Press, 1990).

211 "This move is not a reflection": *San Francisco Chronicle,* April 25, 1987.

211 "A genius in coaching": *San Francisco Chronicle,* April 25, 1987.

211 "I'm not here": *San Francisco Chronicle,* May 15, 1987.

211 "Joe is doing things": *USA Today,* March 2, 1987.

212 "The biggest part": *Football News,* April 1987.

212 "If I had wanted to retire": *San Francisco Chronicle,* May 15, 1987.

212 "I have to lose it": *San Francisco Chronicle,* May 15, 1987.

212 "Sure, you wonder": *San Francisco Chronicle,* May 15, 1987.

212 "I want to make it as difficult": *San Francisco Chronicle,* May 15, 1987.

213 "Anytime you have": Jerry Rice and Michael Silver, *Rice* (New York: St. Martin's Griffin, 1996).

214 "You're not going to get it": Michael MacCambridge, *America's Game* (New York: Anchor Books, 2004).

214 "I was hoping that neither": *San Francisco Chronicle,* October 12, 1987.

215 "We aren't like steelworkers": Ronnie Lott with Jill Lieber, *Total Impact* (New York: Doubleday, 1991).

216 "Eddie DeBartolo has treated us": David Harris, *The Genius* (New York: Random House, 2008).

216 "I could feel the 49ers": Ronnie Lott with Jill Lieber, *Total Impact* (New York: Doubleday, 1991).

217 "To tell you the truth": *San Francisco Chronicle,* December 28, 1987.

217 "I've got one of those nice": *San Francisco Chronicle,* January 15, 1988.

218 "The only thing is": *San Francisco Chronicle,* December 28, 1987.

218 "May have been his greatest": *San Francisco Chronicle,* December 28, 1987.

219 "He made it obvious why": *The Sporting News,* January 12, 1988.

219 "Young or Montana": *San Francisco Chronicle,* December 28, 1987.

219 "It was the wrong way": *San Francisco Chronicle,* December 28, 1987.

219 "There are times": *San Francisco Chronicle,* December 28, 1987.

220 "Could you just move": *San Francisco Chronicle,* December 28, 1987.

220 "I'm killing Bubba": *San Francisco Chronicle,* January 11, 1988.

220 "We're going with Steve": Bill Walsh with Glenn Dickey, *Building a Champion* (New York: St. Martin's Press, 1990).

220 "That's bullshit": David Harris, *The Genius* (New York: Random House, 2008).

221 "Explosive": *USA Today,* August 4, 1988.

221 "I was in a strange mood": *San Francisco Chronicle,* January 11, 1988.

222 "Provincialism": *San Francisco Chronicle,* November 17, 1987.

222 "Montana isn't even the best": *San Francisco Chronicle,* November 17, 1987.

222 "We may have a quarterback": Bill Walsh with Glenn Dickey, *Building a Champion* (New York: St. Martin's Press, 1990).

223 "Walsh tried to play mind games": Joe Montana and Dick Schaap, *Montana* (Atlanta: Turner Publishing, 1995).

224 "Nothing drives me nuts": *USA Today,* August 4, 1988.

224 "They are two great quarterbacks": *USA Today,* August 4, 1988.

224 "I threw the ball into": Jerry Rice and Michael Silver, *Rice* (New York: St. Martin's Griffin, 1996).

225 "At that point": Bill Walsh and Glenn Dickey, *Building a Champion* (New York: St. Martin's, 1998).

226 "Laying down like dogs": New York *Daily News,* August 24, 1995.

227 "We couldn't get the pressure": *San Francisco Chronicle,* January 2, 1989.

227 "I think a lot of the things": *NFL Preview,* 1989.

228 "This could have been Joe's greatest": *Colorado Springs Gazette Telegraph,* January 9, 1989.

228 "What's going on out there": *Sports Illustrated,* January 30, 1989.

228 "This has been by far": Japan Times, August 4, 1989.

229 "Playing the game over and over": Jerry Rice and Michael Silver, *Rice* (New York: St. Martin's Griffin, 1996).

231 "An economical respect," *The Atlanta Journal,* January 23, 1989.

231 "We've got 'em now": *The Sporting News,* January 23, 1989.

232 "Look, isn't that John Candy": Joe Montana and Dick Schaap, *Montana* (Atlanta: Turner Publishing, 1995).

232 "In the third": *Sports Illustrated,* August 6, 1990.

232 "He just gave me one": ESPN SportsCentury documentary, July 30, 1999.

232 "Because Montana is so cool": Bill Walsh and Glenn Dickey, *Building a Champion* (New York: St. Martin's, 1998).

233 "The second we took the field": Jerry Rice and Michael Silver, *Rice* (New York: St. Martin's, 1998).

233 "If they'd blitzed": *Sports Illustrated,* January 26, 1996.

233 "Thirty-four seconds", *The Atlanta Journal,* January 23, 1989.

234 "Montana is not human": *The Sporting News,* January 23, 1989.

234 "I've seen him do this": *The Sporting News,* January 23, 1989.

234 "As far as Joe Montana's concerned": *Sports Illustrated,* January 23, 1989.

236 "Outside of my dad": David Harris, *The Genius* (New York: Random House, 2008).

237 "Confidence-wise, it helps": *The Sporting News,* January 15, 1990.

238 "We're not going to stop him": *The Miami Herald,* October 31, 1993.

239 "I think he is playing": *The Sporting News,* January 15, 1990.

240 "Do things under pressure": *NFL Preview,* 1979.

242 "I got in Banks's way": *The New York Times,* November 29, 1989.

242 "Montana has everyone in the NFL": *Akron Beacon Journal,* January 30, 1990.

242 "There's not an adjective": *Akron Beacon Journal,* January 30, 1990.

243 "I saw Joe's little smile": *San Francisco Chronicle,* January 30, 1990.

243 "The way Montana was playing": *San Francisco Chronicle,* January 30, 1990.

243 "Okay, Daddy": *Sports Illustrated,* January 26, 1996.

243 "Off the field": *San Francisco Chronicle,* December 28, 1987.

244 "Yeah, I think we can say": *San Francisco Chronicle,* January 30, 1990.

244 "Later in the evening": *Sports Illustrated, San Francisco Chronicle,* January 30, 1990.

246 "We had the world's best": *The Tuscaloosa News*/Associated Press, September 11, 1990.

246 "I tried to bury Montana's butt": *San Francisco Chronicle,* August 27, 1990.

247 "Glad you got here": ESPN SportsCentury documentary, July 30, 1999.

247 "We couldn't wait": New York *Daily News,* October 8, 2005.

247 "In order to win": *The New York Times,* November 29, 1989.

248 "The only way Montana": *The New York Times,* December 5, 1990.

249 "Overrated": Ronnie Lott with Jill Lieber, *Total Impact* (New York: Doubleday, 1991).

249 "When I hite": *The National,* January 21, 1991.

249 "We thought he'd killed": Bill Parcells and Nunyo Demasio, *Parcells* (New York: Crown, 2014)

249 "He's like: *The National,* January 21, 1991.

250 "At the time": *Sports Illustrated,* August 13, 1990.

250 "He grabbed my hand": *Sports Illustrated,* April 24, 1995.

250 "It was a big play": McClatchy News Service, January 24, 1991.

250 "Before Steve arrived": *The Sporting News,* April 24, 1995.

## NINE: ELBOWED

253 "There's no reason why": Gannett News Service, August 15, 1991.

253 "Can I get in on this": Gannett News Service, August 15, 1991.

253 "The transitions are hard": *USA Today,* May 9, 1991.

253 "There was a little bit": *Houston Chronicle,* October 1, 1991.

254 "Technical success": *San Francisco Examiner,* October 11, 1991.

254 "Not to be too cocky": *San Francisco Examiner,* October 11, 1991.

254 "I couldn't stand to stand": *San Francisco Chronicle,* September 8, 1991.

255 "Don't come back too soon": *San Francisco Chronicle,* September 8, 1991.

255 "I'm hurting, Jimmy": Associated Press, October 10, 1991.

256 "Everyone knows their limit": Associated Press, October 10, 1991.

256 "I think he's got a lot": *San Francisco Chronicle,* September 11, 1991.

256 "If I still feel my ability's 100 percent": *San Francisco Chronicle,* November 19, 1991.

256 "You don't put the franchise quarterback": *San Francisco Chronicle,* November 19, 1991.

256 "It's like to learning to walk": *San Francisco Chronicle,* April 11, 1992.

257 "For a long time": *San Francisco Examiner,* May 14, 1992.

257 "Sometimes, I want to kick myself": *The Sporting News,* May 12, 1992.

258 "There should have been no qualms": *Newsday,* July 27, 1993.

258 "I don't think this team will ever": New York *Daily News,* January 15, 1993.

259 "Sure he's been miserable": *The New York Times,* December 22, 1992.

259 "The most difficult situation": Joe Montana and Dick Schaap, *Montana* (Atlanta: Turner Publishing, 1995).

260 "We're trying to stay": *San Francisco Examiner,* March 10, 1993.

260 "I'm just looking for an opportunity": *USA Today,* April 9, 1993.

263 "There was a period": *Cleveland Plain Dealer,* April 15, 1995.

263 "Designated starter": *The Washington Post,* April 19, 1993.

263 "It took George some time": *Sports Illustrated,* April 26, 1993.

263 "It was a farce": Associated Press, April 15, 1995.

264 "[Joe] has a deep heart": *The Washington Post,* April 19, 1993.

264 "Steve is comfortable in his role": Associated Press, April 19, 1993.

264 "There is a big desire to prove": Associated Press, April 22, 1993.

266 "The heart of what I'm doing": *San Francisco Examiner,* April 22, 1993.

266 "We're not here to watch": Associated Press, July 21, 1993.

266 "Sometimes it gets carried away": Associated Press, July 21, 1993.

267 "This is not now": *The Kansas City Star,* April 21, 1993.

267 "There was something about Joe": *The Kansas City Star,* August 23, 2013.

268 "More zip on the ball": *Gameday,* December 26, 1993.

268 "It's aggravating to me": Associated Press, October 5, 1993.

268 "I just got squashed": *USA Today,* September 22, 1993

268 "A real cheap shot": *Chicago Sun-Times,* Oct.ober 5, 1993

269 "He had a real fire": ESPN SportsCentury documentary, July 30, 1999.

270 "I don't know if it was": *The Kansas City Star,* January 24, 1994.

270 "I asked him if he was okay": *USA Today,* January 24, 1994.

271 "Everything went white": *The Kansas City Star,* January 24, 1994.

271 "I'm not sure how satisfying": *The Kansas City Star,* August 23, 2013.

272 "We thought they'd concede": *The New York Times,* October 18, 1994.
272 "He's out there trying to high-step": *Pro Football Weekly,* October 9, 1994.
272 "One of sixteen games": Associated Press, September 6, 1994.
273 "I don't know if any quarterback": Associated Press, September 9, 1994.
273 "You get on the field": *The Washington Post,* September 9, 1994.
273 "It was like playing your brother": *The Kansas City Star,* August 23, 2013.
274 "Like the Doublemint Twins": *The Washington Post,* January 2, 1995.
274 "We are struggling": Associated Press, February 28, 1995.
275 "I didn't think I would ever lose": *The Kansas City Star,* April 19, 1995.
276 "The greatest football player": ESPN SportsCentury documentary, July 30, 1999.
277 "My career was like living": *USA Today,* April 19, 1995.

## TEN: HOMEWARD BOUND

282 "I miss the excitement": *San Francisco Chronicle,* December 15, 1997.
282 "What makes him comfortable": *Sports Illustrated,* December 24, 1990.
282 "Ghost of Joe Montana": *USA Today,* January 4, 1990.
283 "I wasn't going to stay there": *Florida Today,* May 13, 2006.
283 "I don't like looking back": *San Francisco Chronicle,* December 15, 1997.
284 "I can't wait 'til": *San Francisco Chronicle,* December 15, 1997.
285 "Thankfully, there was a dryer": *The Repository* (Canton, Ohio), July 29, 2000.
285 "Joe Montana, simply stated": Induction Ceremony Transcript, Pro Football Hall of Fame.
286 "Like I'm in my grave": Induction Ceremony Transcript, Pro Football Hall of Fame.
286 "I've now seen the light": Induction Ceremony Transcript, Pro Football Hall of Fame.
289 "Sometimes in a lifetime": *Pittsburgh Post-Gazette,* September 2, 2006.
291 "A tremendous, tremendous job": Induction Ceremony Transcript, Pro Football Hall of Fame.
291 "I'm just an average Joe": *The National,* July 25, 1990.
291 "Vince Lombardi": *The National,* July 25, 1990.
291 "I think Montana's": *The New York Times,* January 22, 1990.
291 "Overall, Joe Montana": *The New York Times,* January 22, 1990.
291 "There hasn't been": *The New York Times,* January 22, 1990.

# Index